applied typing

THIRD EDITION

applied typing

THIRD EDITION

A. M. Drummond
Matthew Boulton Technical College, Birmingham

I. E. Scattergood
British School of Commerce, Birmingham

McGRAW-HILL Book Company (UK) Limited

London · New York · St Louis · San Francisco · Auckland · Beirut
Bogotá · Düsseldorf · Johannesburg · Lisbon · Lucerne · Madrid
Mexico · Montreal · New Delhi · Panama · Paris · San Juan
São Paulo · Singapore · Sydney · Tokyo · Toronto

07 084223 8

Typeset by William Clowes and Sons Limited, London, Beccles and Colchester
Printed in Great Britain at the University Press, Cambridge

Preface

Applied Typing is the second *main* textbook in a series of learning/teaching aids that will help you to become an efficient typist. The series consists of:

Typing First Course which covers the keyboard and takes you well beyond the standard required for
(a) junior office typists;
(b) the elementary stage of any typewriting examination.

Keyboard Instruction Tapes which are a series of tapes covering the presentation of the keyboard. These are suitable for
(a) individual practice at home or in the classroom;
(b) class teaching;
(c) reinforcement of keys previously practised.

Loose-Leaf Handbook and Solutions Manual has sections dealing with
Skill Teaching
Syllabuses
Schemes of Work
Lesson Plans
Solutions to exercises in Typing First Course
Programmed Learning Guides
Headed paper and forms which can be easily copied.

Practical Typing Exercises—Book One which contains further examples of exercises introduced in Typing First Course. Many of these exercises give the exact layout of typed documents and, therefore, are very easy to follow.

Applied Typing presents a systematic and comprehensive programme for perfecting and applying typing skill up to the standard of the intermediate and advanced stages of any typing examination.

Loose-Leaf Solutions Manual giving the solutions to all exercises not displayed in Applied Typing and headed paper and forms which can be easily copied.

Practical Typing Exercises—Book Two. Because of the wide variety of documents and theory covered in Applied Typing, it was not always possible to give, in that textbook, the additional exercises for which many teachers and students have asked. Therefore, we have prepared Practical Typing Exercises—Book Two which contains further examples of exercises introduced in Applied Typing.

The third edition of Applied Typing has been completely and thoroughly revised, and is an up-to-date standard reference book on type-writing theory. The exercises are also up-to-date and great care has been taken to include modern methods of display—fully-blocked letters and tabulation, open punctuation, etc.—which are now acceptable in business and by typewriting examiners. It will meet the typing needs of candidates for Stages II and III of any type-writing examination—

The LCC Private Secretary's Certificate and Private Secretary's Diploma
The RSA Diploma for Personal Assistants and Teacher's Certificate in Typewriting
The Faculty of Teachers' Typewriting Diploma

While your aim, no doubt, is to gain an examiner's certificate, we have also kept well to the fore the needs of business, and many exercises are based on material, layout and standards required by an employer. However, we would mention that, while this textbook gives the best advice, layout, and exercises that are possible after a great deal of research into office requirements and examiner's needs, you will find that your employer, or examiner, may ask you to display a document in a slightly different style from that given in the textbook. Every employer, every examiner, may, for a great variety of reasons, require certain matter to be set out in what could be considered an unusual style. But that is their prerogative! All you have to do is to follow the layout of a previously typed document or follow instructions. In business you must conform to the wishes of your employer; in an examination you follow instructions. In both you must be consistent in layout, spelling, punctuation, etc.

Applied Typing, third edition, thus combines realistic, modern, production work with the carefully planned unit structure of the previous editions. Each of the units is divided into three sections:

SKILL BUILDING

In order to be able to carry out the varied kinds of typing required in an office, or in an examination, you will have to improve your basic typing ability, and this section provides a constant review of the typing and machine techniques that are essential to accurate and speedy production work. Skill Building units contain:

(a) A review of the alphabet keys which is an excellent warm-up drill and, at the same time, gives intensive practice on the alphabet keys; this in turn improves accuracy and speed.

(b) Intensive drills on
Common Phrases
Common Prefixes
Common Suffixes
Common Words
Concentration
Figures
Fluency
Letter Combinations
Shift Keys
Shift Lock
Special Characters

(c) Accuracy/Speed practice graded according to syllabic intensity (SI), speed, and timing. We believe that a controlled but random and unselected vocabulary is the most effective way of building typing skill and, therefore, the difficulty of copy in Accuracy/Speed exercises has been graded according to the syllabic intensity. Syllabic intensity is the average number of syllables per word contained in a passage and gives you an indication of the relative difficulty of copy. In Applied Typing you are presented with graded and controlled copy so that you build speed with accuracy and sustain your speed for gradually lengthening periods of time.

The following table shows the controlled development of speed and accuracy:

Page	Timings in minutes	Number of words	Syllabic intensity	Error tolerance
1	1	70	1.10–1.30	1
8	2	140	1.13	2
12	3	210	1.27	3
18	4	280	1.25	3
23	5	350	1.27	3
32	1	80	1.19–1.24	1
38	2	160	1.20	2
43	3	240	1.28	3
50	4	320	1.34	3
59	5	400	1.28	3
71	1	80	1.25–1.27	1
79	2	160	1.24	2
85	3	240	1.33	3
90	4	320	1.37	3
98	5	400	1.30	3
110	1	80	1.26–1.29	1
119	2	160	1.30	2
131	3	240	1.32	3
137	4	320	1.37	4
142	5	400	1.38	5
147	1	80	1.30–1.32	1
155	2	160	1.33	2
163	3	240	1.40	3
178	4	320	1.37	4
184	5	400	1.38	4
192	5	400	1.50	4

Begin by typing as much as possible of the first accuracy/speed passage on page 1 to establish your speed. Then:

(a) if in the first timing, you have not more than one error, your aim should be to increase by 5 words a minute the speed reached in the first typing. For example, if your present speed, with not more than one error, is 35 words a minute, your starting point for building speed will be 40 words a minute;

(b) if you have more than one error in the first timing, continue to practise the passage at the speed reached in the first timing until you can type it with not more than one error. As the length of timing increases by one minute in each of the next four units, you should continue to practise at the selected speed up to the end of Unit 5.

At the beginning of Units 6, 11, 16, and 21, endeavour to increase your speed by five words a minute. Each time the speed is increased, practise the one-minute timing until you reach the goal within the error tolerance, and then continue with the next four units at the same speed. Your ultimate goal should be a minimum of 80 words a minute with not more than 4 errors.

These units provide a thorough review of all machine and typing techniques and develop them to the higher levels required for fast and accurate production typing. The first exercise on all new work is set out clearly, and the essential features are emphasised. Blocked and centred styles: In order to save time, many organisations are now using blocked rather than centred styles. In business you must follow the house style preferred by your employer; in examinations, you should follow the layout and instructions. Typists taking the advanced stage of any type-writing examination should be capable of using any style.

PRODUCTION TYPING

The purpose of *Applied Typing* is to develop quick and accurate production typing. Each job has a target time based on average timings of a variety of students. We have included timed pro-duction targets to emphasise the importance of accuracy, speed, theory, and good machine techniques in all typing. The businessman expects a document to be typed speedily, accurately, and sensibly the first time—no second or third attempts—because he strongly objects to the wastage of paper and time. At the top of the page on which a production job is to be typed, you should type the job number and the time allowed, e.g., Production Job 5—10 minutes. If at the first attempt you do not com-plete the job in the stipulated time, continue your practice until you do.

Before you start to type an exercise, it is *essential* that you read it through first to

(a) get the sense;
(b) correct any spelling or grammatical mistakes;
(c) amend the script so that you carry out all instructions without hesitation.

Review Quizzes. The five review quizzes give a thorough and rapid review of punctuation, styling and display. Self-checking answers are given on page 211.

Secretarial Aids. The five secretarial aids give you useful information about:

Proof-reading
Stationery
Personality
Responsibility
Care of the Typewriter.

The good typist must turn out production work quickly and accurately. However, the operator who can, in addition, carry out success-fully the many other jobs connected with the work is invaluable to an employer. The typist who hands the perfect document to her employer for signature; who knows how to prepare corre-spondence for despatch; who knows how to look after stationery supplies; who handles the job with composure and poise, etc., is the typist who will progress and will be given preference when the opportunity for promotion arises. You are responsible for the accuracy of any document you type. Therefore, you must check at each stage to see that names are correctly spelled, addresses, dates, and figures accurate. When typing columns of figures you add up each column to make sure that the total is correct before typing the total. In other words, you accept responsibility for your typing.

Most of us have to work with other people. Are you the kind of person that 'other people' will be happy to have as a colleague in the office? Do you speak clearly and pleasantly, dress appropriately, treat others with courtesy, and work quietly and efficiently? If not, now is the time to start acquiring the attributes of a competent typist who will be an asset to an employer.

Acknowledgments

We wish to express our gratitude to Mrs. Hilary Dorman and Mr. P. C. Pratt for their kind per-mission to use extracts from their plays *Bloggs' Big Day* and *Imprint For Murder*; Mrs. Norah Holt-Turner for permission to use an extract from *Travellers' Tales*; Messrs. Marsh and Soulsby for permission to use extracts from their publication *Outlines of English Law*; Mr. Jack Nobbs for permission to use an extract from his book *Advanced Level Economics*; the many organisations who allowed us to study the contents of documents, style and layout.

Finally, we sincerely thank our colleagues for their valuable help and suggestions as well as for assisting with the copying of the manuscript work.

We have endeavoured to give as comprehensive and complete coverage of typewriting theory and practice as space will allow. We hope you have enjoyed your typewriting course and that your expertise in using the typewriter will bring you satisfaction and a rich reward.

A. M. Drummond

I. E. Scattergood

Index to Contents

Introductory Notes

Reminders before starting to type

1. Insert paper by means of interliner and remove by means of paper release.
2. Set margins according to instructions given in each Unit. Bear in mind that right-hand margin must never be wider than left-hand.
   In Production Typing, if margins are not stated, select what you consider to be the most suitable for the particular job.
3. Set line-spacing.
4. Clear previous tab. stops and re-set where required.
5. Date all your work.

Keyboard techniques

At the beginning of each Unit there are keyboard reviews. Type each of these as instructed. Whenever you have time, repeat any which cause you difficulty.

Folders

We suggest you should keep the following folders:

1. Production Jobs.
2. Reference Notes.
3. Miscellaneous completed exercises which you are required to keep.

Skill building

Type each line or sentence (A, B, and C) *three* times, and, if time permits, complete your practice by typing each group once as it appears. Margins: Elite 22–82, Pica 12–72.

A. Review alphabet keys

1.	On the journey they visited an extremely quaint cottage where a wizened old woman kept an aviary of many fine birds.

B. Review shift key

2. June York Aden Ward Mary Fife Kate Peter Roger Nancy Tom Pat

3. June, Mary, Kate, Peter, Roger, Nancy, and Tom left for Ayr.

4. Telephone Mr. L. H. Ward about the Annual General Meeting of The National Union of Teachers which will be held on Friday.

C. Improve fluency

5. Why not let her try the new hat and fur she has got for you?

6. Now the boy has cut his leg and his arm on that old tin can.

7. She did not say why she had put her big red bag in the road.

8. The lad can now pay you for the new pen nib you got for him.

Accuracy/Speed Practice

Read page v in Preface under heading 'Accuracy and Speed Practice'. Then, having selected your starting point for building speed, practise the following passage as far as you can in one minute at that speed until you can do so within the Accuracy Standard indicated.

One-minute timing	Not more than 1 error
	words

AS.1	As he came close to the town, he met a crowd of folk he	11
did not recognize. This was strange, for he thought he knew	23
all of the people on that side of the town. When he came to	35
the main street, he found all of his old haunts had gone and	47
rows of shops stood in their place. Then it struck him that	59
all that was some 30 years ago — a fact he had forgotten.	70

(S.I. 1.10)

AS.2	You should be prompt to time not only at work, but also	11
when you arrange to meet anyone. To keep someone waiting is	23
very bad manners. Some people are always late, but are wild	35
if they themselves are kept waiting. If you know you cannot	47
be in time to keep your appointment, you should endeavour to	59
let the person know, and explain why you cannot do so.	70

(S.I. 1.30)

UNIT 1	1

Telegrams

Take a carbon copy and type in capitals with THREE spaces between words. Use a telegraphic address if there is one. Do not abbreviate name and address to the extent that they will be difficult to identify. Essential figures should be in words. Do not use abbreviations. Most telegrams are confirmed by letter. Telegrams may be telephoned or despatched by telex to a telegraph centre.

Telex messages

Telex calls can now be made to almost all countries of the world. Organisations with teleprinter facilities have their own design of telex forms on which the typist will type a telex message which is then passed to the teleprinter operator for despatch. The advantage of a telex message is that both sender and receiver have an immediate copy of the message, and there is no possibility of misunderstanding as may be the case when the telephone is used. Further, there is no need to send a letter of confirmation.

Window envelopes

Some firms use envelopes from which a panel has been cut out at the front. This is known as a 'window' envelope. The object of window envelopes is two-fold:

1. It saves time in typing the name and address on both letter and envelope.
2. It avoids the possibility of error in copying the address on the envelope.

When a window envelope is used, the name and address of the addressee must be typed in full on the letter itself, and in such a position that, when the letter is folded, the position of the address will coincide with the cut-out portion on the envelope. To help the typist, the position of the cut-out is sometimes marked on the letter heading either by marks in the corner or by a ruled box. Window envelopes may also be provided with a transparent cover over the cut-out part.

This type of envelope is not normally used for personal letters. It is used without the transparent cover mainly for statements, invoices, form letters, etc.

Word division

General

1. If possible, avoid dividing a word at the end of a line.
2. If it is necessary to do so to avoid an irregular right-hand margin, you should not divide on more than two consecutive lines.
3. Divide according to syllables *provided that the pronunciation of the word is not thereby changed*.
4. Wherever possible, let the portion of the word left at the end of the line indicate what the word is.

Specific

DIVIDE:

5. After a prefix and before a suffix. Examples: inter-sect, absorp-tion.
6. *Before* the repeated consonant if the final consonant is doubled (to apply spelling rule). Example: shop-ping.
7. *After* the repeated consonant if the root word ends in a double consonant. Example: miss-ing.
8. Between the two consonants (usually) when a consonant is doubled medially. Example: bag-gage.
9. After a single-letter syllable in the *middle* of a word. Example: manu-script.

10. Between two *different* consecutive consonants in the *middle* of a word. Example: desig-nation.
11. After the first of three consecutive consonants in the middle. Example: magis-trate.
12. At the original point of junction in compound words and words already hyphenated. Example: fisher-man, pre-eminent.
13. Between two separately sounded vowels. Example: radi-ator.

DO NOT DIVIDE:

14. Words of one syllable or their plurals. Examples: course, courses.
15. After one or before two letters only. Examples: again, aided.
16. Proper names. Example: Wilson.
17. Sums of money, sets of figures, or contracted words. Examples: £14.32, isn't, 123,456,789.
18. At a point which alters the pronunciation. Examples: prod-uct (*not* pro-duct), kin-dred (*not* kind-red).
19. The last word of a paragraph or a page.
20. Foreign words—unless you know the language and where to divide.

Technique development

Horizontal centring

Headings and displayed items may be centred on the paper or on the typing line. In either case, find the centre point and back-space once for each two letters and spaces that the typed line will occupy (ignore any odd letter) and begin typing at the point to which you have back-spaced. To centre *Amount* as a heading, back-space AM OU NT. To centre *The Amount*, back-space TH E-space AM OU NT. To centre *The Total*, back-space TH E-space TO TA (ignore odd L). Say the letters to yourself as you back-space.

Special Notes: When the paper is inserted so that the left edge is at 0, note the scale-point at which the right edge appears; half that number is the centre of the paper. For example: A4 paper extends from 0 to 100 (Elite) or 0 to 82 (Pica); the centre would be 50 (Elite) or 41 (Pica). If margins have already been set, to find the centre point of the typing line, add the margins together and divide by 2. For example, with margins of 20 and 85 the centre point of the typing line is: $20 + 85 = 105 \div 2 = 52$ (ignore fraction left over).

1. Practise horizontal centring. Read the above explanation, then
   (*a*) display the headings below on A5 landscape paper (210 × 148 mm)
   (*b*) display another copy on A5 portrait paper (148 × 210 mm) with margins of Elite 10–65, Pica 10–55.

<pre>
                    NEW ERA SUPPLIES
         Phoenix Place, Brighton, Sussex, BN1 5NA
                       Stationery
                       Envelopes
                    Duplicating Paper
                     Carbon Paper
                   Typewriter Ribbons
               QUICK DELIVERY GUARANTEED
</pre>

2. Practise word-division. Type one copy of the following words, inserting a hyphen at the most suitable point if the word can be divided. If necessary, review rules, page 222. Margins: Elite 22, Pica 12.

<pre>
incompetent condemnation Bristol inspection doorway UNICEF
niece occurrence disastrous non-existent gauges mortgage
infatuation although shouldn't children brilliant 5,000,000
can't problem university transcription appropriate coated
</pre>

3. Practise line-endings. Type a copy of the following in double-line spacing. Use indented paragraph. Margins: Elite 22–82, Pica 12–72.

Words to be divided are: facilitate, educational, disseminating, practice.

<pre>
     The object of the Department of Research was to facilitate and
co-ordinate, wherever possible, all aspects of educational research.
Its aim is, moreover, to avoid duplication of effort by developing
a rapid means of collecting and disseminating research results, and
of decreasing the great time lag between research and application
of the results in practice. Documents of significance are sent to
the clearing centre.
</pre>

Further exercise on line-end division is given on page 12 of **Practical Typing Exercises, Book One**.

Specifications

Size of paper
A4 (210 × 297 mm)

Ribbon
Normally a black ribbon is used.

Parts of Specification
Three, viz. Main heading; Body; Marginal headings.

Spacing
Main heading in double-line spacing. Body typed in double-line spacing if the Specification is a short one, or in single-line spacing, with double spacing between paragraphs, if it is long.

LAY-OUT
1. *Main heading*. The word 'SPECIFICATION' in heading at top is typed in spaced capitals, starting at 30 Pica, 35 Elite.

2. Subsequent lines of heading are indented 5 spaces, i.e., 35 Pica, 40 Elite.

3. The name and address of architect are typed two single-line spaces underneath the heading, in single-line spacing, either in indented form, when each line of the address is indented five spaces, or it may be blocked.

4. Date, usually at left margin, two single-line spaces below last line of Architect's address. It is sometimes typed on right-hand side underneath Architect's address.

5. *Body*. Left-hand margin set at 63 mm from edge of paper, i.e., 25 Pica, 30 Elite. Right-hand margin 13 mm.

   Paragraph indentation 5, unless blocked style used.

6. *Sub-headings in body*. The word PRELIMINARIES (when used) is usually typed in spaced capitals, centred on typing line, and underscored.

When a section or trade is started, the name of the trade is centred in typing line, typed in closed capitals, and underscored.

7. *Marginal headings*. These start 25 mm from left-hand edge of paper (to allow room for binding if necessary). They are typed in closed capitals and underscored (each line, if more than one). Single-line spacing is used, and no full stop is typed at end of marginal headings.

   Note: The margin release is used for marginal headings. It is a good plan to return the carriage to 0 on scale by means of the margin release and to set a tab. stop 25 mm from edge of paper for start of headings.

8. It is now modern practice to block headings at left margin.

9. *Continuation sheets*. On continuation sheets, the heading is repeated above the marginal headings and underscored, as follows: Specification (Contd.), and unless the section on the previous page was completed, the sub-heading is also repeated underneath the word Specification, e.g. Bricklayer (Contd.).

10. *Numbering of pages*. At bottom, in centre. In a long specification the marginal headings are also numbered.

11. *Endorsement*. This contains brief details of work to be done, date, name of person for whom it is to be carried out, and name and address of Architect. In the case of a short specification the endorsement is typed on the back of the last sheet in such a way as to be read easily when the sheets are folded (lengthways down middle). The folded edge should be to the left and the open edges to the right.
    It is usual for long specifications to be bound, and in this case the endorsement is typed on the front cover.

Tailpiece

This is an ornamental arrangement frequently used at the end of a chapter or section of a book, and is made up by combining characters, such as hyphen, colon, etc.

Longhand abbreviations

Abbreviations are often made in letters or matter written by hand for the typist to copy. In such cases the writer may make his own abbreviations, such as the following: / or (full stop) for *the*, g for *ing*, w for *with*, wh for *which*, wd for *would*, shd for *should*, sh for *shall*, amt for *amount*, abt for *about*, tog for *together*, mfr for *manufacturer*, ōr for *other*, th for *that*, and so on. The typist must, of course, type these words in full, and common-sense will decide what the word is.

4. Practise use of longhand abbreviations. Read the above explanation, then type a copy of the handwritten draft below, spelling in full all words that are abbreviated. Margins: Elite 22–82, Pica 12–72.

> We hv rec'd yr ltr of 4th Mar., regarding / non-dely by / rly co. of the gds wh were sent fwd to you a mth ago. We wd. point out th these gds were handed to / driver, who signed for them as being packed & labelled correctly, & we are surprised th they hv not bn deld. to you. We are askg the rly co. to look into / matter & we will write to you again as soon as poss.
>
> Meanwhile we wl, w yr permission, obtain a further supply fr the mfr for despatch w yr ōr order.

Standard abbreviations

Apart from longhand abbreviations which anyone writing a rough copy may adopt, there are certain standard abbreviations which are always used, and others which may be used in certain circumstances. Study the list of these abbreviations and their uses which is given on page 212.

5. Practise standard abbreviations. Read the above explanation, then type a copy of the following in double spacing, using abbreviations or writing these in full where necessary.

> We are returning yr invoice number 102, as / price charged, viz 60p per kg, shd be c.i.f., and not f.o.b. English port, as shown in P.S. of yr ltr of / fifth Sept. The amt. b/f from yr last a/c is incorrect, & we wd ask you to check this, as we think you hv not deducted the 5% dis. wh was agreed. The Dr & Cr items shd be typed in 2 separate columns as usual.

Paragraphing

There are three different styles of paragraph layout:

1. *Indented*: The first line usually starts on the sixth space to the right of the second and subsequent lines of the paragraph. It should be noted that you *must* have *at least five clear spaces* before starting the indent.
2. *Block or flush*: All lines start at the same point on the scale.
3. *Hanging*: The second and subsequent lines of the paragraph are typed two spaces to the right of the first line.

Spacing between paragraphs
(a) When indented or hanging paragraphs are used with *single* OR *double* spacing, leave *double* between paragraphs.
(b) When blocked paragraphs are used with *single* spacing, leave double between paragraphs.
(c) When blocked paragraphs are used with *double* spacing, turn up one extra space between paragraphs, i.e., turn up 3 single spaces.

Further exercises on longhand abbreviations are given on pages 22, 23, 24 of **Practical Typing Exercises, Book One**. Further exercises on paragraphs are given on page 25 of **Practical Typing Exercises, Book One**.

Ribbons

(a) Bichrome (two colour—usually black and red) and Monochrome (one colour) ribbons are the most common. They are referred to as FABRIC ribbons and may be made from cotton, nylon, or silk.

(b) A carbon ribbon is made from carbon-coated paper or plastic film. It can be used once only and is thus expensive. However, it gives very sharp and even impressions and is used when typing offset-litho masters.

(c) A correcting ribbon is used for correcting typing errors. It may be the bottom half of the carbon ribbon or it may be completely separate on additional spools. To correct a typing error, switch to the correcting ribbon, type the same error (the correcting ribbon will 'lift' the impression from the paper). Switch to normal ribbon and type correct letter(s).

Roman numerals

1. *Units:* I (1); X (10); C (100); M (1000)
   Fives: V (5); L (50); D (500).

NOTE: I can be placed *only* before V or X;
X ,, ,, ,, ,, ,, L or C;
C ,, ,, ,, ,, ,, D or M.

2. The four *unit* symbols can be repeated to express 2 or 3 units of the *same* symbol.

   Examples:

1 = I;	2 = II;	3 = III;
10 = X;	20 = XX;	30 = XXX;
100 = C;	200 = CC;	300 = CCC;
1000 = M;	2000 = MM;	3000 = MMM.

3. The symbol I may be used or repeated (up to III) *after* any of the above units or fives, in which case it *adds* to the symbol in front. Examples:

I = 1;	VI = 6;	XI = 11;	LI = 51;
II = 2;	VII = 7;	XII = 12;	LII = 52;
III = 3;	VIII = 8;	XIII = 13;	LIII = 53;
CI = 101;	DI = 501;	MI = 1001;	
CII = 102;	DII = 502;	MII = 1002;	
CIII = 103;	DIII = 503;	MIII = 1003.	

4. To express 4, 9, 40, 400 and 900, take the symbol immediately *above* and put the appropriate unit symbol *in front*, which means that it is *subtracted* from the higher symbol. Examples:

4 = 5 − 1 = IV;	9 = 10 − 1 = IX;
40 = 50 − 10 = XL;	90 = 100 − 10 = XC;
400 = 500 − 100 = CD;	900 = 1000 − 100 = CM.

5. To express numbers other than those in Rule 4, take the unit or five symbol immediately *below* and *add* to it the remaining symbols by putting these *after* the unit or five symbol. Examples:

6 = 5 + 1 = VI;	14 = 10 + 4 = XIV;
7 = 5 + 2 = VII;	15 = 10 + 5 = XV;
8 = 5 + 3 = VIII;	16 = 10 + 6 = XVI;
	17 = 10 + 7 = XVII;
	18 = 10 + 8 = XVIII;
60 = 50 + 10 = LX;	600 = 500 + 100 = DC;
70 = 50 + 20 = LXX;	700 = 500 + 200 = DCC;
80 = 50 + 30 = LXXX;	800 = 500 + 300 = DCCC.

6. A horizontal line drawn over the unit symbol means that the unit is multiplied by 1000. Example:

   $\overline{M} = 1000 \times 1000 = 1,000,000.$

7. To convert Arabic figures into Roman numerals, take each figure in turn. Example: To convert 467, proceed as follows:

400 = 500 − 100 = CD;	60 = 50 + 10 = LX;
7 = 5 + 2 = VII;	
467 = CDLXVII.	

Except in tabulation and display work, when using A4 paper the left margin must never be less than 12 Elite, 10 Pica, and when using A5 portrait paper (148 × 210 mm), the left margin must never be less than 6 Elite, 5 Pica. Whichever paper is used, the right margin must *never* be wider than the left.

6. Practise typing headings and indented paragraphs.
Type a copy of the following on A4 paper (210 × 297 mm) in double spacing, using margins of Elite 20–85, Pica 10–75. Leave 6 clear line-spaces at top. Keep your typed copy for future reference in Folder No. 2.

<u>HEADINGS IN TYPESCRIPT</u>

Of the many kinds of headings, the 3 which are most commonly used are: main, shoulder, and paragraph.

MAIN HEADINGS

These may be blocked at left margin or centred on the typing line, and they are usually in CLOSED capitals or SPACED capitals. When typed in closed capitals, one space is left between words. When spaced capitals are used, there is ONE space between letters and 3 spaces between each word. Any heading typed in lower case (except in tabulation) with initial capitals MUST be underscored. It should be noted that only after main headings at the <u>beginning</u> of an exercise should 2 blank lines be left. The title of this exercise is a main heading.

SHOULDER HEADINGS

These are generally typed in all-capitals at the left margin, preceded and followed by one blank line. The heading above this paragraph is a shoulder heading. There is never a full stop after a main heading or a shoulder heading unless the last word is abbreviated. Main headings and shoulder headings may be single-underscored but double or treble underlining must NEVER be used.

PARAGRAPH HEADINGS

<u>Paragraph headings</u> may be typed with initial capitals and lower-case letters and underscored or in closed capitals with or without the underscore. The first 2 words of this paragraph are a paragraph heading.

<u>Second Style</u>. Paragraph headings may be run into the first sentence of the paragraph, as in the paragraph above, or the heading may be displayed as in this paragraph.

Legal documents

Folding
A4 documents are folded into two lengthwise or into four horizontally. Documents which are larger than A4 are folded into four.

To fold into two lengthwise:
Place the sheet or sheets face upwards on the table, and turn left-hand side over to meet right.

To fold into four:
Place the sheet or sheets face upwards on the table, turn bottom edges to meet top, crease flat, then take folded edge, turn upwards, and crease again.

Endorsement
When the document is folded, the endorsement is typed on the uppermost side, with the open edges to the right and the fold to the left.
It is advisable to make a pencil mark to show the top of the endorsement before the document is inserted into the machine for the typing of the endorsement.

Details for Endorsement
1. Centre date across top on approximately the seventh single-line space from top edge, starting with the word 'Dated'.

2. Where two parties are concerned the name of the first party (in capitals) is centred about 9–12 single-line spaces below the date.

3. The word 'and' (centred) on the third single-line space below the name of the first party.

4. Name of second party (in capitals) centred on the third single-line space below 'and'.

5. Nature of document in spaced capitals and under-scored, centred in middle of page, followed by description of subject-matter in double-line spacing below the title of document (each line centred if more than one).

6. Name and address of solicitors at foot, first line to start about 51 mm from bottom edge.

Paper sizes—reference table

Paper	Size		Horizontal spacing				Vertical spacing	
			Number of horizontal spaces		Centre point of paper		Total number of single-line spaces	Number of single-line spaces from top edge to centre of paper
	inches	millimetres	Pica	Elite	Pica	Elite		
International								
A4	$8\frac{1}{4} \times 11\frac{3}{4}$	210 × 297	82	100	41	50	70	35
A5 Landscape	$8\frac{1}{4} \times 5\frac{7}{8}$	210 × 148	82	100	41	50	35	17
		or						
A5 Portrait	$5\frac{7}{8} \times 8\frac{1}{4}$	148 × 210	59	70	29	35	50	25
A6	$5\frac{7}{8} \times 4\frac{1}{8}$	148 × 105	59	70	29	35	25	12
$\frac{2}{3}$A4	$8\frac{1}{4} \times 7\frac{4}{5}$	210 × 198	82	100	41	50	47	24

Poste Restante

Poste Restante means TO BE CALLED FOR. The words are typed after the name of the addressee who will collect from the post office named in the address. Used for inland and overseas mail.

7. Type the following on A4 paper (210 × 297 mm) in double spacing. Use shoulder headings, block paragraphs and margins of Elite 24–84, Pica 15–75.

EQUAL OPPORTUNITIES

As from January, 1976, the main provisions of the Equal Pay Act and the Sex Discrimination Act came into operation.

EQUAL PAY ACT

A woman is entitled to the same pay as a man doing the same or broadly similar work, or work rated as equivalent under job evaluation.

SEX DISCRIMINATION ACT

Under this Act it is unlawful to discriminate against a woman when choosing an applicant for a job; when offering terms of employment; when promoting or training employees; when dealing with the provision of housing, services and facilities, etc., such as mortgages and credit facilities.

INDUSTRIAL TRIBUNALS

Claims for equal pay and complaints about discrimination (in employment) should be presented to an industrial tribunal.

8. Type the following on A5 landscape paper (210 × 148 mm) in double spacing, centring the main heading and using indented paragraphs. Margins: Elite 22–82, Pica 12–72.

POST OFFICE GUIDE

The Post Office Guide is the official book of reference regarding postal information and post offices throughout the United Kingdom. It is a wise plan always to keep a copy in the office for use when needed. Two of the services provided by the Post Office are given below:

Express Letters. If a letter is marked 'Express' and an extra fee is paid, it receives priority and is delivered by special messenger.

Business Reply Service. For this service a licence must be obtained from the Post Office. By this means a person may receive replies from his customers without their having paid the postage, this being collected from the receiver.

Half-space correction

1. When reading through your typescript before removing it from the machine, you may find that you have omitted a letter from a word, e.g., typed 'If you' instead of 'If your'. To 'squeeze' in the extra letter you must type the word 'your' a half space to the left so that a half space precedes and follows it. Proceed as follows:

(a) Erase the word that has to be altered ('you' in this case).

(b) Move the carriage so that the printing point is on the clear space after the word 'If'.

(c) Press space bar and HOLD IT DOWN.

(d) Type the letter 'y'.

(e) Release space bar.

(f) Press space bar and HOLD IT DOWN.

(g) Type letter 'o'.

(h) Release space bar.

(i) Type 'u' and 'r' in the same way.

2. It may be that you have typed 'your' instead of 'you'. In that case you should move the word 'you' a half space to the right so that one-and-a-half spaces precede and follow it. Proceed as follows:

(a) Erase the word.

(b) Move the carriage so that the printing point is where the 'y' of 'your' was previously typed.

(c) Press space bar and HOLD IT DOWN.

(d) Type the letter 'y'.

(e) Release space bar.

(f) Continue in the same way for letters 'o' and 'u'.

NOTES:

(a) Some typists prefer to use the back spacer.

(b) 'Squeezing' or 'spreading' is not possible with an electric typewriter unless it has a half-space space bar.

Justifying

The right-hand margin in typewriting cannot be completely regular as in printing, but for purposes of display it may be made regular by adopting the printer's method. This is known as 'justifying'—i.e., the space between the words is adjusted, so that each line is brought out to the same margin point. (The printer can adjust the space between letters, as he has different sizes of spaces.)

For this purpose a draft must be typed, and the additional spaces indicated at suitable points. The first line should be the required length, and the other lines should have spaces suitably adjusted to bring them to the length of the first line.

A typewriter which has a special device for this justifying can be obtained. It equalises the spaces between every word when the draft has been made, and the required number of spaces to be added to each line is known. This device is known as the Automatic Right Margin Justifying Device, and it is mainly used for the preparation of matter such as bulletins, booklets, etc.

In addition to the main heading above, there is a sub-heading. It gives more information than the main heading indicates and may or may not be included. In the above example the sub-heading takes up 2 lines with no spacing between the lines. Where a heading or sub-heading is split between 2 or more lines, we suggest that these lines be typed in single spacing.

Side Headings

These headings are typed inside the left margin and usually in closed capitals with or without underscore. When typing side headings, the following steps should be taken.

(a) First decide on left and right margins.
(b) Set right margin.
(c) Where you intended to set left margin, set a tab stop.

(d) From tab stop, tap in once for each character and space in the longest line of side headings plus 3 extra spaces.
(e) At this point set left margin.
(f) To type side headings, use margin release, bringing typing point to tab stop set in (c).

9. Type the following exercise on A4 paper using single spacing. Set margins at Elite 25–85, Pica 15–75, and type the main and sub-headings and first paragraph. After you have typed the first paragraph, from the left margin tap in once for each character and space in the longest line of the side headings (NATIONAL SAVINGS BANK) plus 3 extra spaces. This will bring you to scale point Elite 49, Pica 39. At this point set the left margin, and at Elite 25, Pica 15 set a tab stop.

<u>S A V I N G S</u>

<u>Saving money through a bank</u>

  The amount of money you save usually depends on how much you earn. It is a good plan to save a proportion of your salary each month and any of the following will be glad to pay interest on your savings.

NATIONAL SAVINGS BANK A Post Office service. You can open an account with a very small sum and you will be given a bank book in which to record your deposits and withdrawals.

TRUSTEE SAVINGS BANK Offers similar facilities to those of the National Savings Bank. There are 3 types of account: Ordinary, Current, and Special Investment.

BUILDING SOCIETIES If you wish to take out a mortgage to buy a house, then you stand a better chance of getting the mortgage if you already have a savings account with the Building Society.

Further exercises on headings are given on pages 26–28 of **Practical Typing Exercises, Book One**. Also page 29 of Book Two.

Dead keys

Some machines are provided with keys which, when depressed, do not cause the carriage to move forward the usual single character space. These are known as 'dead keys'. They are usually fitted for foreign accents, so that the accent can be struck first and, without the necessity of back-spacing, the letter key is then struck.

Building firms also sometimes have dead keys fitted on the machine for the denominator of certain fractions which they use frequently, and the typist merely inserts the numerator, e.g., $\frac{}{16}$ or /16.

Draft

If your employer asks you to type a DRAFT COPY of a document, it would be wise for you to enquire whether the document is likely to be radically revised or whether the DRAFT is to show how the document will look when completed.

If the document is likely to be extensively revised after typing, then the DRAFT should be in double or treble spacing with wide margins. On the other hand, if the DRAFT is to show how it will look when finished, then it should be typed in the style required for the finished job.

The word DRAFT should always be typed in capitals at the top left-hand margin at least one clear space above the start of the document.

'Fit' (manuscript)

1. It is sometimes necessary to divide a long manuscript among several typists. If the manuscript is in chapter form, the division should be made at the end of a chapter. If, however, the matter is continuous, the division must be made in such a way that the last line of each typist's section comes to the bottom of a page, so that it may run on without a break to the start of the next typist's section. This is known as 'fit'. To do this, it may be necessary to make some adjustment to the line-spacing on the last page.

2. When a manuscript is divided in this way, care must be taken to see that each typist adopts the same margins, style for headings, etc., and that the ribbons and type-faces on all machines match.

Figures and Words

(a) Use words instead of figures for the number ONE on its own and numbers at the beginning of a sentence.

(b) Use figures in all other cases.

NOTE: These are the basic rules but other methods may be used.

Type the following manuscript in double spacing on A4 paper with suitable margins, bearing in mind that the right margin should never be wider than the left. Centre the main heading and use paragraph headings for the others. Insert necessary apostrophes and spell out abbreviations where needed.

FORMATION OF LIMITED COMPANIES

→ Indent

Formation. When a limited co. is formed it is necessary to submit to the Registrar of Cos certain docs., in wh connection fees & stamp duties are payable.

Registration of a co. Some of the docs. required by the Registrar are given below.

Memorandum of Assoc. This controls the powers of the co. & states the cos. objects. It also tells the shareholders & other persons dealing w. the co. in what activities the co. may engage, & also its capital, etc.

Articles of Assoc. These concern / regulations applg. to / internal management of / co., but they cannot grant powers to / management wh are not laid down in the memorandum.

Registered Office. There must be kept a register of directors, secretaries, & directors' holdings of shares, as well as a Minute Book of general meetings.

Prospectus. A prospectus is defined by the Companies Act as any prospectus, notice, circular, advert. or other invitation offering to the public for subscription or purchase any shares or debentures of a co.

Issuing Shares. Shares may be issued by a new co. to raise / capital needed to commence business, or they may be issued by a co. already established in order to raise more capital for expansion.

To distinguish a copy of a document from an original, type the word 'COPY' at the top, and the word 'SIGNED' before the signature (if any).

Combination characters

Brace	Brackets typed one beneath the other	( ) ( ) ( )
Caret	Underscore and solidus	/
Cedilla	Small c and comma	ç
Cent	Small or capital c and solidus	¢ ₵
Diaeresis	Quotation mark	ü

Divide into	Right bracket and under-score on line above	) ‾
Paragraph	Capital I and small c	⁊
Section	Two capital S's or small s's	§ §
Square brackets	Solidus and underscore	[ ]
Square root	Small v and solidus, followed by underscore on line above	√‾

Correction signs

Sign in margin	Meaning	Mark in text	
l/c or l.c.	lower case = small letters	—	under letter to be altered, or / struck through letter or word
u.c. or caps	upper case = capital letter	—	under letter to be altered or / struck through letter or word
⌀	delete (take out)	—	through letter or word
⌒	close up (less space)	⌒	between letters or words
trs.	transpose	∿	between letters or words
N.P. or //	new paragraph	[	placed before first word of new paragraph.
Run on /	no new paragraph—carry straight on	∿	between paragraphs.
Stet/	let it stand—as it was originally	...	under word(s) struck out. These words to be put in as originally.
//	straighten margin		
ital.	italics	———	(underscored)
⊙	insert full stop		
;/	„ semi-colon		
⊙	„ colon		
,/	„ comma		
⸜	„ apostrophe		
/‑/	„ hyphen		
|—|	„ dash		
⸜ ⸜	„ quotation marks		
#	„ space		
⋏	„ words		
(/)/	„ brackets		

Double underscore underneath words usually means that such words are to be typed in unspaced capitals.

Treble underscore underneath words usually means that such words are to be typed in spaced capitals (one space between each letter, and three spaces between words).

Type each exercise (A, B, C, and D) *once* for speed, and finally *once* for accuracy.
Margins: Elite 22–82, Pica 12–72.

A. Review alphabet keys

1.   Hire Purchase is a vexed question which dozens of young married couples have solved by just visiting a bank manager.

B. Review figures

2. w2e3 we23 e3r4 er34 t5y6 ty56 y6u7 yu67 u7i8 ui78 i8o9 io89.

3. The 240 men, 137 women, 58 girls, and 69 boys were on board.

4. The estimated expenditure for 1963/64 was: Primary £745,000; Secondary Schools £8,360,000; Further Education £10,275,000.

C. Build accuracy on common prefixes

5. dispose, display, discount, district, discussed, disappoint.

6. I am disappointed that the discount is so low. I hope to be in your district on Tuesday, when we can discuss it further.

7. We have just discovered that there is a display next Monday.

D. Practise common letter combinations

8. the they that this thank their month thought through nothing

9. We think that their order was not sent through as usual. At least there is nothing we can do about it now as this is the last day of the month. Thank them for settling the account.

Accuracy/Speed Practice   Two-minute timing   *Not more than 2 errors*

	words
AS.3 Some time ago you asked us about some chairs and stools	11
of a style which you could use in your branch shops. At the	23
time we had none in stock to suit you. Now we have just had	35
in a supply of the type of chair and stool which we think is	47
just what you want. Not only is the style suitable for your	59
purpose, but the price is right. As you have always come to	71
us for all your needs, we are giving you the first option on	83
these goods. We do not, of course, wish to keep them in our	95
store too long, so we would ask you to call and inspect them	107
as soon as you can, and decide if they are what you require.	119
In the meantime, we are not putting the goods on show in our	131
shop until you have decided if you want them. (S.I. 1.13)	140

Yours sincerely

Helen M Grant

Mrs Helen M Grant
Secretary to J Black, Director

12. *Titled persons*. The use of very formal salutations and endings are now rare. For example, when writing to The Rt Hon The Earl of Newtown
The formal salutation is: My Lord
The complimentary close is: I have the honour to remain, Your Lordship's obedient servant,

This is now being replaced by less formal wording such as:
Dear Lord Newton
I am, Sir,
Yours sincerely/respectfully, faithfully, etc.

NOTE: In order to display a letter to advantage the spacing between the various parts may vary from those given above. For instance, with a very short letter on A4 paper, more space could be left after the heading and before typing the date. Also more space could be left between the parts—a maximum of three clear—and more space left after the end of the letter and before typing the word ENCLOSURE. With a long letter you may wish to leave less space between the various parts—minimum of one clear space. Be consistent.

FOLDING LETTERS
Letters and papers should be neatly folded to fit the particular size of envelope used.

    *   *   *   *   *

Steps in typing a letter

1. Ascertain number of copies required.
2. Assemble paper and carbon. (a) Insert paper with left edge at 0 on carriage-position scale; (b) Adjust if necessary.
3. Turn down three spaces after last line of heading or allow 9 spaces (38 mm) for heading.
4. Decide margins and set margin stops.
5. If necessary, set tab. stop for 5 indents.
6. If necessary, set tab. stop for centre of writing line.
7. Set line-spacing.
8. Insert reference(s).
9. Back-space from right-hand margin for each character or space in date. Type date. This does not apply to fully-blocked letters, in which the date starts at left margin.
10. Turn up 3 single-line spaces.
11. Type name and address of addressee in single-line spacing.
12. Turn up 3 single-line spaces.
13. Type salutation.
14. Turn up 2 single-line spaces.
15. (a) If there is a heading—from tab. stop in centre of writing line, back-space once for every two letters or spaces in heading. Type and underscore heading. Note: In fully-blocked letters the heading starts at left margin. (b) If there is no heading—indent if necessary and type first paragraph.

OVERSEAS MAIL

1. *Airmail—countries outside Europe*. In the letter, the words AIR MAIL are typed 3 spaces after the last line of the printed heading. On the envelope the words PAR AVION (BY AIR MAIL) are typed in the top left hand corner.
Example:
PAR AVION (BY AIR MAIL)
    Mr J de Munck
    88–46 West Street
    Elmhurst
    NEW YORK
    NY 11373
    USA

2. *The All-up European Service*. Letters (including letter packets) and postcards for countries in Europe are sent by air whenever this will mean quicker delivery. It is not necessary to type the words BY AIR MAIL on the envelope.

3. *Letters to the Irish Republic*
    R. O'Connor, Esq.,
    24 Kenmore Road,
    KILLARNEY,
    Co. Kerry,
    IRISH REPUBLIC

4. *Letters to United Kingdom*
    Ms A Halcrow
    12 Scotland Avenue
    PENRITH
    Cumbria
    GREAT BRITAIN
    CA11 7AA

16. *Leave double spacing between paragraphs*, irrespective of whether the letter is in single or double spacing, except when using blocked style in double spacing, when an extra space must be left.
Note: If $1\frac{1}{2}$ spaces are used, leave only $1\frac{1}{2}$ spaces between paragraphs.
17. Continue to type body of letter.
18. After last line of last paragraph, *turn up two single-line spaces only* and type complimentary close, commencing approximately at middle or slightly to the right of typing line. In fully-blocked letters, type at left margin.
19. If applicable, type name of firm *immediately below* complimentary close.
20. Turn up 5 single-line spaces and type name and/or official status of person signing letter.
21. Check to see if there is an enclosure. If so, type 'Enc.' near bottom left-hand corner. If more than one enclosure, type 'Encs.'
22. Read letter through very carefully *before* removing from machine, making any necessary corrections neatly on top and carbon copies.
23. Remove papers from machine by means of paper release.
24. Type envelope(s).
25. Attach enclosure (if any) and envelope to letter.

Proof-correction signs

Alterations in printers' proofs are indicated in the original copy by standard correction signs recognized by all who are concerned with this type of work. The letter or word to be altered is struck through, and the appropriate sign is written in the margin against the line in which the correction is to be made, followed by the solidus (/), which marks the end of the marginal note. Refer to page 216 for the most common of these correction signs.

1. Practise correction signs. Read the above explanation and then type a copy of the following on A5 portrait paper (148 × 210 mm) making the required corrections. Use double spacing and margins Elite 12–62, Pica 5–55.

stet   We regret to ~~inform~~ *advise* you that we are extremely dissatis-

dw/ fied with/delay which has occured in conection with the r/ n/

l.c. delivery of our /utumn /atalogue, which should have been in

A/ the hands of our customers in the third week of /ugust and

trs.,/ which a/tually reached them in the course of last week/long

/ after the ~~publications~~ *receipt* of the ~~receipt~~ *publications* of /other wholesale houses.

Run on   You will find that you gave a definite delivery promise

\# of one month, and had/we known you would have exce/eded this

stet N.P. period, we ~~would~~ *should* have placed the printing elsewhere. [As a

,/ result of the delay/ we have already lost a great deal of

⊙ business/

2. Type a copy of the following on A5 landscape paper (210 × 148 mm), making the required corrections. Use double spacing and block paragraphs. Margins: Elite 22–82, Pica 12–72.

stet   Late ~~on that~~ *on the* afternoon, John's father persuaded Norah & John to drive out w. him to see the child.

N.P. [Norah gave one look at the child, & whatever doubts she *still* had vanished. ["It wasn't just her curly hair & brown eyes and the ears wh were just like mine," Norah " recalled./It was everything abt her.

run on / I wanted to run and take her up in my arms, but John wouldn't let me." "If you

'/ go to her," he said, "we'll both break down.

,/ It won't be any good for the girl/ & it won't be any good for us."

Further exercises on correction signs are given on pages 28–29 of **Practical Typing Exercises, Book One.**

1. *Reference*. If words OUR REF. are already printed on the letterhead, type reference in alignment with print, and leave ONE character space clear before typing reference. If OUR REF. is not printed, turn up three single-line spaces after heading and type at left margin.

2. *Date*. Typed three single spaces after reference and blocked at left or right margin.

3. *Name and address of addressee*.
(a) Typed in single spacing on the third single-line space below reference or date and blocked at the left margin.
(b) Typed in single spacing at the foot of the page at left margin and ending one inch (25 mm) from bottom of page.
 (i) If letter finishes with complimentary close, turn up seven single spaces before typing name and address.
 (ii) If letter finishes with name and designation of signatory, turn up two single spaces before typing name and address.
 (iii) If you are using a continuation sheet and the name and address of addressee has not been typed before the salutation, then it MUST be typed at the bottom of the FIRST page, two single spaces after last typed line and ending one inch (25 mm) from bottom of page.
 (iv) If you type the name and address of addressee at the bottom of the page and the letter is marked for the attention of a particular person, the attention line is typed in the usual place before the salutation. Similarly, PRIVATE, CONFIDENTIAL, etc., must be typed in the usual place and not at the bottom of the page.
 (v) In a one-page letter with the name and address of the addressee at the bottom, the enclosure notation should be placed two spaces after the last line of the address. See further notes about ENCLOSURES below.

4. *Salutation*. On third single space below last line of address or two single spaces after the attention line. Always blocked at left margin. If the correspondent wishes to write in salutation in ink, leave plenty of space. It is suggested that you turn up nine single-line spaces after the last line of address (of addressee) before starting first line of body of letter.

5. *Body of letter*. Start on second single space below salutation or on second single space after subject heading.

6. *Complimentary close*. On second single space below last line of body. A letter with the salutation Dear Sir(s), Madam, should end 'Yours faithfully' which is usually followed by the firm's name. When a letter starts Dear Mr., Dear Miss, Mary, John, etc., the complimentary close should be 'Yours sincerely', or 'Yours truly'—the latter is rarely used. NEVER type company's name after 'Yours sincerely'. Whether you type name and designation of writer will depend on how well the writer knows the addressee. Follow style in previous correspondence or ask writer.

7. *Name of firm*. Typed one single space after complimentary close.

8. *Name of signatory*. After complimentary close, or name of firm, turn up minimum of five single spaces and type name of signatory; turn up one space and type designation. In business letters a male person does not append the word 'Mr.' before his name. However, it is common practice for ladies to put 'Miss' or 'Mrs.' before their name, or in brackets after.

9. *Enclosures*. After last line of typing, turn up a minimum of two spaces and type 'Enclosure' at left margin. 'Enc.' is the abbreviation normally used. If there is more than one enclosure then type 'Enclosures' or 'Encs.'. Some organisations list the enclosures. A few employers, and some examining bodies, prefer the word 'Attached' or 'Att.' when the word 'attached' is used in the body of the letter; e.g., 'We attach a copy of our price list.' Another method of indicating an enclosure, or enclosures, is to type three unspaced dots in the left margin opposite the line(s) in which the enclosure(s) is mentioned.

10. *Signing letters on behalf of the writer*. Your employer may ask you to type and sign a letter on his behalf. The complimentary close in this case would be:

Yours faithfully   Yours faithfully,
J R BLACK & CO LTD J. R. BLACK & CO LTD.

Helen M Grant   OR *Helen M Grant*
for
John Black   Dictated by Mr. Black
Director   and signed in his
              absence

11. Your employer may ask you to write a letter on his behalf and sign it, or circumstances may necessitate your writing on behalf of your employer; e.g., 'Mr Black has asked me to thank you for your letter dated 21st June, etc.'
The complimentary close would be

Yours faithfully
J. R. BLACK & CO. LTD.

Helen M Grant
Helen M. Grant (Mrs.)
Secretary to J. Black, Director
OR

The interliner lever (sometimes called ratchet release) releases the platen temporarily from the line-spacing mechanism. It is usually on the left side of the carriage. Locate it on your machine. When the interliner is returned to its normal position, the platen goes back to the original writing line.

The interliner is used for typing:
(a) Inferior and superior characters.
(b) Double lines underneath totals.
(c) Certain combination characters.

Superior (raised) characters

Some characters have to be typed above the normal typing line, such as degrees (small o), mathematical formulae, and raised reference marks. These are called 'superior' characters. To type them you should proceed as follows:
(a) Turn platen back half a space.
(b) Type superior character(s).
(c) Return platen to original typing line.

Note: If no half-line spacing is provided on your machine, use interliner as follows:

(a) Release platen from line-spacing mechanism by means of the interliner lever.
(b) Turn platen back about half a space.
(c) Type superior character(s).
(d) Return interliner to normal position.
(e) See that platen returns to original typing line.

3. Practise superior characters. Read the above explanation, then type one copy of the following in double-line spacing. Margins: Elite 22–82, Pica 12–72.

$$9y^2 \text{ x } 5y^2; \text{ } a^2b^2 \text{ x } a^5b^4; \text{ } a^2 \text{ x } a^2b \text{ x } 5ab^4; \text{ } 5a^2 - 3b^2 \text{ x } 3ab^2c^4.$$

They said that 160° C. equals 367° F. and they were correct.

$$b.h.p. = 0.85 \text{ x } CR^{0.34} \text{ x } d^{1.75} \text{ x } S^{0.4} \text{ x number of cylinders.}$$

Inferior (lowered) characters

Inferior characters are those which have to be typed below the normal typing line as in chemical formulae. To type these, follow the same steps as for superior characters, but turn platen *forward* half a space instead of backward.

4. Practise inferior characters. Read the above explanation, then type one copy of the following in double-line spacing. Margins: Elite 22–82, Pica 12–72.

$$O_2; \text{ } H_2; \text{ } T_1°T_2° \text{ } (T_1 - T_2) \text{ } T_1; \text{ } C_{12}H_{22}O_{11}; \text{ } W_a \text{ x } R; \text{ } t_1 - T; \text{ } C_nH_m$$
Symbols: Water H_2O; Hydrogen H_2; Oxygen O_2; Sugar $C_{12}H_{22}O_{11}$.

Typing Columns of Figures with Totals

5. Type a copy of the following, using the interliner for the double lines. Set margin at 20 and tab. stops for second and third columns at 35 and 50.

	1,643	4,585	3,120
	2,456	3,219	286
Do not turn up →	1,021	3,222	5,012
Turn up 2 spaces →			
Turn up 1 space →	5,120	11,026	8,418

Further exercises on Inferior/Superior characters are given on page 52 of **Practical Typing Exercises, Book One** and on pages 31 and 32 of **Book Two**. A further exercise on double underscore is given on page 37 of **Book One**.

UNIT 2

c/o	= care of. Used only in addresses. (Sometimes the word 'at' is used instead of c/o.)		E. & O.E.	= Errors and omissions excepted.
c/f	= carried forward. Used in accounts, statements, etc.		f.o.b.	= free on board. Used in commercial matter.
Co.	= company. Used in names of firms.		Junr., Jnr.	= Junior. Used in addresses.
c.i.f.	= cost, insurance, freight. Used in commercial matter.		Ltd.	= Limited. Used in name of company.
			M.A.	= Master of Arts. Degree after person's name.
c.o.d.	= cash on delivery. Used in commercial matter.		O.H.M.S.	= On Her Majesty's Service. Usually abbreviated.
Dr.	= debit, debtor. Used in accounts.		PS.	= Postscript. Used at foot of letter—never in body.
Cr.	= credit, creditor. Used in accounts.		Senr., Snr.	= Senior. Used in addresses.
D.Sc.	= Doctor of Science. Degree after person's name.		v.	= versus. Abbreviated or typed in full.

Bills of Quantities

The following notes will be a guide to the typing of Bills of Quantities:

1. The name of each trade is centred, and in the case of a lengthy Bill of Quantities each trade begins on a new sheet. In shorter Bills of Quantities the document is continuous, i.e., a fresh sheet is not used for each trade. At the end of the document the total of each separate trade is carried to a final summary sheet.

2. The main heading giving details of the Bill of Quantities is set out as in the specimen copy, each line being centred and the important lines underscored.

3. The name of the architect is typed in the same way as on a Specification.

4. The date is also typed in the same way as on a Specification.

5. The preliminary details headed PRELIMINARIES —usually in spaced capitals—are generally typed right across the page (irrespective of the columns ruled), with indented paragraphs, while the details of measurements, etc., are kept to the corresponding columns.

6. The separate items are typed in single-line spacing with double between the items, and are usually numbered as in the case of a Specification, the space at the left of the ruled columns on the left-hand side of the sheet being used for this purpose.

7. The pages are numbered at the foot in the centre.

8. Short Bills of Quantities are folded lengthwise from left to right in two folds and endorsed on the uppermost side, i.e., with folded edge to the left. The endorsement is worded in a similar manner to that of a Specification. Long Bills of Quantities are bound and endorsed on the front page.

9. There is a growing tendency to block headings at left margin.

Borders (Ornamental)

Display work, such as programmes, menus, etc., can be made more artistic by the use of a suitable ornamental border or corners, such as the following. You should be able to make up other artistic borders, but in doing so take care not to make the border too heavy, as this will detract from the general appearance.

```
*  *  *  *  *  *  *        0 : 0 : 0 : 0 : 0

                               :              :
*                *             :              :
                          0 : 0 : 0 : 0 : 0
*  *  *  *  *  *  *

      ***                      ***
       *                        *

       *                        *


       *                        *
       *                        *
      ***                      ***
```

Production typing

Job 2

Type the following on A5 portrait paper in double spacing, inserting any necessary apostrophes and quotation marks, and dividing at line-ends as required. Abbreviations should be typed in full where necessary. Use a hanging paragraph.

We hv recvd a letter fr a customer who complains abt an electric iron, which, he states, is unsatisfactory after only 2 wks use. He says: I am returning the iron to you, & in view of the 6 mnths guarantee y gave me, I must ask y to send this iron back to the manfrs ws / request th they give it a thorough exam & test. We are sending the iron to y by tomorrows post & hope y wl give this complaint yr immediate attention.

Job 3

Type the following on A5 portrait paper in double spacing, making any necessary corrections as indicated. Use block paragraphs.

Every month, for over 3 yrs, I hv purchased yr radio magazine & this is my first complaint. [This is the situation: Excellent as yr mag is, I do not care personally for / combination of light & heavy / matter; & I am confident th all of readers feel / as I do / the same few really splendid mags are directed particularly to those of us who are interested in / our own radio building. On the ot hand, there are several gd publications for those of us who want the / popular / point of view.

Job 4

Type the following as it appears on A5 landscape paper in double spacing. Make your own line-endings. Remove from machine and mark in ink any necessary corrections with the recognized signs. Then type the passage again, making the corrections indicated by you. Indented paragraph.

```
    I often passed a house where 2 little boys of about 8 and 10
lived, they invariably came dashing out to pet my dog & they seemed
to have such fun with him that I asked, havent you ever had a dog of
your own.  They shook there heads, Dad wont let us have one.  So I
was surprised, a few days later, to find the two children romping
about on there lawn with a puppy.  Well, I said, so Dad bought you
a dog after all.  The children grinned.  No, hes Dads dog.  We gave
him to Dad for his birthday — but he lets us play with him.
```

Abbreviations

Many abbreviations used in English are made up of separate letters, each of which stands for a single word. Some of these have a full stop between each letter, while others may be written without a full stop, although there is a growing tendency for the full stop to be omitted in all cases. The full stops are always omitted in open punctuation. A few of these abbreviations are listed below. In your work from time to time you will probably come across others, in which case you should look up their meaning in a dictionary, and then add them to the list we have given.

Common abbreviations

Cantab. = of Cambridge.
C.B.E. = Commander of the British Empire.
D.S.O. = Distinguished Service Order.
EFTA = European Free Trade Association.
G.L.C. = Greater London Council.
G.M.T. = Greenwich Mean Time.
L.R.C.P. = Licentiate of the Royal College of Physicians.
M.B.E. = Member of the Order of the British Empire.
M.P. = Member of Parliament.
M.P.S. = Member of the Pharmaceutical Society.
m.p.h. = miles per hour.

O.B.E. = Officer of the Order of the British Empire.
P.C. = Privy Councillor.
R.S.V.P. = Please reply (Répondez s'il vous plaît).
T.U.C. = Trades Union Congress.
UNO or U.N.O. = United Nations Organization.
U.N.E.S.C.O. or UNESCO = United Nations Educational Scientific and Cultural Organization.
U.N.R.R.A. or UNRRA = United Nations Relief and Rehabilitation Administration.

Standard abbreviations

A list of the most common standard abbreviations with their uses is given below.

I. *Always Used*

ad lib = ad libitum = at pleasure
e.g. = exempli gratia = for example
Esq. = Esquire = courtesy title
etc. = et cetera = and others
et seq. = et sequentes = and those that follow
i.e. = id est = that is
Messrs. = Messieurs = courtesy title
Mr. = Mister = courtesy title
Mrs. = = courtesy title
N.B. = nota bene = note well

II *Used with Figures only*

a.m. = ante meridiem = before noon
h.p., H.P. = horse power
No., Nos. = number, numbers
p.m. = post meridiem = after noon
% = per centum
Vol. = volume
*in. = inch or inches
ft. = foot or feet.

*yd = yard or yards
*oz = ounce or ounces
*lb = pound or pounds (weight)
*qr = quarter or quarters (weight)
*cwt = hundredweight or hundredweights
*m = metre, metres
*mm = millimetre, millimetres
*cm = centimetre, centimetres
*g = gramme, grammes
*kg = kilogramme, kilogrammes

* These do not require 's' in plural.

III. *Used in Cases Indicated*

*& = ampersand = and
@ = at, at the price of
B.A. = Bachelor of Arts. Degree after person's name.
Bros. = Brothers. In names of firms or companies only.
b/f = brought forward. In accounts or statements.

* Used in names of firms and numbers (such as Nos. 25 & 26—Never in ordinary matter).

Skill building

Type each line or sentence (A, B, and C) *three* times, and, if time permits, complete your practice by typing each group once as it appears. Margins: Elite 22—82, Pica 12—72.

A. Review alphabet keys

1. The clerk excelled at his job, which is very exhausting and for which special organizing ability is mainly required.

B. Practise common prefixes

2. prefer, prepaid, prepare, present, prevail, prevent, predict
3. They prefer not to predict the outcome of their predicament.
4. Be prepared to prevail upon your President to act forthwith.
5. All present must try to prevent the predicted rise in price.

C. Practise common phrases

6. we are, we may, we did, we will, we hope, we have, we should
7. We should like to know if we may visit you on Saturday next.
8. We are not sure when he will have the suite you asked about.
9. We hope that we have sent you the correct shade of material.

Accuracy/Speed Practice	Three-minute timing	Not more than 3 errors
		words

AS.4	Did you know that more than 80 per cent of all business	11
	is carried on, at least in part, by mail? It is not surpris-	23
	ing, therefore, that most firms deal with thousands of letters	35
	every year. Add to these figures the many internal memoranda	48
	written in each firm, and you can see why every worker needs	60
	to know how to write letters.	66
	A business letter is not a descriptive essay: it is a	76
	polite statement of facts, easy to understand. In most cases	88
	you do not know the person to whom you are writing; so you	100
	should use simple words, short sentences and short paragraphs.	112
	Do not say, "We are in receipt of your note of the 12th instant,	125
	the contents of which have been noted." Say, "Thank you for	137
	your note (or whatever was sent to you) of the 12th May." If	149
	you have had the letter, one assumes that you have read it and	162
	you know what the writer had to say. Do not use words which	174
	are not needed. It is a waste of the dictator's time and that	186
	of the typist. It also takes up the receiver's time. No one	198
	in business can afford the time to read superfluous words.	210

(S.I. 1.27)

Answers to Review Quizzes

No. 1 (page 29)
1. 35, 50
2. 10, 12
3. 25 mm, 13 mm
4. Left margin
5. 13 mm
6. Capital I
7. 25 mm
8. Interliner
9. Below
10. +
11. Let it stand
12. Read, Before
13. Left, Capitals
14. Same
15. 3, Spaced, Unspaced
16. 5
17. 2, Right
18. One, 3

No. 2 (page 64)
1. Underscored
2. Left, Upper case, Underscore
3. 2
4. Left, Right
5. Single-line, Reference Mark, One, Close
6. Agenda
7. Minutes, Minute Book
8. Not, Top
9. Dropped Head
10. Small Roman
11. Third, Past
12. 3

No. 3 (page 103)
1. 5
2. 2, Left
3. Left
4. 2
5. Enc, Left, Designation, . . ., At
6. £, p, Not
7. Centred, Above, Below
8. Addressee's, Page, Date, Same
9. Separate
10. Last, Punctuation
11. Unless
12. Second, Left
13. Third

No. 4 (page 123)
1. Above
2. Underscored
3. 8
4. Not, One
5. Dead
6. Tailpiece
7. Continuous Dots, Hyphens, Edge, Edge
8. Sufficient
9. Below
10. Not
11. Reversed
12. Single, Double

No. 5 (page 170)
1. Top, Bottom
2. Deepest
3. Equal
4. Underneath
5. One
6. Beyond
7. Once, Twice
8. 5 hyphens
9. No, One
10. Raised
11. Headings, Descriptive
12. Following
13. Continuous

Answers to exercise on page 118

(Corrected errors are underscored)

1. <u>Messrs.</u> Barrett & Patterson,<u>_</u>   Date
2. Newport, <u>Gwent.</u> (County must be stated—there are other towns 'Newport'.)
3. Dear <u>Sir,</u>
4.   It has <u>been</u> kindly suggested to us by the Oldham Manufacturing
5. Co. of <u>Oldham,</u> Lancashire, that we invite <u>your advice</u> on the following
6. <u>problem.</u>
7.   We are re-modelling or 2-storey factory in Cardiff <u>and</u> wish <u>to</u>
8. instal the most <u>up-to-date</u> automatic <u>sprinkler</u> equipment <u>procur-</u>
9. <u>able.</u> We should appreciate your answer to the <u>following</u> <u>ques-</u>
10. <u>tions:—</u>1. What would be the <u>approximate</u> cost of <u>installing</u> a <u>satis-</u>
11. factory sprinkler <u>system</u> on both <u>floors? 2.</u> How soon after you
12. receive <u>our</u> order could <u>installation</u> be completed? <u>3.</u> <u>Judg-</u>
13. <u>ing</u> by <u>your experience,</u> what is the average <u>percentage</u> of <u>saving</u> in
14. insurance costs resulting from such <u>installations?</u>
15.   <u>We</u> are <u>enclosing</u> the floor plans of the <u>factory.</u> If you <u>require</u>
16. further information in order to answer the <u>foregoing,</u>
17. please <u>let us</u> know.
18.   <u>Your</u> early reply will be <u>appreciated.</u>

<u>Yours</u> faithfully,
J. M. STEEL & CO.

(5 spaces)

J. Haywood
Secretary.

<u>Enc.</u>

Questions should
be displayed one
underneath the
other and indented.

Technique development

Numbers

Cardinal numbers are Arabic numbers—1, 2, 3, etc.

NOTE: The figure 1 is expressed either by the lower-case letter L or by the figure 1 if this is provided on the typewriter, but these must not be mixed, i.e., the same key must be used for figure 1 throughout an exercise. *Never* use capital I for the cardinal number 1.

Ordinal numbers denote order or sequence, e.g., 1st, 2nd, etc. They may be typed in words or figures.

NOTE: These are not abbreviations and must not, therefore, be followed by a full stop.

Roman numerals are formed from seven symbols known as Units and Fives, viz.

Units: I (1)   X (10)   C (100)   M (1,000)
Fives: V (5)   L (50)   D (500)

1. Practise formation of Roman numerals. Read the above explanation and study notes on page 220; then type the following in double spacing: (a) In words and Roman numerals; (b) in words and Arabic numbers.

(a) 1865   1964   386   1999   444

(b) MCDXXXIV   CIX   LVII   DXCIV   XLIX

Uses of Roman numerals

1. For Monarchs, Form and Class numbers.
   George VI, Form IV, Class II.
2. For chapters, tables or paragraphs instead of Arabic figures.
   Chapter III, Table II.
3. Sometimes to express the year.
   1961—MCMLXI
4. In enumerations to distinguish between sets of figures.
   Article I, Clause 1, Paragraph (i).
5. Small Roman numerals used for preface, sub-sections, Biblical references.
   1 John iii. 23.
   See page xi of preface.

NOTE: When used for numbering sections or paragraphs, the Roman numeral is usually followed by a full stop and 2 spaces.

2. Practise using Roman numerals. Study the above rules and then type the following, using Roman numerals for Arabic where applicable.

Forms 3 and 4 have been told to read Chapters 6, 9, and 12,

and to study Tables 19 and 20 (Chapters 16 and 17).

The year of its erection, 1125, was cut into the stonework.

And a certain man drew a bow at a venture. 1 Kings 22 34.

Inset Matter

If matter is to be inset from the left margin, the longest line of the inset portion should end the same number of spaces from the right margin, so that the space from the left margin to the start of the inset portion equals the space from the end of the longest line to the right margin.

A further exercise on Roman Numerals is given on page 51 of **Practical Typing Exercises, Book One.**

He put forward the theory that food production increases only in an arithmetical progression (2, 4, 6, 8 . . .) whereas population increases in a geometrical progression (1, 2, 4, 8, 16, 32 . . .). This has been rightly criticized by Professor Cannan as a 'misleading mathematical jungle'. Similarly, it is clear that man is not necessarily doomed to live at a level that entails scraping a bare existence. We ought to be able to organize our resources in order *to challenge scarcity* and improve the conditions of those unhappy persons who, according to Malthus: 'in the great lottery of life have drawn a blank'.

Since human wants are never ending, the so-called level of subsistence moves ever upwards. The minimum number of calories necessary to sustain a life, where even a sedentary occupation can be performed, is often quoted as 2200 a day. Yet it is possible for people to exist on far fewer. Neo-Malthusians might well argue that the upgrading of calorific standards makes it an almost hopeless plight for the human race to 'catch up'. Man is chasing his own tail, especially as the population of the world is doubling every generation.

If the population growth is not contained, even enormous efforts by the Food and Agriculture Organization during its World Plan Period to 1985 will have been in vain. The World Health Organization has been keeping people alive for longer than the Food and Agriculture Organization can feed them. The ultimate goal must be to check the production of people; in the long run this may be more expedient than to increase food production. But even if science provides the methods of birth control, mankind has to be persuaded to accept them. This involves overcoming superstition & religious objections as well as educating thousands of millions of people. In the meantime, the economist must be concerned in increasing the world's food supply to prevent over 30,000,000 people a year dying of starvation. Scarcity can be decreased given a better distribution of the world's foodstuffs.

NB [There are prophets of doom. Lord Snow predicted a major catastrophe in the world because of the 'food population collision'. Lord Snow contended: 'We ought, in the rich countries, be surrounded by a sea of famine, involving hundred of millions of human beings'. Can we prevent Malthus from being right, in the long run?

(in a lecture given in the USA in '68 & published by Oxfam in the UK in '70)

Before the end of the century

An enumeration is a set of paragraphs or lines, which are usually displayed as follows:

1. The numbers usually project to the left of the first line of the paragraph, and the second and subsequent lines are blocked underneath the first line (as in this paragraph). Leave 2 spaces after full stop following numeral.
2. In some cases the numbers are put in brackets, e.g., (2), in which case 2 spaces are left after the final bracket.
3. Letters may be used in place of numbers.
4. Where there are subdivisions of enumerated items, these can be distinguished in order of importance as follows:

Capital Roman numerals for main division. I
Upper case letters for first subdivision. A
Arabic numbers, small letters or small Roman numerals.
5. When Roman numerals are used in enumerations, these may be blocked on *left* or *right*.

Left	*Right*
I.	I.
II.	II.
III.	III.
IV.	IV.

3. Practise typing inset enumerations. Type the following on A4 paper (210 × 297 mm) using margins Elite 20–85, Pica 10–75. Leave 6 clear line-spaces at top of paper and follow layout. Block Roman numerals on right. Keep your typed copy for future reference in Folder No. 2.

HIRE PURCHASE

Hire Purchase is a system of buying goods over a period of time. You hire the goods and payment is made by instalments over a fixed period. The goods are not your property until the last instalment has been paid. Let us look at the advantages and disadvantages of this system.

   I. ADVANTAGES

       (a) You can afford to buy more costly goods.

       (b) You can have the goods straight away.

       (c) Payments by instalments are simple and
            may be made:

              i. weekly;

             ii. monthly; or

            iii. at other agreed intervals.

  II. DISADVANTAGES

       (a) You pay more than you would if you paid
            cash.

       (b) You can acquire the goods when money is
            plentiful — husband and wife both work-
            ing. But what will happen if either or
            both are not working?

       (c) Goods may be out of date before the
            final payment is made.

NOTE:
The Roman numeral I is here inset one space to right of paragraph indent to allow for the Roman numeral II, and to be consistent the small Roman numeral i has also been inset 2 spaces to right to allow for the small Roman numeral iii.

Further exercises on enumerations are given on pages 10, 23, 43, 46, and 61 of **Practical Typing Exercises, Book One**, and on page 6 of Book Two.

Job 92 Production Target—*20 minutes*

The exercise starts with page 16 and should be typed in double spacing with a typing line of 65 spaces. It is essential that your typing does not at any time extend beyond the 65 spaces and, at the same time, the right-hand margin should be as even as possible.

spaced caps / closed caps

2 MACROCOSM—*Thinking big**

closed caps at left margin

UNIT 4. Population

Introduction—Why the economist is interested in population problems

The economist is interested in population problems, either on an international or national scale, for two main reasons:

(a) Production of goods and services depends on the labour force.

(b) Consumption depends upon the demand of the population for goods and services.

Figure 4.1 illustrates the world population from 1750 with projections to the year 2150. Population statistics, particularly before 1900 and after 1980, are subject to errors as large as 10 per cent, but they do indicate the enormous increase in world population and give some intimation of the exceedingly difficult problems to be faced. Whether or not we can find employment for all those who are physically and mentally capable of work. How shall we cope with the 6500 million people who are expected to be alive in the year 2000?

Typist - please leave 3" (76 mm) clear vertically for Figure 4.1.

u/c at left margin

Topic 4.1 Malthus and the neo-Malthusians

Although the Reverend Thomas Robert Malthus (1766–1834) is usually associated with drawing the public's attention to the importance of population growth, he was not the first economist to have been concerned with the problem. Adam Smith believed that the demand for men regulated the production of men. The importance of Malthus lies in the fact that he inculcated a pessimism about the population problem under the shadow of which man still exists. Neo-Malthusians, or those who believe that the ghost of Malthus still lurks among us, might argue that we are still haunted by intense scarcity, malnutrition, and famine because the ideas of Malthus were not realistically accepted and that the pockets of affluence which exist in the western world have lulled Europeans and North Americans into a false sense of security.

Malthus has been a much-maligned man. He did not advocate famine, war, disease, vice, and misery, but rather he believed that these tragedies would strike the human race if population continued to outstrip the food supply. And even though, in the last few years, improved genetic strains of wheat, rice, and other major foodstuffs have brought new hope to mankind, it is still too early to say that Malthus will not prove to be right in the long run. Indeed, Malthus contended that it might take several centuries for the effects of his theories to be fully felt.

However, Malthus was wrong to attempt to prove that there was an exact mathematical correlation between the supply of food and the supply of people.

Words are sometimes deliberately omitted at the beginning, or end, or in the middle of a sentence. Such omission is indicated by the use of three spaced full stops, as follows: . . . If the omission occurs at the beginning of the sentence, the full stop at the end of the previous sentence is typed as usual, followed by one space after full stop and 3 spaced dots (one space only between each) (as here). . . . If the omission occurs just before the end of the sentence, the three spaced dots are followed by a fourth dot to show the end of the sentence, as follows: . . . .

4. Practise ellipsis. Read the above explanation, and then type the following on A4 paper in double spacing, centring the main headings. Leave 6 clear spaces at top. Block Roman numerals to left. Margins: Elite 20—85, Pica 10—75. Keep your typed copy for future reference in Folder No. 2.

CHAPTER XII

MONEY

The substance chosen for money must have certain characteristics, some of which are given below.

I.   ESSENTIAL PROPERTIES OF SUBSTANCES USED FOR MONEY

    (1)   Acceptability

        It must be generally acceptable.

    (2)   Portability

        (a) It must be easy to carry.

        (b) The cost of transport must not be too great.

    (3)   Durability

        (a) It must be hard-wearing.

        (b) It must not deteriorate easily.

    (4)   Divisibility

        It must be divisible into smaller units . . . in Great Britain pounds are divided into pence.

II. FUNCTIONS OF MONEY

    (1)   Measure of Value

        (a)   Money establishes a definite standard of value.

        (b)   It thus enables the relative value of other commodities to be compared. . . .

    (2)   Medium of Exchange

        It is universally accepted, and can thus be exchanged for . . .

NOTE:
After the full stop following the Roman numeral I an extra space, i.e., 3 spaces in this case, must be left to allow for the Roman numeral II to be blocked to the left.

Further exercises on ellipsis are given on pages 7 and 29 of **Practical Typing Exercises, Book Two.**

Spaced caps [

ADVANCED LEVEL ECONOMICS

Typist - Please block all headings at left margin

Second edition
Jack Nobbs, JP, BSc(Econ) ← *u/o*

CONTENTS ← *closed caps & u/o*

In addition to the methods of enumeration explained on page 14, it is modern practice to use the decimal point, followed by a figure, for sub-divisions. For example, 4(a) and 4(b) would become 4.1 and 4.2; 4(a) i and 4(a) ii would become: 4.1.1 and 4.1.2. When using open punctuation, the decimal point for decimalised enumeration must be inserted. If there is a full stop after the last figure, leave 2 clear spaces; if there is no full stop, leave 3 clear spaces.

5.

Leisure Attitude Survey *- caps & u/o*

Report *- spaced caps*

Table of Contents *- caps*

Section

1   Introduction

2   Analysis and Survey Methods
     2.1   Purpose of Survey
     2.2   Method of Survey
     2.3   Analysis of Survey Data

3   Results obtained from the Survey
     3.1   Sociological Data
     3.2   Rural Entertainments
     3.3   Urban Entertainments *trs*

4   Trip Generation to Leisure Areas around the Conurbation
     4.1   *Introduction*
     4.2   Trip Generation by Social Class and Type of Area
            4.2.1   Trip Generation by Social Class and Type
                     of Area (Non-car Trips)
            4.2.2   Trip Generation by Social Class and Type
                     of Area (Car Trips)

5   Future demand for Leisure Facilities

6   Conclusions
                    _____

References

Appendix I — Present & Future Demands
Prepared by J R Duffell and G R Goodall
       Dept. of Transportation.

Type the above exercise on A4 paper. Margins: Elite 22–82, Pica 12–72.

A further exercise on decimalised enumeration is given on page 7 of **Practical Typing Exercises, Book Two**.

Display the following exercise on a sheet of A4 paper.

YORKTOWN SCHOOL

ARITHMETIC TEST   Time ~~30~~ 45 minutes   DECEMBER 1978

ALL QUESTIONS TO BE ANSWERED. The answers to Question 1 are to be written in the space provided on this sheet. Other questions to be answered on the paper provided.

1. Calculate

     $761 + 94 - 15 \div 2 =$ £ _____
     $203 - 3 + 76 \times 3 =$ £ _____
     $896 + 4 + 20 \times 4 =$ £ _____
     $345 - 145 \times 5 \div 2 =$ £ _____

2. Reduce to lowest terms

     (a) $\dfrac{96}{100}$ (b) $\dfrac{50}{350}$ (c) $\dfrac{120}{360}$

3. Change the following improper fractions to whole or mixed numbers

     (a) $\dfrac{876}{25}$ (b) $\dfrac{148}{12}$ (c) $\dfrac{175}{13}$

4. Change to improper fractions

     (a) $18\dfrac{2}{3}$ (b) $56\dfrac{5}{9}$ (c) $52\dfrac{7}{11}$

5. Simplify

     (a) $4\dfrac{1}{2} - 2\dfrac{1}{3} + 1\dfrac{1}{4}$ (b) $8\dfrac{2}{9} - 5\dfrac{1}{6} + 3\dfrac{1}{3} + 1\dfrac{2}{3}$

     (c) $\left(\dfrac{7}{8} \div 2\dfrac{1}{3}\right) \times \left(1\dfrac{1}{8} \text{ of } 8\dfrac{2}{3}\right)$

6. Find the difference between

     $1/2 + 3/4 \times 5/6 - 5/12$ and $\left(1/2 + 3/4\right) \times 5/6 - 5/12$

Job 5   Production Target—*10 minutes*

Type the following on A4 paper (210 × 297 mm) in single spacing, with double between numbered and lettered items.

Economic Report   (Typist - all words double underscored in closed caps and underscored, please)

Britain earned a record in motor export - 11 per cent higher than last yr. The followg is a summary of / yr just ended:

I. General

uc.   1. Early in the new year, prices rose sharply and

stet   many articles disappeared from the market ~~shops~~.

The reasons given were/-

(a) Widespread ~~stc~~ strikes.

(b) Lack of price controls.

market/   2. There was a sharp increase in ~~fo~~ fresh

trs   quotations for forei~~gn~~ currency.

II Finance

1. The % age ratio of gold & convertible

foreign ⌐   exchange reserves ~~rose by 8 per cent~~. again improved.

2 Foreign exchange reserves rose by 8 percent.

\# III   Commerce & Industry

1. Exports

l.c.   (a) American market: The demand for all types of motor vehicles increased considerably w. emphasis on:

lc   i. ~~+~~ Racing models;

lc   ii. Saloon cars in / £10,000 range.

(b) European market: there was little change from / previous month.

2. Imports (a) There was an overall fall in imports.

(b) Imports of cotton rose as follows/ i Egyptian by 4 per cent. ii. American by 5 per cent.

Typist. Please display as above

Type the following table on a sheet of A4 paper and rule.

TELEPHONING FROM EUROPEAN COUNTRIES TO THE UK

Please first countries in alphabetical order + type UK in full

Country	International Coinbox Identification	Coins you can use (Note 1)	Minimum charge (Note 2)	What to dial (Note 3)
AUSTRIA	3 coin slots	1, 5, 10 sch	9 sch	00 44
DENMARK	2 or 3 coin slots	25 ø, 1 Kr (5 Kr)	50 ø	009 44
SWITZERLAND	4 coin slots	10, 20, 50 C, 1 F	40c	00 44
NETHERLANDS	Accepts 25c coins	(10c) 25c	25c	09 ... 44
FRANCE	metallic grey colour	25, 50c 1, 5 F	40c	19 ... 44
NORWAY	—	1 Kr. (5 Kr)	1 Kr	095 44
Germany	Green Sign	10, 50 pf	20pf	00 44
Sweden	3 coin slots	10, 25ø	50ø	009 44
Spain	3 " "	5, 25, 50 pta	50 ptas	07 ... 44

Notes: 1. If there is a choice of coin wh can be inserted, use the highest denomination. Coins /*shown in brackets/* are the ones accepted in certain coin boxes.

2. Insert before dialling.

3. Dial the code given, then the UK STD code (w'out the initial '0') then the UK tel. no.

4. Where 3 unspaced dots are shown in the last column, wait for a second dial tone before continuing.

Skill building

Type each exercise (A, B, and C) *once* for practice, *once* for speed, and finally *once* for accuracy. Margins: Elite 22–82, Pica 12–72.

A. Review alphabet keys

1.   We think it expedient to modernize our works by acquiring an adjacent factory which will at least give more space.

B. Review shift lock

2. UP-TO-DATE, FORTY-ONE, SELF-CONFIDENT, NEVER-TO-BE-FORGOTTEN

3. The COMMANDER-IN-CHIEF was a SELF-CONFIDENT and RELIANT man.

4. CASH IN BANK £1,571; CASH IN HAND £105; GOODS IN STOCK £324.

C. Practise concentration

5. 'Feet' in poetry: (a) The TROCHEE (trochaic rhythm); (b) The
SPONDEE (spondaic rhythm); (c) The TRIBRACH; (d) The IAMBUS;
(e) The ANAPAEST (trisyllabic); (f) The AMPHIBRACH.

Accuracy/Speed Practice

Note: From now on, you must make your own line-endings

Four-minute timing   Not more than 3 errors

	words

AS.5   As winter draws near, many birds are preparing to leave us and set   13
off on their long flight south in search of sunshine, while some stay   27
behind.   To them a winter of snow and frost will mean a bitter struggle   41
for survival.   Last year hunger and cold drove many to seek shelter and   55
food close to homes, and people who had taken no interest in them before   70
helped them.   Perhaps the most endearing all-the-year round resident is   84
the robin, whose red breast becomes bright in winter-time and who can   98
become very tame.   Sparrows remain with us, so do the starlings.   You can   112
still hear the blackbird singing in the frosty sunshine.   The finches —   126
some so brightly coloured — stay, but they do not often become as tame as   141
the other birds.   The delightful blue tits also are always to be seen.   155
Some of the birds who stay behind in the winter are useful, eating pests   169
which damage the crops, but others do harm.   Harmful or not, they all   183
find surviving the bitter cold a problem.   The ground is hard, and they   198
cannot dig out worms and other food.   There is no fruit, and there may   212
be few berries.   215

      Many of you may want to help them during this bad time.   Food scraps,   228
such as fat, bacon rind, and bits of bread, are always welcome.   Strings   242
of nuts may be hung from the branch of a tree.   Half a coconut provides a   257
wealth of food for the blue tits.   But birds must also drink, so when the   272
ground is frozen, put out water for them.   (S.I. 1.25)   280

Typist. The following is a bit jumbled. Please prepare 3 lists for me. On the first sheet type all items marked 'A' (in alphabetical order). Use heading: <u>SECRETARIES — SHORTHAND)-TYPISTS — TYPISTS</u>. All items marked 'B' on another sheet of paper in alphabetical order. Heading: <u>CLERKS</u>. All items marked 'C' on a third sheet of paper in alphabetical order. Heading: <u>OTHERS</u>.

<u>JOB</u>	<u>DESCRIPTION</u>
Ⓒ JUNIOR CASHIERS	Record cash receipts & disbursements. Prepare daily cash reports. In charge of Petty Cash.
Ⓑ POSTAL CLERKS	Open mail, date stamp, sort & distribute. Prepare outgoing mail.
Ⓑ SHIPPING CLERKS	Prepare shipping documents; compute transportation costs, and trace lost or delayed shipments.
Ⓐ SHORTHAND)-TYPISTS	Take dictation in s'hand & transcribe notes to produce finished correspondence. Use telephone. May do some filing.
Ⓒ SWITCHBOARD) OPERATORS	Operate company switchboard & equipment. Keep records of calls. Take telephone messages.
Ⓐ TYPISTS	Type forms, reports, & or business papers. Prepare stencils, lists, etc.
Ⓐ SECRETARIES	As for s'hand typists, plus: Receiving & entertaining visitors. Making travel arrangements. Keeping employers diary. Attending meetings & recording minutes.
PAY-ROLL CLERKS Ⓑ	Compute pay-roll fr. time & piecework records. Issue pay cheques & envelopes.
PUNCHED CARD) OPERATORS Ⓒ	Prepare & verify punched cards fr business papers & or data.
Ⓒ RECEPTIONISTS	Greet & direct callers. Use tel. Keep reception area neat & tidy. Keep records.
Ⓑ FILING CLERKS	Check papers for release for filing. File & find papers. Help in transfer & storage.
Ⓒ DUPLICATING M/C OPERATORS	Operate stencil & spirit duplicators. Use photo-copying equipment.
Ⓑ INVOICE CLERKS	Price orders. Prepare invoices. Check computations.
Ⓑ PURCHASING CLERKS	Locate source of supply. Issue letters of enquiry. Maintain records and verify estimates.

Technique development

1. Type a copy of the following in double spacing, paying particular attention to the difference in spacing for hyphens and dashes. Use A5 landscape paper. Margins: Elite 22–82, Pica 12–72.

His son was only 31 years of age when he was re-elected — by virtue of his far-sighted views — as secretary of the Company. The Company is moving its factory – now at 9 High Street – to new premises at 30 Broad Street, where up-to-date machinery has been installed. The firm is engaged chiefly in the sale of ready-to-wear suits of first-class quality & up-to-the-minute style.

Combination characters

When you have to type a symbol which is not included on your typewriter keyboard, you should construct it by combining two characters, i.e., type one character, back-space, and type the other. On some machines it may be necessary to raise or lower the platen before typing the second character, in which case you should use the *interliner* (ratchet release), so that, when you have returned the interliner to its normal position, the platen goes back to the original line of writing. The most common of these combination characters, as they are called, are given below, and an additional list is given on page 216.

2. Practise the combination characters given at the right-hand side of the following exercise. Type the complete exercise on A4 paper in double-line spacing. Use a left margin of Elite 20, Pica 10, and set tab stops at Elite 37, Pica 27 (for the second column) and Elite 85, Pica 75 for the third column. Keep your typed copy for future reference in folder No. 2.

COMMON COMBINATION CHARACTERS AND SPECIAL SIGNS

Asterisk	Small x and hyphen	x̵
Dagger	Capital I and hyphen	I̵
Degree	Small o raised half a space	o
Division	Colon and hyphen	÷
Dollar	Capital S and Solidus (Oblique)	$
Double Dagger	Capital I raised half a space and another capital I typed slightly below; or capital I and equation sign	I̵
Equation Sign	Two hyphens — one hyphen slightly above the other	=
Exclamation	Apostrophe and full stop	!
Feet	Apostrophe typed immediately after figure(s)	'
Inches	Double quotation marks typed immediately after figure(s)	"
Minutes	Apostrophe typed immediately after figure(s)	'
Multiplication	Small x with space either side	x
Plus	Hyphen and lowered apostrophe	+
Seconds	Double quotation marks	"

3. Practise combination characters and special signs. Type a copy of the following on A5 landscape paper. Margins: Elite 22–82, Pica 12–72.

"Hello!", he said. "I am surprised to meet you here again."
Position:— Longitude 21° 12' 15" E. — Latitude 15° 5' 20" N.
240 — 120 ÷ 2 x 3 — 100 + 20 = 300 + 100 — 200 x 2 ÷ 5 + 20.

There is a large body of legislation which aims to prevent cheating and to protect the public against defective goods. The following are the more important matters which are controlled.

1 *False trade descriptions.* Any person who, in the course of a trade or business (a) applies a false trade description to goods, or (b) supplies or offers to supply goods to which a false trade description is applied, shall be guilty of an offence under the Trade Descriptions Act 1968. It is also an offence, in the course of any trade or business, to give false indications that the goods supplied have Royal approval, or are of a kind supplied to some celebrity. It should be noted that these rules only apply where the description was applied or the goods supplied in the course of a business. A false

H/   description applied by a nondealer wl not be an offence under these sections, & may not be an offence at all unless the victim can prove the MENS REA necessary to constitute an offence of fraud. [Other Acts prohibit mis-   *N.P.* descriptions of special classes of gds. For example, under Section 2 of the Food & Drugs Act 1955, if a person sells, to the prejudice of the purchaser, any food or drug] substance or quality of the food or drug demanded by the buyer, the seller commits an offence. The Fair Trading Act 1973 gives the Sec of State for Trade & Industry power to make regulations prohibiting other misleading practices.

which is not of the nature

MENS REA

2   Some false or misleading indications as to the price of goods are offences under Section 11 of the Trade Descriptions Act.

3   Weights & Measures are subject to legislative controls .... There are criminal sanctions for giving short weight or measure.

---

* Extract from OUTLINES OF ENGLISH LAW
        (Second Edition)
        Marsh and Soulsby
Published by McGraw-Hill Book Company (UK) Limited
Produced with permission

4. Practise using words and figures. Study notes on page 217, then type the following in single-line spacing, noting where words or figures are used. Margins: Elite 22–82, Pica 12–72. A5 landscape paper.

```
There were only 4 or 5 girls in the large room at 8 o'clock.
There are over 9 million inhabitants, though very few voted.
The lunch-time period will be one hour — from 12.30 to 1.30.
We will allow a discount of 5 per cent for cash on delivery.
We hope you can send the goods to us within the next 5 days.
His son arrived on 1st June — on his seventy-fifth birthday.
```

5. Type the following on A5 landscape paper (210 × 148 mm) in single-line spacing, altering words to figures or vice versa as required. Margins: Elite 22–82, Pica 12–72.

```
200 children are to spend 1 week's holiday abroad.
It took us almost two hours to walk about 5 or 6 miles.
We shall do our utmost to deliver your order in three weeks.
A trade discount of 25% is allowed on all our goods.
Many of the boys are between sixteen and eighteen years old.
The box offices are always opened promptly at 11 o'clock.
```

Internal telephone index

It is usual to keep a list of names and addresses and telephone numbers which are frequently required. For this purpose use is made of the strip-indexing method, whereby each name and address and telephone number is typed on a separate strip. The strips are usually supplied in sheets, and the details are typed on the strips, which are afterwards separated from the sheet, and then they are inserted alphabetically in devices or frames specially made to take them. These strips can be moved up or down to allow of additional strips being inserted in their correct order, or to remove strips containing obsolete names. The surname is usually typed first, and in upper case letters, followed by the initial(s) and then the address, all on one line if possible. If two lines are needed, these must be in single-line spacing, as the strip is usually not more than 6 mm in depth. In order to carry the eye from the end of the address to the telephone number, continuous dots may be inserted as in the first line of example (leaving one clear space before the first dot and one clear space after the last dot).

NOTE: A comma is typed after surname, and after initials, in an index or alphabetical list.

Example of method of typing strip

```
BROWN, A. J., 46 Thomas Street, Leeds.  LS2 9JT ............ 0532 21375
FISHER, L., & Co. Ltd., 20 Clitton Road, Northampton.  NN1 5BQ 0604 6868
```

6. Practise typing internal telephone index. Read the above explanation; then type the following names and addresses in alphabetical order according to the surname (if a personal name) or the first word of the name (if an impersonal name). Leave double spacing between each name. Left margin: Pica 5 spaces, Elite 5 spaces. Right margin to be blocked 5 spaces from right-hand edge of paper.

```
White & Bradbury Ltd., Empire Way, Northampton.  NN1 5BQ  0604 8686
Mardon's Ltd., Green Lane, Wolverhampton.  WV2 4DB  90 20035
Adelphi Ltd., 96 Park Lane, Croydon, Surrey.  CR9 1TP  01-688 3814
Ronaldson, H., Ltd., Broad Street, Liverpool.  L1 6BJ  051-486 1217
Bradley & Bliss Ltd., Kings Avenue, Leeds.  LS1 3AE  0532 21735
MacAndrew Ltd., 31 High Street, Kirby, Liverpool.  L3 8XF 051-727 2409
G. B. Kent & Sons, 8 Burnett Street, Blackpool.  FY4 3DW  0253 32244
```

Further exercise on words and figures is given on page 39 of **Practical Typing Exercises, Book One**.
Further exercises on telephone and telex indices are given on page 8 of **Practical Typing Exercises, Book Two**.

Type on A4 paper in single spacing. Use a dropped head for: UNIT 30. DEFECT-IVE GOODS. The main heading and the sub-headings at the right-hand side should end so as to leave 13 mm clear between the last letter and the right-hand edge of the paper. There should be a minimum of 5 clear spaces, and not more than 8, between the end of the right margin and the last letter of the sub-heading.

Unit 30.   Defective Goods*

A   The Problem

As in the last Unit, an attempt will be made here to show how common situations can raise legal problems which cut across the boundaries of contract, tort, crime and other branches of law.

Consumer protection, like safety on the roads and at work, is governed by legislation which is aimed primarily at the prevention of cheating or loss. The legislative controls are administered largely by inspectors appointed for the purpose, and criminal sanctions are provided for breach.

Compensation for the victim who has bought faulty goods is normally another matter. If the supplier will not give compensation voluntarily, the victim may have to start separate civil proceedings for breach of contract, misrepresentation, or in tort. Not all consumers are so determined, or indeed can afford the time, energy and money to do this.

Consider these transactions:

1 Soulsby buys a box of *X*'s chocolates from Marsh's Confectionery Shop. Some of the fillings contain impurities. Soulsby, and his guests to whom he has given chocolates, become ill after eating them.

2. Soulsby buys a second-hand car from a neighbour, Marsh, who tells him that it is a '70 model. In fact, unknown to Marsh, the car is a 1968 model, the registration book of wh has bn falsified by a previous owner. The car proves to be in poor condition, & Soulsby incurs considerable expense in repairing it.

3. Soulsby buys a second-hand car from Marsh (Motor Dealers) Ltd., who tells him th it is a '70 model. (in the course of negotiations) The rest of the facts are as in the previous situation.

Job 6 Production Target—*10 minutes*

Starting 7 spaces from the top of a sheet of A5 paper (148 × 210 mm), display the following; i.e., centre each line horizontally. List the items in alphabetical order. Type in double spacing with two clear spaces after every third item.

Office ~~Pract~~ Practice ← caps & underscored

Course Content ← l.c. with initial caps
& underscored

Working in a Modern Office

u.c. Getting along w. people

u.c. Automation in the office

Dictating (Machines) & Transcribing

of ~~Internal~~ Communications

of (Methods) of Duplicating

u.c. Post Office Services

Filing

~~l.c.~~ u.c. Sales Office procedure

Purchasing Office "

of Cash Handling

Wages Office "

Stock & Stock Control

(Office) Personnel

Reception Work

Job 7 Production Target—*7 minutes*

Type the following names in alphabetical order, to be used as an internal telephone index, using single-line spacing.

E. M. Hinks Ltd., Chichester Road, Belfast. N.I. BT1 4LA
0232 22957

Maverick & Sons, Gateway, Leicester, LE2 1DL 0533 13147

L. C. Clare Ltd., 21 George Str., Edinburgh. EH2 2LZ
031-225 1847

Brown & Shell Ltd., Berkley Str., London. W7X 6AA
01-262 5847

Walgarth & Co. Ltd., 39 Hazel Rd., Reading, Berks. RG1 3EZ
0734 11645

Broadway & Co. Ltd., Brook Str., Bradford,
West Yorks. BD1 ~~1HZ~~ 1HY
0274 51781

J. A. Clarke Ltd.,
1 High Street, Stratford, London. ~~EH3~~ E15 3BH
01-794 2112

UNIT 4

21

Display the following on a sheet of A4 paper. Justify the right-hand margin so that there is exactly 38 mm clear after the right margin.

Spaced caps → # Outlines of English Law

Underscore → **Second Edition**

Caps → S. B. Marsh

B.Com., LL.B., Ph.D., Barrister-at-Law

Head of Department of Law
Manchester Polytechnic

and

Caps → J. Soulsby

LL.B., Solicitor

Principal Lecturers in Law
Manchester Polytechnic

This portion to be typed so that the last line finishes 13 mm from bottom of page.

McGraw-Hill Book Company (UK) Limited

London · New York · St Louis · San Francisco
Düsseldorf · Johannesburg
Kuala Lumpar · Mexico ·
Montreal · New Delhi · Panama ·
Paris · São Paulo · Singapore ·
Sydney · Toronto

Type the following exercise on A4 paper in double spacing, making any
necessary corrections. Use shoulder headings and indented paragraphs.

T. J. Anderson & Co. Ltd. ← *centre, caps & underscore*

Annual Report ← *centre, initial caps & u/o*

u.c. The Directors hv pleasure in submitting the Co's fifty-second
Annual Report together w the audited a/cs f the yr ended 31 Dec 77.

I.　PROFIT

The profit and loss ~~a/c~~ statement appears on p.8.

II. DIVIDEND

Final dividend of 2.50p per share, making a total ordinary dividend for the yr of 3.75p per share.

III. Share Capital   *caps*

At an extraordinary general meeting of the Co. *u.c.* held on 20 July 1976, the authorised share capital was increased to £7,000,000. There now remains unissued 23,782 ordinary shares, & the Directors consider it desirable to increase the margin of unissued share capital, & accordingly it is proposed to ask shareholders to approve the following special resolution:

"That the capital of the Co be increased fr. £7,000,000 to £8 million by the creation of an additional 1,000,000 shares of £1 ea. & th, accordingly, Article 12 (A) of the Articles of Association be altered."   *Use block paragraph*

IV FIXED ASSETS

There has bn no ~~major~~ significant change to fixed stet assets during the yr.

V TRAINING

Management & staff training was given in finance, marketing, collective bargaining and other topics. This involved over 2,000 off-the-job hours.

AGREEMENT No. ————

Dated the ——— day of ——————————— 19 ——

Name of Purchaser ——————————————— (Mr./Mrs./Miss)

Address of Purchaser's Premises ———————————————

———————————————

the purchaser's "I," being the occupier of the premises specified, hereby agree to purchase from BARKER, JENKINS & CO. LTD

(a) (Hereinafter referred to as the "Sellers") the goods,

of appliances and/or apparatus (hereinafter) herein

"y y" referred to as "the apparatus") set out below on the terms & conditions described in the schedule overleaf.

Signature of Purchaser ——————————— Occupation ————

Witness ——————————— Address of witness ————

Signed on behalf of Sellers ———————————

List Price Total		Value Added Tax		Description of Apparatus – Maker, Model, and Serial number

Total Purchase Price	Initial Payment	Amount remaining	Interest on amount remaining	Total amount remaining

Type each line or sentence (A and B) *three* times, and, if time permits, complete your practice by typing each group once as it appears. Margins: Elite 22–82, Pica 12–72.

A. Review alphabet keys

1.   Much to the delight of the viewers a brilliant question completely baffled the expert quiz jury who quickly retired.

B. Improve fluency

2. Did you buy all the tea and pay the boy the sum you now owe?

3. The man saw the lad was not yet fit for the job you got him.

4. Few can now say why she and her son did not get off the bus.

Accuracy/Speed Practice	Five-minute timing	Not more than 3 errors
		words

AS.6   When you choose books to read, you should make a point of selecting 13
them as you would your friends. If you constantly read poorly written 27
books, this will have just the same effect on your character and manners 42
as if you mix always with the wrong kind of people. There is no need to 56
be afraid of books which are called great. Much of the best literature 70
is found to be of interest to young and old alike. Some of the famous 84
classics are tales which used to be told to children long ago, such as 98
stories about animals, and tales of goblins and elves and fairies which 112
were said to live in the woods and mountains. Some well-known books, 126
such as, for instance, 'Robinson Crusoe', were not really written for 140
children, but they still remain great favourites with them. 152

    Whatever may be one's taste, there are good books to be found which 165
can satisfy it. One most fascinating book is the 'Arabian Nights', that 180
carries the reader on a magic carpet to the mystic Orient. Some of the 194
great books take us into the world of mythology, to ancient Greece, where 208
Zeus, king of the gods, and Apollo, god of light and music, once dwelt. 223
Reading books of the life story of some great man or woman, or of a hero 237
who achieves something worth while in the face of extreme difficulty, of 251
the deeds of such people and of their human relationship, seems to bring 266
one on intimate terms with the great. 273

    In choosing the right books, it is a help, of course, to seek the 286
aid of some older person who knows what is good, although, in many cases, 301
we can judge for ourselves whether a book is bad or good. To decide if a 316
book is good or bad, you must have some standard to guide you, and the 330
best way to gain such a standard is first to read those books which have 344
proved themselves to be good.   (S.I. 1.27) 350

ink for ruling and a fine-nibbed pen (preferably not a ball-point pen). Insert B.

6
to
27
6. If any portion of a letter or MS is required to be inset, the no. of spaces on ~~the~~ right-hand side may be equal to th. on the left or the inset may end at the right margin. The number indented depends on the longest line of the inset portion.

9
H.
7. When a letter or MS requires a continuation sheet, you shd divide the matter at a suitable point, w'out, however, leaving too great a space at the foot of the

lh
1st page. (At least 2 lines of a para shd appear at the bottom of the first p. & at the top of a continuation sheet.) The

l.c.
usual heading for a continuation sheet of a letter is: Name of addressee, page no., date, but where a letter is addressed

u.c.
to "the manager", or or official of a firm, the name of the firm must appear in

u.c.
addition to "the manager".

When typing on the back of a page, e.g., page 2 on back of page 1, it is usual to reverse the margins. Margins of 12-94 Elite,

27
10-77 Pica, ~~on pages~~ would become 6-88 Elite, 5-72 Pica on the reverse side.

8
to
8. In hyphenated words no space shd be left before or after the hyphen. Do not separate numerical adjectives, whether in words or figures, fr the words to wch they refer, i.e., six metres, 6th May — both must be typed on the same line. (Typist—put this at end of No.5

27
to
(Words printed in italics shd be underlined.)

10. Enclosures must be indicated in letters & memos.

'B'
~~A~~ You shd also take a sheet of carbon paper w. you, altho this may be provided.

'A'
Headings may be underscored w. a single line, never w. a double or treble line.

* It is better to use an eraser rather than eradicator wh are not always satisfactory.

Footnotes are used:

(a) To identify a reference or person quoted in the body of a report.

(b) To give the source of a quotation cited in a report.

(c) For explanations that may help or interest a reader.

Each footnote is:

(d) Preceded by the reference mark which corresponds to the reference in the text.

(e) Typed in single-line spacing.

The reference mark in the text must be a superior character. In the footnote, it is typed either on the same line or as a superior character. In the text NO space is left between the reference mark and the previous character. In the footnote ONE SPACE is left between the reference mark and the first word. The position for the typing of footnotes is explained below.

The reference mark may be a number, asterisk, dagger or double dagger. Refer to page 19 for combination characters.

1. Type the following on A4 paper (210 × 297 mm) in double spacing, and keep your typed copy for future reference in Folder No. 2. Margins: Elite 20–85, Pica 10–75.

FOOTNOTES IN TYPESCRIPT

In ordinary typewritten work, the footnote is ALWAYS placed on the page on which the corresponding reference appears in the body and typed in <u>single</u> spacing. Care must be taken to leave enough space at the bottom for the footnote, and, if a continuation page is needed, a clear space of 25 mm must be left after the footnote at the bottom of the page. The footnote is separated from the main text by a horizontal line from margin to margin. The horizontal line is typed by underscore one single-line space after the last line of the text, and the footnote typed on the second single space below the horizontal line. If more than one footnote, turn up 2 single spaces between each.

2. Practise typing footnotes in typescript. Type the following on A5 (210 × 148 mm) paper in double spacing, with single spacing for footnotes. Keep your typed copy for future reference in Folder No. 2. Margins: Elite 20–85, Pica 10–75.

Whether you work in a large or small office, you are expected to turn out a day's work each working day.* The unit cost of typewritten work having risen sharply over the last few years, all typists must realize the necessity of increasing their production rate if they are to keep their jobs.†

_____

* In many firms, standards of measurement of typed work have been set up, and salaries are paid accordingly.

† To do this, analyse the whole typing job, and decide on the most time-saving way of doing it.

Type a copy of the following notes for duplicating, making all necessary corrections.

Examination Hints – spaced caps & w/s

2. Do not be satisfied w. slipshod work. Never overtype. See th you hv a clean pencil rubber & typewriting rubber, & erase all errors neatly.

h. If, after erasing the error, the letters on either side of the erasure appear faint, type lightly over these.

4. If you are not sure how to set out any piece of work typing, follow the setting of the test paper wh is usually a good guide as to what is wanted. [Follow carefully the method of paragraphing, i.e., a hanging paragraph may have be used bn used for insets. Be consistent in spacing, spelling, etc.

N.P.S/ no.5h

1. Always read carefully all instructions for ea. question before you start to type.

3. Before starting to type, read thru to gain an idea of the subject matter, & note any peculiarities of handwriting & special instructions. Be careful w spelling and punctuation. Use common sense both in deciphering MS & also in arranging matter.

H

7. Note any instructions given regarding headings. Usually words underlined shd be typed in closed caps, & words treble underlined in spaced caps. (Insert A)

double/

9. Always check thru yr work before removing it from the machine.

u.c/

12. Always be in the exam room in plenty of time to test yr m/c, &, if anything is wrong w.it, report it to the invigilator before the start of the exam.

u.c/

particularly w. words wh. can be spelt in two ways, such as "realise".

13. Take w. you to the exam..a pencil, ruler, pencil rubber & typewriter eraser,* also

3. Type the following exercise on A4 paper, leaving one inch (25 mm) clear at the top of the page. Use (a) margins of Elite 20–85, Pica 10–75; (b) double-line spacing—remember to type the footnotes in single spacing with double between footnotes; (c) indented paragraphs; (d) shoulder headings as in copy, i.e., not underscored. Centre main heading on typing line.

TELECOMMUNICATIONS

RADIO PAGING

This is a comparatively new service offered by the Post Office. It operates in certain areas & the pagers are used by a variety of people, directors, maintenance engineers, salesmen, etc. The P.O. will supply a pocket size paper which has its own pageing number, & pro-vided you are within a coverage area, [1] a tel. call from anywhere in the United Kingdom will start the pager.

KEYPHONE

On this tel. the rotary dail has been replaced by a separate key for each digit.

TAPE CALLMAKER

Frequently used tel. nos (up to a total of 400) are stored on a tape. Select the no., press a button, & the no. will be dialled auto-matically. [2]

CARD CALLMAKER

The tel. nos. are punched into cards. To dial a no., select the punched card with the no. you want, slot in into the callmaker which sits beside your tel. or telex — the no. will be dialled auto-matically. [2]

---

(1) It should be noted that a pager will not work if you are in a basement.
(2) With both these sistems the possibility of dialling a wrong digit is eliminated.

Further exercises on footnotes are given on pages 11, 28, and 50 of **Practical Typing Exercises, Book Two**.

Someone once said that your face is your fortune. It may not make you a fortune, but a well-cared-for face can be a great asset in every way. Cleanliness is the foundation of complexion care. Your skin, like a flower, grows and changes as time goes by. If you do not cleanse your skin daily, dead cells and oil accumulate, pores clog, and before long your skin ceases to breathe.

What kind of skin do you have? Dry skin tends to have fine lines, looks taut and may flake. Oily skin looks shiny with large pores and absorbs make-up. You may be lucky and have normal skin — soft and just moist enough to look dewy.

Choose a suitable freshener because this will make your skin feel delightful. It conditions, tightens pores and stimulates. It also ensures that no make-up or cleanser is left on the skin.

If you have an oily skin, do not use a moisturizer.

(35 wpm) Otherwise, look for a light cream that sinks into your face. Mist moisturizer is good because it works well on normal and most combination skins.

(40 wpm) No matter what type of skin you have, an eye cream is essential. Eyes are the focal point of the face and wrinkles start first around the eyes. Remember: cleanse, refresh, and moisturize one after the other every night and morning.

(50 wpm) If your skin is extremely oily, blemished or sensitive, you may have many problems. In severe cases see a specialist and follow his advice. A mild case of spots can be easily dealt with in an old-fashioned way. Boil some water and, with

(60 wpm) a large towel over your head, hold your face over the steaming water for five minutes. This treatment helps rid your skin of impurities by opening the pores and causing perspiration to flow.

Your face is the first thing at which people look. It

(70 wpm) will give away your age more than anything else; therefore, you must take care of it.

198

4. Type a copy of the following exercise on A4 paper, using margins of Elite 20–85, Pica 10–75. Use single spacing with double between lettered items. Type the heading and the first line at the left margin. The bracketed letters should be typed at the left margin and the paragraphs blocked as in copy. Keep your typed copy for future reference in folder No. 2.

TYPING MEASUREMENTS

In typing measurements, the following points should be noted.

(a) One space is left after the number(s) and before the unit of measurement. Example: 8½ (space) in; 148 (space) mm; 2.5 (space) cm.

(b) Never add an 's' to the symbol to form the plural — symbols are the same in the plural as they are in the singular, e.g., 20 metres — 20 m; 14 inches — 14 in.

(c) When the signs for feet and inches are used, no space is left between the figures and the sign, but one space is left after the sign, e.g., 2 ft 3 in = 2' (space) 3".

(d) Full stops are NEVER used in abbreviations of metric measurements, but they may or may not be used in ft (foot/feet), yd (yard/yards), etc. To be consistent it is suggested that you do not use the full stop after any abbreviated unit of measurement unless at the end of a sentence.

(e) The letter 'x' (lower case) is used for the word 'by'. Example: 210 mm x 297 mm (space before and after the 'x').

(f) At line ends NEVER separate the figure(s) from the symbol.

(g) Most symbols are small letters, but there are a few in upper case such as C and M which stand for Celsius and Mega. Certain keyboards (teleprinters for example) have upper case letters only, and when using such machines the unit should be typed in full, e.g., 15 MILLIMETRES.

(h) As it may cause confusion, the symbols l (lower case L) for litre(s) and t (lower case T) for tonne(s) should not be used — better to write the words in full. If, for some reason, the abbreviation for litre is essential, then insert it in ink and use a looped 'el', i.e., ℓ.

(i) ml for millilitre is not acceptable. Either type the word in full or insert the 'el' with a loop.

Miscellaneous items

Elision is the omission of a letter (usually a vowel) when pronouncing a word, e.g., wouldn't, can't, don't. This form of abbreviation must NOT be used in typescript unless you are quoting direct speech, i.e., using quotation marks.

The hyphen—used to replace the word 'to' in certain instances. Examples:

The firm's address was 19–23 North Street. He lived from 1901–1976. This date could also be typed 1901–76, but you must be careful if the dates spread over 2 centuries, e.g., 1707–1806 (NOT 1707–06).

Minus and plus signs—placed close to the figure to show a minus or plus quantity, e.g., -78, $+22$. However, when used to show subtraction or addition the dash (space either side) and the $+$ sign with a space on either side are used, e.g., $218 - 118 + 50 = 150$. The following is an example of the 2 uses of the minus sign:

$$20 - 10 = 10; 10 - 20 = -10.$$

Job 82

Type a fair copy of the following Will which has been drawn up for Mrs. Janet Hay Honeybourne, 17 Russell Square, London, WC1 2RT. Her executrix is Miss Andrea Ward, 19 Edgware Road, London, W2 3QT.

all caps → This is the last Will and Testament of me ----- of ----.

L. justly → First I direct the payment of all my debts funeral and testamentary expenses.

all caps → I appoint ----- of ----- to be my executrix.

all caps → I give devise and bequeath the following legacies

To my brother William Geo. Howell the sum of £5,000. As to all the rest residue and remainder of my real and personal estate or any other estate at the time of my decease [and bequeath I GIVE] over wh. I have disposing power the same to the said Andrea Ward of ----- as her absolute property.

all caps → I hereby revoke all former Wills + other testamentary writing and declare this to be my last Will and Testament.

all caps → In Witness whereof I have hereunto set my [thereto made by me] hand this ----- day of ----- one thousand nine hundred and ----.

caps → Signed by her last Will as the testatrix in the presence of us present together who in her presence + in the presence of ea. other have subscribed our names as Witnesses

Job 83

Write the following letter and encl. a copy of the above To: Mrs. Honeybourne 15 York Rd, Leeds 9 [address as above]

Dear Mrs Honeybourne, I enclose a fair copy of the Will you suggested when you called here last week. If you agree with the contents, perhaps you wd. be good enough to call, as arranged, at this office on Monday next at 2 p.m.

Type the following exercise on A4 paper in double-line spacing, making corrections indicated. Use suitable margins. Leave 6 clear spaces at top of page.

Erasing – *centred in caps*

uc   The good typist does a minimum of erasing. it

, however,   cannot be assumed th any person can type for a whole day w'out making an error now + ~~then~~

N.P.   then. [Erasures must be made to correct these

lc   occasional errors : But the erasures * must be well done so th they cannot be detected in casual reading. move the carriage to / left or to the right so th the particles fr the rubber will

LO uc   not fall into the type basket∧ insert a card behind the original copy + in front of the carbon sheet .)

Run on /   Erase / error on the original, blow the particles off the sheet + away fr the m/c . Place

;h   the card behind the carbon∧ erase the error

∽   on the ~~carbon~~ copy . ~~t~~ Then remove the card ‡ + return the carriage to the point on the paper at wh the error was made. Type the correction.

∽P   If / typed letters on either side of / correction are faint, strike over them lightly. [note : altho' there are a no. of eradicating products on / market to correct an error instead of using an eraser, these methods are not always satisfactory, + you will be well advised to use an eraser

(marginal note, circled:) Continue in this way until all copies hv bn erased.

---

*   Always keep a ~~gt~~ gd rubber within easy reach. If necessary tie it to yr typewriter w. a piece of string.

‡   If y use ordinary paper, it is necessary to put a piece of paper btwn the shiny side of ea carbon sheet + / carbon copy. Remember to

the ∧   remove the paper before typing∧ correction.

At the top, usually printed, appear the words 'THIS IS THE LAST WILL AND TESTAMENT', starting at 15. A Will is usually typed on double paper, both sides of each sheet being used, and in double-line spacing.

Certain words must be capitalised in the text of a Will, such as the following:

NAME (of testator); AND; I APPOINT; I BEQUEATH; I DEVISE; I DEVISE AND BEQUEATH; I GIVE AND DEVISE; I GIVE AND BEQUEATH; I DIRECT; I GIVE; I REVOKE; IN TRUST; IN WITNESS WHEREOF; SIGNED.

Wills are folded and endorsed in the same way as Agreements.

4. Practise typing, folding and endorsing a Will. Type the following on A4 paper, in double spacing; then fold and endorse.

THIS IS THE LAST WILL AND TESTAMENT

— of me —

ELSIE CARTER of 25 Old Road Solihull in the County of Warwick the Wife of JAMES CARTER. --

1.   FIRST I DIRECT the payment of all my just debts funeral and testamentary expenses by my Executors hereinafter named.

2.   I APPOINT my Husband the said James Carter and my Son JOHN CARTER to be the JOINT EXECUTORS AND TRUSTEES of this my Will. --

3.   I GIVE all my clothing and apparel my personal jewellery trinkets and articles of personal use or adornment UNTO my Daughter JANE CARTER absolutely. ----------------------------

4.   I GIVE AND BEQUEATH UNTO my Brother TOM DAVIES the sum of ONE HUNDRED POUNDS if he shall be living at my death. --------

5.   I GIVE DEVISE AND BEQUEATH all my real and personal estate whatsoever and wheresoever not hereby or by any Codicil hereto otherwise specifically disposed of and of which I can dispose by Will in any manner I think proper (hereinafter called 'my Residuary Estate') UNTO my Husband the said James Carter for his own use and benefit absolutely. ------------------

6.   LASTLY I hereby REVOKE all former Wills. --------------------
IN WITNESS whereof I have to this my Will set my hand this Thirty-first day of December One thousand nine hundred and seventy-seven. --

ELSIE CARTER

SIGNED by the said ELSIE CARTER as and for her last Will in the presence of us both being present at the same time who in her presence at her request and in the presence of each other have hereunto subscribed our names as witnesses. --------------------

B. Johnson,   I. Wilkins,
The Manor House,   12 Falstaff Road,
Solihull, Warwickshire.   Shirley, Solihull,
Company Director.   Secretary.

Type the following on A4 paper in single-line spacing with double spacing
between paragraphs. Use shoulder headings for paragraph headings. Numbers
above one to be in figures; ordinal numbers in words. Leave six clear spaces at
top of paper.

TIPS FOR TYPISTS

Side margins. When using A4 paper, see th the left/hand margin
is not less than 25 mm, i.e., 10 Pica, 12 elite. With A5 paper the left
margin should (be less than 12mm (not) (5 Pica, 6 Elite). No matter
what size of paper is used, the rt-hand margin must NEVER be
wider than the left-hand margin.

Top margin. When using headed paper, start 3 single-line
spaces after last line of heading. W. plain paper, leave 6
clear spaces at top, i.e., turn up 7 single-line spaces.
Bottom margin. Leave 25 mm or 6 clear single-line spaces.

Before inserting paper, it is a gd plan to put a light
pencil mark 25 mm from/ btm edge of the paper as a
warning signal. Later, of course, this is erased.

Spacing. Use single-line spacing for business letters & dble
spacing of legal documents, short specifications + literary
work. Draft copies are usually typed in dble spacing, or,
treble spacing may be used. (If extensive revision is necessary)

Page nos. In typing from MS, the first page is not numbered.
On or ff. the no. is usually placed on the fourth single-
line space from the top in/ centre of the typing line,
with a dash at either side, e.g., - 2 -

* This is important when/ matter is cont'd on a subsequent
page.

‡ Many typists use a backing sheet wh is a little
wider than the typing paper.

‡ If the letter is short, you may use double spacing
+ a shorter writing line. When using single or
dble/ line spacing, leave one clear space only between
paragraphs.

On the backing sheet make a mark 25 mm
from/ bottom edge of the typing paper.

2. Type the following Agreement in double spacing, copying and noting the display.

A N   A G R E E M E N T   made this First day of December One thousand nine hundred and seventy-seven   B E T W E E N   JOHN BERK of 22 Water Street in the City of Liverpool (hereinafter called "the Licensor") of the one part and CHARLES PAGE of 37 Bogmoor Road, in the City of Glasgow (hereinafter called "the Licensee"), of the other part.
WHEREBY IT IS AGREED as follows:

1.   IN CONSIDERATION of the royalties hereinafter stipulated the Licensor grants to the Licensee a sole licence to manufacture the washing machine in accordance with the patent of invention No. AB 824, 568 filed on the Tenth day of May One thousand nine hundred and sixty in the United Kingdom and to sell the said machine within the United Kingdom during the continuance of the aforesaid Patent.

2.   THE LICENSEE agrees to pay to the Licensor an annual royalty of Two per cent on the nett selling price of the machines made by the Licensee and invoiced by him to his customers, the said royalty to be payable on the Fourteenth day of July and the Fourteenth day of January of each year for the entire duration of the said Patent.

3.   THE LICENSEE shall keep proper books of account in regard to the said washing machines manufactured and sold by him under the aforesaid Patent, which books shall at all reasonable times be made accessible to the Licensor for inspection by him or his agent.

AS WITNESS the hands of the parties the day and year first before written.

SIGNED by the said JOHN BERK   )
in the presence of:—   )   JOHN BERK
(Name of witness)   )
(Address)   )
(Occupation)   )

SIGNED by the said CHARLES PAGE)
in the presence of:—   )   CHARLES PAGE
(Name of witness)   )
(Address)   )
(Occupation)   )

3. Practise folding and endorsing a legal document. Study instructions for folding and endorsing legal documents on page 219. Then fold your typed copy of the above Agreement in the correct manner and type the endorsement.

Proof-reading

Proof-reading is not easy. Our eyes have a way of passing over the line of typescript and seeing what the mind thinks is there, and not what the fingers actually put there. Moreover, the time devoted to proof-reading is non-productive, and the typist feels it necessary to get on with another job. Yet proof-reading is the sole responsibility of the typist.

There are several common types of errors for which you should look:

1. Spelling, punctuation, grammar.

2. Word substitution—*from* for *form*, *is* for *it*, *as* for *is*, *in* for *on*, *you* for *your*.

3. Transposition of letters—r and t, v and b, i and e.

4. Substitutions that are difficult to detect: n for m, d for s, u for y, or vice versa.

5. Omission of a line or lines which does not outwardly affect the meaning. Check finished work with original.

6. Dates, proper names and place names, and figures.

Composing at machine

Type the following on A5 paper in double spacing, and insert the correct vowel wherever there is a hyphen. *Do not write on this book.*

```
        W- are gl-d t- kn-w th-t it w-ll b- p-ss-bl- f-r you t-
sp--k -t a m--t-ng -f --r Cl-b -n Fr-d-y, 21st N-v-mb-r.   Th-
m--t-ng st-rts -t 6.30 p.m.
        W- -r- s--k-ng th- s-rv-c-s -f a sp--dy -nd -cc-r-t-
typ-st f-r --r s-n--r -ng-n--r.   S-m- pr-v---s -xp-r--nc-
-n th-s typ- -f w-rk -s -ss-nt--l.
```

Review Quiz No. 1

To speed up your production typing, you must be able to apply quickly important details such as spacing after punctuation, correct use of apostrophe, points of typewriting theory, and so on. This is the first of a number of Review Quizzes which you should complete by typing the following in double spacing, and supplying the missing word or words needed to give the correct answer. Do not write on your textbook.

1. There are . . . single-line spaces on A5 landscape paper and . . . single-line spaces on A5 portrait paper.
2. There are . . . Pica characters and . . . Elite characters to an inch (25 mm).
3. Except in display and tabulation, the left margin on A4 and A5 landscape paper must never be less than . . . . . . and the right margin never less than . . . . . .
4. In no case must the right margin be more than the . . . . . .
5. On A5 portrait paper the left margin must not be less than . . . . . .
6. Use the . . . . . . to type the Roman numeral one.
7. The top and bottom margins should not be less than . . . . . .
8. To type double lines underneath totals use the . . .
9. An inferior character is typed . . . the normal typing line.
10. The combination character for a double dagger is . . .
11. 'Stet' means . . . .
12. Always . . . your typescript . . . removing it from the machine.
13. Type a shoulder heading at the . . . margin usually in . . .
14. Footnotes are typed on the . . . page on which the reference occurs.
15. To show an ellipsis in the middle of a sentence type . . . . . . dots.
16. In an indented paragraph there must be . . . clear spaces before starting the indent.
17. In hanging paragraphs the second and subsequent lines of a paragraph are typed . . . spaces to the . . . of the first line.
18. When blocked paragraphs are used with double spacing, turn up . . . extra line-space between paragraphs, i.e., turn up . . . single-line spaces.

Turn to page 211 and check your answers. Score one point for each correct entry. Total score: 34.

In addition to the main rules on the previous page, you should note the following:

Certain words, such as the following, are typed in spaced or unspaced capitals, to make them more prominent:

SPACED CAPITALS: A N   A G R E E M E N T
                        B E T W E E N
                        A L L   T H A T
                        A L L   T H O S E
                        A N D   W H E R E A S
                        T O   H O L D

CLOSED CAPITALS: TOGETHER
                        PROVIDED
                        PROVIDED ALSO
                        IN WITNESS

Also Names of Parties the <u>first time these appear</u>, ~~for~~ the first word or words of each recital, and ~~for~~ the words: SIGNED SEALED AND DELIVERED, also money items, such as THREE HUNDRED POUNDS.

There are 2 clauses which appear at the end of all legal documents, viz.

<u>Testimonial Clause</u> — This appears at end of wording of document and reads: "IN WITNESS whereof the said parties to these presents have hereunto set their hands and seals the day and year first above written." (Note: In the Draft this clause may be abbreviated to: "In witness, etc.").

<u>Attestation Clause</u> — This starts in the margin at 5, and is bracketed at 40 as follows:

SIGNED SEALED AND DELIVERED   )
by the within named (Name in   )
capitals)   )
in the presence of (Name in   )
capitals)   )

(Witness's signature and address and occupation)

NOTE: The wording of the Attestation Clause may vary slightly in the different documents, but the typist in a solicitor's office always has a copy to guide her.

Insert at 'A' [The first word of each paragraph commences at the 20th degree of the scale (or 51 mm from left edge). If numbered, type the figure at the 15th degree (or 38 mm from left edge).

Type the following in single spacing on A4 paper, unless otherwise instructed.
Paragraphs enumerated (a), (b), etc. should be hanging paragraphs where
applicable.

(from their eighteenth birthday)

Family Law Reform Act 1969   ← — Caps + underscore
People's Act 1969

For hundreds of yrs a person has not become an adult
until his/her twenty-first birthday. On 1st Jan, '70, above Acts
came into force + all young people are to be treated as
responsible adult citizens. This means th/ following points are
/ right of all persons eighteen + over, instead of 21 + over as
previously.

(Typist: Double spacing between numbered item)

I.   MARRIAGE
    (a) W permission fr yr parents or guardian y can marry
          after the age of 16.
    (b) At 18 yrs y are free to marry w'out anyone's consent.
    (c) Power to make you a ward of court has bn abolished
        f persons over 18.

II.   VOTING   *(if you wish to do so,)*
    As fr yr 18th birthday y can vote at Parliamentary + Local
    Elections.

III.   PUBLIC OFFICES
    Until y are twenty-one y cannot stand as a candidate
    for
    (a) Parliament
    (b) Local Elections

(Please display lettered items as above)

IV.   OWNERSHIP OF PROPERTY + LAND   As fr yr 18th birthday y
    can (a) buy yr own house, property, and land;
    (b) take out a mortgage on a hse.

V.   MISCELLANEOUS
    Fr yr 18th birthday you can (a) hv yr own passport
    w'out consent of yr parents or guardian; (b) make a
    valid will; (c) Inherit money or property; (d) buy
    gds on H.P. or credit sale *

VI   There has bn a change in/ description of persons
    not of full age. Under Para. 14 of / Family Law
    Reform Act of '69 a person who is not 18 yrs of
    age is now described as a minor instead of
    an Infant.

---

* Finance companies will no longer hv to insist on an
older person giving a guarantee for th payments
wl be kept up.

1. Type a copy of the following notes in single spacing, with double spacing between paragraphs. Use A4 paper. Keep your typed copy for future reference in Folder No. 2. Make all necessary corrections.

<u>LEGAL WORK</u>

Although you ~~will~~ may not be required to type legal documents unless you are employed in a solicitor's office, you should have a general idea of the way in which the most common of such documents are typed and endorsed. A legal document is usually typed 3 times. The first typing is a rough copy, known as a /draft/ The second typing is a /Fair Copy/ which is a neatly typed copy of the rough corrected draft for submitting to a solicitor or client. The final copy is the 'Engrossment' for signature by all the parties concerned.

There may be slight variations in form in ~~various~~ different legal offices, but there are certain basic rules which apply to the typing of all legal documents, the most important of which are as follows:

1. A black ribbon is generally used.

2. A wide left-hand margin is required. (Insert 'A')

3. The Draft is typed in treble spacing to allow room for corrections. This copy may contain abbreviations, & numbers, sums of money and dates may be in figures instead of in words.

4. Punctuation marks are usually omitted to avoid possibility of a double or ambiguous meaning being conveyed, which might lead to lawsuits.

5. All pages are numbered at bottom in centre.

6. If the matter contains numbered clauses, a full stop appears at the end of each clause.

7. In certain documents, such as a Will or Engrossment of a deed, a red ink line is ruled to fill in any long blank spaces at end of clause, or sometimes a series of unspaced hyphens may be used (----------).

8. The Fair Copy is typed in double spacing and must not contain any abbreviations, alterations or erasures. Figures, money items and dates must be in words.

9. The Engrossment is typed in double spacing and on both sides of the paper. Here also no abbreviations, alterations or erasures are allowed. No words may be divided at line-ends. All figures, money items & dates must be typed in words (House nos. may be in figures).

10. The last page is left blank, as this will bear the Endorsement when the document is folded.

Continued on next page

Type the following on A4 paper (210 × 297 mm) in double spacing. Leave 6 clear line-spaces at top of paper. Typing line 60 spaces.

How to start yr Car Engine   ← caps + underscore

Indent hand/ → First ensure th the/brake is applied +th the gear lever is in/ neutral position. Insert the ignition switch key into/ ignition switch.

1. Cold Engine

    1.1 Depress accelerator pedal + then return it to normal posn.

    1.2 Pull the choke control knob fully out.

    1.3 Depress clutch pedal + crank/ engine by turning/ ignition key fully clockwise.

        1.3.1 Keep clutch pedal depressed + the ignition key held ... until/ engine starts.

        1.3.2 If the engine does not start ... return/ key to the 'off' posn, pause + repeat.

2 Warm Engine

    2.1 Crank the engine by turning/ ignition key fully clockwise; keeping/ accelerator pedal in/ halfway posn ....

    2.2 Release the ignition key + the accelerator pedal immediately / engine starts.

Type the following on A5 (210 × 148 mm) paper in double spacing, unless otherwise instructed. Leave 6 clear spaces at top. Centre each line horizontally.

PRACTICAL ACCOUNTING

A teaching portfolio of Notes, Resource Material and Solutions

by

D. C. Austen

This is a valuable aid to teachers, providing an abundance of Resource Material, including Special Stationery which may be photocopied

(Leave ½" (13mm) clear vertically)

Publishers: McGraw-Hill Book Company (UK) Limited

Type the alphabetic review *once* for practice, *once* for speed, and finally *once* for accuracy. Margins: Elite 22–82, Pica 12–72.

Review alphabet keys

The secretary realized that the question as to the kind of performance to be given next June is awaiting a decision.

Accuracy/Speed practice   Five-minute timing   Not more than 3 errors

		words
AS.31	The general tone of business during the year has, on the whole,	13
	been satisfactory. There are, however, straws in the wind to which it	26
	is desirable to draw attention. During the war and post-war years,	39
	failures in business were infrequent. Many failures are largely due	53
	either to fraud or folly, or a combination of both. In the period	67
	in question there was no particular object in indulging in the former,	81
	and no great opportunity of displaying the latter. Markets would	94
	absorb anything that was offered, even ill-made rubbish, and the art	107
	of salesmanship was superfluous. This era shows signs of drawing to	121
	a close, and the less intelligent and less efficient will find it	134
	harder to survive.	138

In some trades capacity to produce is still the only limiting factor to the volume of sales, but this is by no means universal. In many others there is evidence of increasing stocks and a sense of selectivity, both as regards price and quality, which did not exist before. There is no longer the same insatiable appetite.

So long as this tendency does not go too far it is no bad thing. It is salutary that the value of salesmanship should be realized, and that good workmanship and efficient and economic production should come into its own. There is no doubt, however, that in a world where appreciation of the realities of the situation is conspicuously absent, there will inevitably be casualties.

The export position is not unsatisfactory and it is time that some tribute was paid to those who are working continuously to maintain existing and to expand new markets. Appreciation of their efforts will not make them lie down on their jobs: their portion hitherto has more than frequently consisted of reproof for unattained ideals.

Those with the maximum amount of information on the subject profess to see the elimination of the overall adverse balance by the end of the year. It is to be hoped that they are correct. While it would be unwise to question these conclusions, it would be equally unwise to be complacent.   (S.I. 1.50)

words
150
164
177
190
201
214
228
241
255
269
276
290
303
316
330
343
355
369
384
397
400

Skill building

Type each exercise (A, B, and C) *once* for practice, *once* for speed, and finally *once* for accuracy. Margins: Elite 22–82, Pica 12–72.

A. Review alphabet keys

1.   A reasonably-sized bowl of bread and milk is frequently given to children just to relieve their exceptional tension.

B. Review special characters

2. "2" 3/3 4 @ 4/5 £5/£6 7 & 8 '8' (192) (5-4) 8' 2" 6/7 22-15.

3. Credit W. Clare & Co. with 3 lengths of Oak 6' 6" x 3' x ½", @ £3.50 each; on Invoice No. R/79/64 they were charged £5.75 instead of £2.25. Also 12 tins Paint @ 45p each — not sent.

C. Build accuracy on shift key drill

4. Dow-Gow & Co. Ltd., R. & T. Sayers, Ball (U.K.I.) Ltd., Sir,

5. In the High Street at Stratford-on-Avon you will see the Old Tudor House Restaurant Limited owned by Kunzle Catering Ltd.

6. Ask the National Farmers Union Mutual Insurance Society Ltd.

Accuracy/Speed Practice

You should now aim at increasing your speed by 5 words a minute, i.e., if you have been typing at 35 words a minute, your aim is now 40 words a minute.

One-minute timing	Not more than 1 error
	words

AS.7   It has often been said that horses sleep while standing up, which is 14
quite true. Some bigger creatures do the same, and so do birds, for that 28
matter. A horse does not lie down to rest on account of the fact that its 43
heavy body, lying on the hard ground, will make the bones of its ribs sore. 58
Thus Nature has arranged that the joints of its legs should lock, so as to 73
support the body when it is relaxed.   (S.I. 1.19) 80

AS.8   We are most anxious to keep in touch with all our friends so that we 14
can help them by supplying goods to them at a figure well within their 28
power to pay. With this aim in view, we are sending you a list of questions 43
which we shall be glad if you will answer to the best of your knowledge. 57
We are sure you will have no objection to acceding to this request, and you 72
will certainly find it to your advantage.   (S.I. 1.24) 80

Type the following extract of Bill of Quantities in correct form on A4 paper.
Rule necessary columns.

Page 1

BILL OF QUANTITIES (spaced caps)
for the
ERECTION OF A 2-STOREY HOUSE AT
THE OAKS
WOOD LANE, STREETLY, STAFFS
for
MR. J. L. WILKINS

Walter Archer, ARIBA,
Chartered Architect +
Quantity Surveyor,
High Street
SUTTON COLDFIELD

May, 19..

P R E L I M I N A R I E S

Item

CONTRACT CONDITIONS

A   The prices in this Bill of Quantities wl be deemed
to cover the cost of complying w. the clauses   v.c.
contained therein as set forth below:

B   Clause 1. Interpretation.
C   Clause 2. Specification + dimensions.   v.c.
D   Clause 3. Additional or Extra Works.
                        Carried to collection   £

Page 2
Item

SUBSTRUCTURE

EXCAVATING AS GP 103
    Starting fr. natural ground level
A   Surface to reduce levels — — — — — —   860   cu m
    Starting fr. reduced level
B   Surface average 100 mm deep to reduce)
        levels   )   10   sq m
C   Rubble-filled cellar not exceeding 1.5 m)
        deep   )   15   cu m
D   Trench not exceeding 1.50 m deep for   )
        foundation   )   90   cu m
E   Pit not exceeding one cubic metre for)
        ditto   (In no.2)   )   1   cu m
    Starting fr. abt 600 mm below
        natural ground level
F   Rubble-filled cellar not exceeding 1.50 m)
        deep   )   75   cu m
G   Trench not exceeding 1.50 m deep for   )
        foundation   )   100   cu m
H   Pit not exceeding 1.50 m deep for ditto   10   cu m
J   Trench over 1.50 m but not exceeding   )
        3.00 m deep for ditto   )   1   cu m
K   Pit not exceeding one cubic metre   )
        for ditto   (In no.1)   )   1   cu m
    Starting fr abt 1.70 m below natural
        level
L   Trench not exceeding 1.50 m deep for   )
        foundation   )   1   cu m
                    Carried to collection   £

Vertical centring

To centre material vertically:

1. Count the number of lines (including blank ones) that the material will occupy.

2. Subtract that figure from the number of line-spaces on your paper. On A4 paper there are approximately 70 single spaces. On A5 portrait paper (148 × 210 mm) there are 50 single spaces, and on A5 landscape paper (210 × 148 mm) there are 35 single spaces.

3. After subtracting, divide the remainder by 2 (ignoring any fraction) to determine on what line to begin typing. For example, to centre 8 lines of double-spaced copy on A5 portrait paper (148 × 210 mm) (a) You need 15 lines, i.e., 8 typed, 7 blank; (b) 50 − 15 = 35 lines left over; and (c) 35 ÷ 2 = 17 (ignore ½). Start to type the matter on the next line (18).

1. Practise display. Read the above explanation; then type the following announcement on A5 portrait paper (148 × 210 mm) in double spacing, taking steps 1, 2, and 3 above.

```
                    NEW EDITIONS
              To be Released 10th October
              Western European History
              Eastern European History
                   Nuclear Physics
                 Management Control
```

Preparing a 'layout' of a notice

Before typing an unarranged notice, prepare a 'layout', i.e., a rough plan in pencil, showing the best arrangement of the matter and the number of lines required. Keep the 'layout' before you as you type the notice.

As a general rule, the following details each occupy one line, and one space at least is left between each. These details need not be in the same order as that given. 1. Name of advertiser. 2. Nature of notice. 3. Place or address. 4. Any other details (in order of importance). Each line is centred horizontally, and the whole notice vertically. No punctuation is inserted at the end of lines unless the last word is abbreviated when a full stop is inserted. If open punctuation is used then there will be no full stops after abbreviations.

2. Prepare a 'layout' for the following notices and then type them on A5 landscape paper (210 × 148 mm).

(a) W. J. Abbey & Co., Caravan Specialists, Delamere, Northwich. Care-free Holidays for years to come. A fine selection of both new and used caravans. Cash or Hire Purchase terms. Open daily for inspection from 8 a.m. to 7 p.m.

(b) J. H. BROADHOUSE & CO. LTD. 21 Scotland Road, Carlisle. CA2 3PU. STAFF VACANCIES. Sec./S'hand-Typist. Asst. Cashier (Grade B). Sales Clerk (Grade C). Progress Clerk (Grade B). Apply in writing, stating qualifications, to: Personnel Officer.

Further exercises on display are given on pages 1–3 of **Practical Typing Exercises, Book One**.

Job 80　　　　　　　　　　　　　　　Production Target—*20 minutes*

Type an original and one copy of the following portion of Specification in correct form on A4 paper, using a continuation sheet if necessary. Fold the Specification and endorse in the correct position. All items underscored to be in closed capitals unless otherwise instructed.

SPECIFICATION of works to be done & materials to be provided in the erection of a house in Hardwick Rd., Streetly, for Mr. Walter Carroll.

William Dixon, ARIBA,
Architect & Surveyor,
128 Parade,
Sutton Coldfield,
West Midlands

May 1978

PRELIMINARIES

SITE　　　The site is situated adjoining No. 45 Hardwick Road, Streetly, & may be inspected at any time.

SCOPE OF CONTRACT　　　The work included in the contract comprises the erection & completion of a house & garage complete w. all drainage.

CONTRACTOR　　　The contractor must provide all necessary plant, scaffolding, ladders, etc., required for the proper execution of the work for the use of workmen & sub-contractors, & for maintaining same during the progress of the works, & for removing when no longer required.

NOTICES & FEES　　　The contractor is to allow for giving all requisite notices to the local authority, obtaining permission & paying all fees if required.

WATER　　　The contractor shall provide water for the use of the works.

ATTEND　　　Each trade is to attend upon all others & perform all jobbing work throughout.

End of preliminaries

EXCAVATOR AND CONCRETOR

EXCAVATE　　　Excavate for all foundations to raft, walls, piers & for drains as shown on plans.

SAND　　　The sand to be clean, sharp, pit or fresh water river sand & to be of quality & type approved by architect.

FILLING　　　Fill in to foundations & trenches & well ram as the work proceeds.

CEMENT　　　The cement to be 'Super' Cement.

AGGREGATE　　　The aggregate is to be composed of approved clean hard stone, all broken to the gauges described.

FOUNDATIONS　　　The cement concrete raft foundations to comprise . . .

Matter can be effectively and artistically displayed if extra prominence is given to important lines by the judicial use of (a) Spaced capitals (one space between each letter and three spaces between each word); (b) Closed capitals (one space between each word); (c) Underscore for certain words or lines; (d) Initial capitals and small letters with or without underscore.

NOTE: Take care not to overdo any one of these methods; otherwise no line will stand out more prominently than others, thus detracting from the general appearance.

3. Practise effective display. Read the above explanation, and then type the following advertisement on A5 portrait paper (148 × 210 mm) using one or more of the above methods.

```
Carpet Mart Ltd., Camden High Street, London.  Special Offer
of Fitted Carpets.  Tomorrow at 9 a.m.  Sale of A.1 Quality
Axminster at less than half price.  Free fitting and free underlay.
Large selection available.  An opportunity not to be missed.
```

Programmes

Programmes can be displayed in various ways. The specimen below is a simple form of a concert programme. Note that the items at the left-hand margin in this particular form start flush at the margin. The items on the right-hand side end flush with the right-hand margin. To ensure that this is the case, bring carriage to one space beyond the right-hand margin, and back-space the number of letters and spaces in the item. Start at point reached. The items in the middle are centred.

4. Practise typing programme. Read the above explanation; then type the specimen programme below on A5 landscape paper (210 × 148 mm), centring it vertically and following the display precisely. Double spacing between each item. Margins: 12 spaces on each side.

```
                    P R O G R A M M E

Overture        Orpheus in the Underworld        Offenbach
                    THE ORCHESTRA

Song               The Magic Flute                 Mozart
                   NORMAN ALLIN

Pianoforte        Polonaise in A Flat              Chopin
                      SOLOMON

Violin           Dance of the Goblins             Bozzini
                  YEHUDI MENUHIN

Song             May Angels Guard Thee             Verdi
                   ROSA PONSELLE

Selection            Lilac Time                   Schubert
                   THE ORCHESTRA
```

Item	CONCRETE WORK (contd)		£
	mild steel bar as in Appendix B; cutting, bending & securing w. tying-wire, distance-blocks & ordinary spacers. [SPACERS]		
A	12mm diameter bar in lintel.	24	kg
B	10 mm ditto in ditto	250	kg
C	10 mm diameter links, stirrup, binder) or special spacer.	350	kg
D	8mm diameter ditto	297	kg
	Standard grade steel deformed bar as Appendix B; cutting, bending [BENDING] & securing w. tying-wire, distance-blocks & ordinary spacers.		
E	25mm diameter bar in lintel.	32	kg
F	20 mm Ditto in ditto	82	kg
G	16 mm Ditto in ditto	305	kg
H	12 mm Ditto in suspended floor.	42	kg
J	12 mm Ditto in lintel on staircase	444	kg
K	10mm Ditto in ditto	289	kg
of	Welded steel wire fabric as Appendix B; cutting, bending & securing w. tying-wire & distance-blocks.		
L	100mm × 100 mm mesh fabric weighing 0.76 kg per sq. metre w. 200 mm side & end laps; wrapping around horizontal steel beams.)	10	sq. m
M	Horizontal soffit of suspended floor or landing.)	19	sq. m
N	Sloping soffit of staircase	15	sq. m
P	Side or soffit of horizontal beam-casing or lintel.)	255	sq. m
Q	caps — Carried to summary		£

31

Further exercise on typing a Bill of Quantity is given on page 61 of **Practical Typing Exercises, Book Two**.

Programmes are frequently printed in the form of a folded leaflet, in which case the name, place, and date, etc., are printed on the front page (right-hand side, i.e., with fold to the left), and the items are displayed on the reverse side of the paper as shown below. The word 'PROGRAMME' (unless printed on the front page) will be centred across the two middle pages. Sufficient space must be left between the left-hand and right-hand sides to allow for the fold, as well as for a few clear spaces on either side of the fold. Before you start to type the Programme, mark in pencil the centre of the paper, so that, when the paper is folded, the fold will come in the exact centre.

FRONT SIDE OF PAPER (UNFOLDED)
    Front page—right-hand side   Back page—left-hand side

                             Fold

Back page Left-hand	Front page Right-hand

It is advisable to mark these two pages on your paper before inserting it.

REVERSE SIDE OF PAPER (UNFOLDED)
    Page 2—left-hand side of fold   Page 3—right-hand side of fold

Page 2 Left-hand	Page 3 Right-hand

5. Practise typing folded Programme. Read the above explanation; then type the following Programme on A4 paper (folded down centre); follow the layout. Each line is centred horizontally and the whole vertically.

Front page

Y O U T H   C O N C E R T

by the

CITY OF BIRMINGHAM SYMPHONY ORCHESTRA
(Leader: MEYER STOLOW)

at the

TOWN HALL, BIRMINGHAM

on

FRIDAY, 10TH NOVEMBER, 19..

at 7.15 p.m.

Conductor: ERIC ROBERTS

3. Practise typing Bill of Quantities. Type a copy of the following extract of a Bill of Quantities on A4 paper, follow the layout and the rules given on page 213. Please use hanging paragraphs as in copy.

Item	CONCRETE WORK (centre in spaced caps)			£
	IN-SITU PLAIN CONCRETE WORK			
A	1:2:4 Medium Gravel-concrete 50 mm × 55 mm kerb; tamping surface to form key for trowelled bed.)	147	m	
B	Wrought formwork; 50 mm side of kerb.)	147	m	
	IN-SITU CONSULTANT—DESIGNED REINFORCED CONCRETE WORK			
l.c	1:2:4 Medium Gravel-concrete			
C	Casing over 0.10 m sectional area to horizontal steel beam; packing around steel fabric wrapping.)	1	cu m	
D	Horizontal lintel over 0.05 m but not exceeding 0.10 m sectional area.)	3	cu m	
E	Ditto not exceeding 0.05 m sectional area.)	13	cu m	
F	Step and staircase	3	cu m	
G	100 mm Bed; trowelling surface; laying on cork insulation of suspended floor. (Insulation and suspended floor measured separately))	5	sq m	
H	130 mm horizontal suspended landing; tamping surface to form key for screeded bed.)	20	sq m	
J	150 mm horizontal suspended floor; trowelling surface.)	10	sq m	
K	150 mm horizontal suspended landing; tamping surface to form key for screeded bed.)	2	sq m	
L	210 mm Ditto; ditto	3	sq m	
M	Carried to collection			£

30

Before proceeding with pages 2 and 3 below, note the following:

1. Calculate the number of vertical lines required, allowing for the spacing to be left between items. (In specimen below, we suggest leaving two clear spaces.)

2. The margins at the extreme left of page 2 and the extreme right of page 3 should be equal, and the number of spaces before and after the fold should be equal. The left and right margins should be a minimum of 13 mm and a maximum of 25 mm. The space on either side of the fold should be a minimum of 7 mm and a maximum of 13 mm.

3. If the carriage of your typewriter is long enough,

then put the paper in lengthwise, and in typing the table below, the margin and tab stops would be set at the points indicated. However, if you have a short carriage, then each page will have to be typed separately, and in that case your left margin will be 12(10) and the right margin 63(55) for the first page, and 7(4), 58(49) for the second page.

4. With a short carriage you will have to type the heading PROGRAMME so that it runs across the two pages without a break, half on page 2 ending close to the right-hand edge of that page. The other half is typed on page 3, starting close to the left edge of the paper. Before you start to type page 3, make a light pencil mark to show the exact point at which the heading is to be continued.

Fold 70(59)

(Page 2)   (Page 3)

P R O G R A M M E

12(10)   63(55)   77(63)   128(108)

1. Bohemian Festival   6. Marching Song   Holst
     Picturesque Scenes   Massenet   ORCHESTRA
     ORCHESTRA

2. My Name is Mimi   7. None Shall Sleep
     La Bohème   Puccini   Turandot   Puccini
     MARION SMYTHE-WILKES   CHARLES WEST
     Soprano   Tenor
                                                   RICHARD GREY
3. Introduction and Rondo   Baritone
     To the Spring   Grieg   8. Spring Song   Mendelssohn
     ALFRED SADLER   ALFRED WOODS
     Piano Solo   Flute
                                                   WILLIAM CLARKE
4. Toreador Song   Piano
     Carmen   Bizet
     GEORGE GIBSON-BROWNE   9. One Fine Day
     Baritone   Madame Butterfly   Puccini
                                                   JOAN ELLIS
5. Hungarian Rhapsody   Soprano
     No. 6   Liszt
     ORCHESTRA   10. March of the Toys
                                                  Babes in Toyland   Herbert
                                                  ORCHESTRA

     I N T E R V A L
     (Refreshments on Sale)   *   *   *   *   *

Further exercise on a folded leaflet is given on pages 12–13 of **Practical Typing Exercises, Book Two**.

2. Type a copy of the following layout of a Bill of Quantities on A4 paper. Keep your typed copy for future reference in Folder No. 2.

(1) B I L L   O F   Q U A N T I T I E S

for

ALTERATIONS AT 'THE HAVEN'

QUEEN'S ROAD, DUDLEY

for

Mr. H. W. JOHNSON

(2) J. W. WALTERS, A.R.I.B.A.,
Architect,
4 Stoke Road,
DUDLEY.

(3) MARCH 19..

(5) P R E L I M I N A R I E S

(4) Item		(6)	(7)	(8)	(9) £
1	The works covered comprise: extending) ground floor of house a distance of) 1.210 metres at rear and then) building on new Sun Room 9.500 m x) 3.060 m with glass roof and sides.)				
2	The Contractor is referred to the) Conditions of the Contract issued) by the Royal Institute of British) Architects and must allow for com-) plying with them and for any cost) incurred therewith.)				
3	The Contractor can enter the site and) commence work immediately after the) Contract is signed which date) should be a few days after the) acceptance of the Tender.				
	Carried to collection		£		

Columns: (1) Heading. (2) Name and address of architect. (3) Date. (4) Item No. (5) Name of trade centred. (6) Measurements. (7) Nature of measurements. (8) Unit price. (9) Total.

Job 14

Type the following in double spacing on A5 paper, using margins of Elite 22–82, Pica 12–72. Use indented paragraphs.

Please send us 6 1-kg colourless Lacquer, 5 2-kg tins Thinners, & 5 1-kg tins Weather-Resisting

N.P. Enamel. [The above-named shop is holding in 10 days' time a one-week sale of shop-soiled ladies', men's & children's wear of high-grade

N.P quality. [Two days ago he said he was starting in 2 weeks' time on a fortnight's cruise, but we are now told he is taking his daughter's youngest child abroad in his son's car, instead of using his daughter's, as hers is being overhauled.

Job 15

Type the following Programme on A4 paper as a folded leaflet, displaying it as effectively as possible.

Page 1

BOLDMERE JUNIOR SCHOOL

SPORTS DAY (spaced caps)

SATURDAY, 20TH MAY

at

2.30 p.m.

* * *

Proceeds in aid of the

LIBRARY FUND

PROGRAMME   PRICE 10p

EVENTS (spaced caps - pages 2-3)

Page 2
1. Boys 7-8 years
   Hoop Race, 50 yards
2. Girls 7-8 years
   Potato Race, 50 yards
3. Boys 8-9 years
   Sack Race, 50 yards
4. Girls 8-9 years
   Egg & Spoon Race, 50 yds
   DANCE DISPLAY
   * * *

Page 3
5. Boys 9-10 yrs
   Wheelbarrow Race, 60 yds
6. Girls 9-10 years
   Three-legged Race, 60 yds
7. Boys 10-11 years
   Skipping Race, 60 yards
8. Girls 10-11 years
   Obstacle Race, 60 yards
   DISTRIBUTION OF PRIZES
   * * *

Specification (Contd.)

EXCAVATOR AND CONCRETOR

EXCAVATION   Excavate under all walls to a solid foundation.

N.P. British Portland Cement to be obtained from approved
manufacturers and to comply in all respects with the
latest British Engineering Standard specification
for Portland cement*/, + to stand the tests named herein.*

The concrete raft to be cement concrete 153 mm
thick and composed of four parts clean gravel, two
parts sand, and one part of cement, reinforced with
B.R.C. Steel Mesh */ no. 65.*

SAND   Sand to be supplied from an approved Sand Pit.

Ⓐ *+ for providing storage
tanks + tools, + for
removing at completion.*   End of Excavator and Concretor
Ⓑ *CLEANING ON COMPLETION Remove all rubbish
+ surplus material on completion, +
leave site clean + orderly.*

ENDORSEMENT

April, 19..

SPECIFICATION OF WORK

to be executed

at

Coppice Lane,

CHURCH STRETTON

for

Mr. William Simpson

J. Wilkinson & Co. Ltd.,
Architects & Surveyors,
80 High Street,
Church Stretton.

Typed on right-hand
side of middle fold as
specimen opposite, or,
in the case of a bound
Specification, on the
front cover.

Bills of Quantities

A Bill of Quantities is a document showing details and prices of materials to be used in building, etc., its purpose being to obtain tenders for the work to be done and materials required. It enables the architect to make an accurate estimate of the work to be carried out, and it is usually prepared by a surveyor, the Contractor completing it with the prices quoted by him for each item. Ruled sheets are normally used, although the document is sometimes typed on plain paper and ruled afterwards. A specimen is given below, but there may be slight variations in the layout and ruling. For full instructions concerning the typing of Bills of Quantities, study page 213.

Skill building

Type each line or sentence (A, B, C, and D) *three* times, and, if time permits, complete your practice by typing each group once as it appears. Margins: Elite 22–82, Pica 12–72.

A. Review alphabet keys

1. When dazzled by the headlights of the many passing cars the expert driver just pulls to the kerb and quickly brakes.

B. Review shift key

2. Milan Luton Wales Genoa Perth Turin Irish China Japan Newton

3. Miss E. Newton visited China, Japan, Milan, Genoa and Turin.

4. Mr. A. Price, Chief Constable, Southern Division, and Mr. R. Marshall, Assistant Commissioner (Crime), Northern Division, will contest the post of Chief Constable, West Midlands.

C. Practise common letter combinations

5. he when them hear held then other where heard either reached

6. Either one or both may reach the valley where they are held.

7. When they reach there, they will hear about the bad weather.

8. All other helpers were then compelled to seek shelter there.

D. Build speed on common phrase drill

9. they are, they must, they have, they would, they should not.

10. They must leave now if they are to catch the next train out.

11. They should not call unless they have a late train to catch.

12. They will be late for the play which they are hoping to see.

Accuracy/Speed Practice   Two-minute timing   Not more than 2 errors

words

AS.9 The sun shone brightly as the car slid smoothly through the leafy	13
lanes, and the passengers' talk ceased for a while. Shortly they would	27
reach their goal, and all of them were anxious that the first glimpse	41
of it should not be marred by the fact that they were not looking out	55
of the windows. Suddenly, they came round the last corner, and before	69
them lay the village, with its grey stone houses along a street lined	82
with trees, a wonderful view of hills for a background, and a quiet	96
river flowing gently along. The car rolled to a stop. They strolled	110
for a time through the quiet street, past the gardens, so full of	123
flowers, and on to the church. Once or twice a dog barked. Otherwise,	137
all was peace. A day to remember, they thought, as, turning for a	150
last glance, they slowly went back to their car. (S.I. 1.20)	160

Specifications

A Specification is a document detailing the work which a contractor proposes to do on any particular job, and shows the quality and measurements of materials to be used. The description of the work to be done and the materials to be used are divided into the different trades, which follow the order in which the work would normally be carried out. The specimen below shows the general layout of a Specification. Further information about methods of layout is given on page 221.

1. Practise typing Specification. Type a copy of the following extract of a Specification on A4 paper, following the layout and scale-points given. Complete with endorsement.

35(30)

S P E C I F I C A T I O N of works required

40(35) to be executed in the erection of a house

at Coppice Lane, Church Stretton, for

Mr. William Simpson.

J. Wilkinson & Co. Ltd.,
Architects & Surveyors,
80 High Street,
Church Stretton.

30(25)
APRIL 19..

44(39)
P R E L I M I N A R I E S

12(10)

DRAWINGS   *l.c.*   This Specification must be read in conjunction
with the general design of house as shown on drawings
site and/layout already deposited.

NOTICES AND   The contractor must comply with any regulation
FEES   and Bye-Laws of local and other authorities, give
any notices, and pay any fees if required.

MATERIALS AND   The materials and workmanship throughout are
WORKMANSHIP   to be of the best quality of the respective kinds.
N.P.   The work is to be carried out to the satisfaction
of Mr. William Simpson or his Surveyor.

WATER   *v.c.*   The contractor is to allow for giving notice
l.c.   and paying fees for tapping the Water Main and providing all temporary services for the supply of
water to all parts of the works/ *(Insert A)*

INSURANCE   The Contractor must insure all workmen under
the Workmen's Compensation Acts, Health and
Unemployment Acts, etc.

Insert B

FROST   Work executed at a time when frost is likely to
occur is to be adequately covered up and well pro-
tected at night.

ATTEND   Each trade is to attend upon all others and
perform all jobbing work throughout.

End of Preliminaries

Technique development

1. Review use of dash. Type a copy of the following in double spacing. Remember to leave one space before and after dash, but no space before or after hyphen. Use A5 landscape paper and an indented paragraph. Margins: Elite 22–82, Pica 12–72.

> It is some twenty – no, more like thirty – years, since we saw him. The new secretary – Mr. H. Smith-Jones – takes up his duties on Monday. Some passers-by – and there were quite a few – stopped to listen. He said, "To be or not to be – that is the question." The visit of my new-found friend – if I may be so bold as to call him that – has given me great pleasure. He can supply up-to-date models of those chairs.

Menus

The following specimen will be a guide to the general display of a Menu. Note that the courses are separated from one another by extra spaces, and by a few dots or asterisks.

2. Type the following menu to fit on a card measuring 148 × 210 mm. Keep your typed copy for future reference in Folder No. 2.

T H E B E L L H O T E L

WORCESTER

Saturday, 16th August, 19..

LUNCHEON

Tomato Soup

or

Grapefruit

* * *

Fried Fillet of Plaice — Sauce Tartare
Roast Chicken, Sausage and Stuffing
Bread Sauce
Roast and Creamed Potatoes
Spring Cabbage
Garden Peas

* * *

Peach Melba
Fruit Tart
or
Cheese and Biscuits

* * *

Coffee

* * *

Type each line or sentence (A and B) *three* times, and, if time permits, complete your practice by typing each group once as it appears. Margins: Elite 22–82, Pica 12–72.

A. Review alphabet keys

1. The child just spent his pocket money buying five dozen extra special fireworks which very quickly went up in smoke.

B. Build speed on common words

2. He has not said when he will send us his bill for the house.
3. Please supply the ten we ordered at the beginning of August.
4. You will remember that that particular item is not required.
5. It seems to me that the sound came from the other direction.

Accuracy/Speed Practice	Five-minute timing	Not more than 3 errors

words

AS.30   A good rule to follow for a kitchen or for any place in which 12
practical work has to be done is the old saying "A place for every- 26
thing and everything in its place." Different people, however, will 39
have different views as to what is the best place for anything, but 53
an important thing to remember is that utensils and food containers 66
should always be put back in precisely the same place after they have 80
been used. Taking and replacing containers should be an automatic 93
procedure. Many people prefer to keep their kitchen saucepans in 106
cupboards instead of on open shelves, probably because they are out of 120
sight, and so the kitchen looks tidier, but other people like to keep 134
their pans on open shelves because they are easy to see, quick to get 148
hold of, and less likely to be damaged. If you prefer to keep your 161
saucepans in cupboards, it is well worth while to have sets so that they 175
will fit into each other. A lot of time can be wasted if you keep your 190
saucepans in one place and the lids in another, so if you cannot put the 204
lids on top of the saucepans, they may be kept on hooks or racks. 217

    The extent to which work in the kitchen can be done more easily and 230
more efficiently is somewhat limited, but it is possible to arrange 244
working surfaces and storage places in such a manner as to suit individual 259
needs and methods. A row of hooks for small cooking tools saves waste of 273
time in searching, particularly if it is near the kitchen stove. Wall 287
cupboards or shelves are also very convenient. These should be low 301
enough to be within arm's reach without being so low that you run the 314
risk of bumping your head. Colanders should also be kept within reach 328
of the sink or cooker. 333

    Moreover, the preparation and mixing of food can often be made less 346
tiring by having a kitchen stool which is adjustable in height and with 361
a rail or step for one's feet. Many kitchen operations can be made less 375
arduous if a little thought is given to them, but these depend on the 389
individual, as no two persons operate in the same way. (S.I. 1.38) 400

If your employer has appointments outside the office, an itinerary may have to be prepared for him which will enable him to know exactly where he should be at any given time. This schedule of a day's appoint-ments should be typed on a convenient size of paper or, preferably, on a card which he can carry about with him.

3. Practise typing appointments itinerary. Type a copy of the following itinerary on a postcard (148 × 105 mm). Block main and sub-heading at left margin. Use margins of Elite 12–62, Pica 5–55. Leave three spaces between the 2 columns, and set a tab stop for the second column at 25 (Elite) 18 (Pica).

```
I T I N E R A R Y
Mr. P. T. Reade's schedule for 8th May, 1978
 9.30 a.m.    Lewis's Ltd., High Street
              Buyer — Mr. L. F. Wood
11.00 a.m.    L. C. Marcell & Co. Ltd., Broad Street
              Buyer — Miss M. H. Moyers
 2.30 p.m.    A. M. Bushell & Son, Victoria Street
              Buyer — Mr. S. F. Morrall
 3.30 p.m.    R. Young & Co. Ltd., Hagley Road
              Buyer — Miss B. Swann
              Return to office to sign letters
```

Open Punctuation

Many organisations are now using open punctuation in a variety of documents. This is particularly so in business letters which are dealt with in Unit 11. Standard punctuation is employed in sentences except in the following instances:

1. Where an abbreviation ends in a full stop, the full stop is omitted and replaced by a space. Example: Mrs (space) A (space) W (space) Gurney, senior partner in Messrs Gurney & Asquith, will discuss the change of trading name to W R Holt & Co Ltd, etc, when she calls tomorrow.

2. Where abbreviations consist of two or more letters with full stops after each letter, the full stops are omitted and no space is left between the letters, but one space (or comma) after the group of letters; eg, John R Jamieson, Esq, MBE, MP, but see name and address of addressee, page 74.

3. th, rd, st, and nd are omitted from the date as is also the comma after the month and before the year.

4. Full stops are omitted after numbered items (leave three clear spaces) and no brackets are used in lettered items (leave three clear spaces).

4. Practise typing sentence with open punctuation. Type the following exercise on A5 landscape paper using margins of Elite 20–85, Pica 10–75.

```
The Directors of B Robins & Co Ltd are: B T S Abbott, A P W
Ben, The Rt Hon Lord Jenkins, GBE, P Kildare, and Sir Peter
Law, KBE.  The next meeting will be held on either 16 June or
23 June 1978, at 10 am.  If 7 pm would be more suitable, please
let me know. Type the following in abbreviated form: eg, ie,
etc, viz, Mrs.
```

| ANNIE BLOGGS | Morning, Dad. Sorry I can't stop. I'm late already. Let me have that bit of bread, will you? |
| | |

(Takes Mr. Bloggs' piece of bread and butter, gulps his tea, and goes.)

So long!

| MR. BLOGGS | Well, I'm blessed. Young people rush like blinkin' grasshoppers these days. There h'ain't much peace for us old 'uns. |
| | |

two ← (Mr. Slye enters. He is slick — and sly)

| MR. SLYE | Good morning Bloggs. (Sits at table) Pass the bread and butter, please. Thanks. Would you pour me a cup of tea, please? |

Job 79   Production Target—*12 minutes*

Centre the following exercise horizontally and vertically on A5 portrait paper. Justify the right-hand margin in the first paragraph (you will have to type a draft of this first). Otherwise, follow layout.

<u>SUBSISTENCE ALLOWANCE</u>

The revised rates of subsistence allowance are
given below and will operate from 1 November
1977. The appropriate paragraphs in Section XIV
of the Handbook should be amended accordingly.

PARAGRAPH 5(b) (iii)

<u>London</u>	Breakfast	....	£1.00
	Lunch	....	£1.50
	Dinner	....	£2.45

<u>Elsewhere</u>	Breakfast	....	£0.90
	Lunch	....	£1.23
	Dinner	....	£2.32

PARAGRAPH 5(b) (viii)

| <u>London</u> | Bed and breakfast | .... | £9.05 |

| <u>Elsewhere</u> | Bed & breakfast | .... | £8.50 |

5. Practise typing travel itinerary. Type the following exercise on A4 paper in single spacing except where otherwise instructed. Use margins of Elite 20–85, Pica 10–75. Leave 25 mm clear at top of page. Type with open punctuation, as in copy, and make your own line endings. Keep your typed copy for future reference in Folder No. 2.

I T I N E R A R Y

MR J C WASHINGTON'S VISIT TO BRISTOL

12–14 June 1978

Typist: When an 'x' appears, leave one clear line space; two x's = 2 clear line spaces.

MONDAY 12 JUNE   *Typist: Leave 3 clear space*

1325		Taxi from office to New Street Station, Birmingham
1405	depart	New Street Station (Platform 7)
1620	arrive	Bristol (Temple Meads)

Acommodation booked for one night at the Grand Hotel, Broad Street. Telephone 0272 21645
Dinner at Grand Hotel with Mr J Smythe (Avon rep)

TUESDAY 13 JUNE

1000   Town Clerks Office, Council House. Tel 0272 21715
Discussion about new factory — correspondence in file No 1

1130   Appointment with Mr F Squires, Manager, Secure 6 Building Society, 7 Temple Gate. Tel 0272 21715 — correspondence in file No 2

Insert 'A'

1700   depart   Grand Hotel. Mr Smythe will collect your luggage & drive you to Weston Super Mare

1745   arrive   Weston *Super Mare*
Accommodation booked at Grand Atlantic Hotel, Beach Rd. Tel 0934 6543

1930   Dinner at Grand Atlantic Hotel with Mr & Mrs Partridge and Mr Smythe

WEDNESDAY 14 JUNE

0930   depart   Weston Super Mare (Refreshments on train)
1222   arrive   New Street, Birmingham

'A' 1400   Bristol Air Corporation, Filton House, Tel. 0272 31476 — correspondence in file No 3

Further exercise on itinerary is given on page 14 of **Practical Typing Exercises, Book Two**.

Please display on A4 paper

Title Page

BLOGGS' BIG DAY — *spaced caps*
by
HILARY DORMAN

Time — Present

Introductory Page

The Scene is laid in a boarding-house parlour.
The furniture is drab, but clean.   There are varied
pictures, ornaments, etc., & there is no colour scheme.

CHARACTERS

Introductory Page

MR. BERT BLOGGS   *(lodger)*
ANNIE BLOGGS (his daughter)
MR. ARTHUR SLYE (another lodger)
MRS. SIDDELLS — LILY (landlady)
MISS CORA MACDUNIT   (two ladies from the
MISS ZELA MOVIEDRONE   Matrimonial Agency)

BLOGGS' BIG DAY — *spaced caps*

Type in red or underline in red.

of the room
The scene opens with Mr. Bloggs sitting at the table which is
in the centre.   He is *a* middle-aged man, very quiet, & a widower.
He had always longed for his freedom, but, on becoming a widower,
he wishes to re marry & have a "nice little home" again.   He is
a retired railway clerk.   He is alone.   The door opens &
Mrs. Siddells enters with a tray on wh are balanced a teapot &
a plate of bread and butter.

MR. BLOGGS   Morning, Mrs. Siddells

MRS. SIDDELLS   Morning, Mr. Bloggs.   Sorry about the breakfast but the gas is
off and I've had to use the primus.   I only managed to boil
some water, though — as the blinkin' thing konked out.   Do
you mind just plain bread and butter?   I 'aven't anything
else to offer.

MR. BLOGGS   No, I *d*on't mind.   I just 'ope nothing else fades out.   There
h'ain't much left as it is.

MRS. SIDDELLS   (She is rather reefined, a widow with a tendency to overdress
Type & underline in red   and make up)
So do I.   I'm sick of trying to run a boarding — er — guest
house, as things are today.   I reely think I'll have to close
down not havin' a man about the place to 'elp.   Ah! well, I'd
better go and see if the post's come.   (Exits) *in red*

Type or underline in red   (She collides with Annie Bloggs in the doorway; they say
'sorry', etc.)

Job 16
Production Target—*6 minutes*
Type the following Menu on a card measuring 4″ × 6″ (102 × 152 mm).
Centre vertically and horizontally.

Soup - Chilled Fruit Juices - Melon Cocktail

Roast Turkey, Chipolata Sausages, Cranberry Sauce, *[ST]*

Parmentier and Duchess Potatoes, Garden peas and *u.c.*

Sprouts.

Peach Flan with fresh cream - Ice Cream -

Cheese Board - Coffee [Typist - treble line spacing between courses please.]

Job 17
Production Target—*7 minutes*
Display the following as effectively as possible on A5 paper. Insert a simple
decorative border. See page 213.

The Canterbury Singers
present
BLESS THE BRIDE
by A.P. HERBERT
Music by Vivian Ellis   By kind permission
of Samuel French Ltd.
Stage manager: Harry Vincent
Wardrobe Mistress: Mary Brown
Dances arranged by Susan James

The Opera produced by F. Faulkener

Job 18
Production Target—*10 minutes*
Type the following Travel Itinerary for Miss W J Wilkinson's visit to London on
22 January 1978 on A5 paper.

0915		Check in at Glasgow Airport
0935	dep	Glasgow Airport (Flight No 5023)
1045	arrive	Ldn (Heathrow)
1145	"	West London Air Terminal
1430		Reception Dorchester Hotel, Park Lane
3 pm		Display of Christian Dior Spring Collection
1800		Report to West Ldn Air Terminal
1835	dep	W Ldn Air Terminal for airport u.c.
1940	dep	Ldn (Heathrow) (Flight 5064)
2100	arrive	Glasgow Airport

```
SUPER.        There is that, of course, sir; but Brant is only a
              young chap and may well have lost his head.

GENTLEMAN     And how about motive?

SUPER.        Isaacs' records show that Brant had borrowed a sizeable
              sum to start a small business, and was behind with the
              repayment.  Isaacs was not a pleasant chap when one of
              his victims couldn't pay up.  He may well have goaded
              Brant beyond endurance.

                   (Knock at the door)

              Ah!  This may be Scotland Yard's report on the revolver.
              Come in!

                   (Enter a CONSTABLE with a box)

CONSTABLE     From Scotland Yard, sir.

SUPER.        Right, let's have it.

                   (He takes box and removes lid)
                   (Exit CONSTABLE)
```

Further exercise on typing a play is given on pages 58–60 of **Practical Typing Exercises, Book Two**.

Used when typing direct speech; e.g., Tom said, "I must catch the 8.30 train this evening." Quotation marks are usually placed after the comma, question mark, and exclamation mark at the end of a sentence. The full stop is placed inside the quotation marks unless the punctuation is not part of the original sentence or unless the sentence ends with a title which is in quotation marks.

When two or more paragraphs are quoted, the quotation marks are placed at the *beginning of each paragraph* and at the *end of the last paragraph only*—see exercise below.

2. Type the following exercise on A5 portrait paper in double spacing. Use indented paragraphs and margins Elite 12–62, Pica 5–55.

```
       Chairman's Annual Statement  — centre in all caps & U/S
                      C
       In his speech at the (AGM) the Chairman, Mr. David Blanco,
    said                    In full

       "Ladies and Gentlemen:
                                              in all sectors
       "I am delighted to tell you th profits/showed a substantial
    improvement during the. passed yr.
                             past                    5
       "Turnover was up from £145,000 to £170,000 despite the fact
  >/ th home sales were the lowest for yrs.  However/ exports increased
    by over 60%.
                                                    d
       ". . . recommending a final dividend of 7%.  I am sure you
  a/ agree that this is/ fair/." return on yr investment
```

Type each exercise (A, B, and C) *once* for practice, *once* for speed, and finally *once* for accuracy. Margins: Elite 22–82, Pica 10–72.

A. Review alphabet keys

1.   On the card table with the green baize top 6 women were playing a game of bezique, and they looked extremely jovial.

B. Improve control of figure keys

2. 2929 3838 4747 5656 1920 1930 1940 1950 1960 1970 1980 1990.
3. Dates to remember: 1066, 1215, 1603, 1707, 1815, 1918, 1945.
4. For this year, £1,850,000 has been allocated for residential building; £974,640 for houses; £760,230 for other buildings.

C. Improve control of shift lock

5. FIRST-CLASS, FORTY-FOUR, HIT-OR-MISS, PAY-AS-YOU-GO, 60-WATT
6. Were the FORTY-FOUR books in FIRST-CLASS condition when they were sent to you? I <u>must</u> say I do NOT like <u>your</u> PAY-AS-YOU-GO policy and HIT-OR-<u>MISS</u> methods. Send me 7 60-WATT bulbs.

Accuracy/Speed Practice   Three-minute timing   Not more than 3 errors

	words

AS.10

	words
In presenting the accounts for the past year, we very much dislike	13
having to put before you something that is not very bright. At the out-	28
set I would like to say to you that this is due to a change in policy on	42
the part of your Directors.	47
As you know, there have been changes in the directorate. The idea	61
of the old Board was to save the Company's cash without having regard	74
to what the new Board think is the most essential point of our policy —	88
namely, that of keeping the plant, etc., at the maximum point of good	102
repair. I do not mean to say that these assets of the Company had been	117
allowed to fall into a bad state, but what I do mean is that we now see	131
that, in order to make the best return to our members, we must bring	144
ourselves up to date.	149
I am not holding out any strong hopes of reaping a benefit from	161
these changes at once — even when we have our plant in order it will	175
still take some time before the full effect will be felt. However, I	189
can assure you that, with the new plant, and by keeping a very careful	203
watch on our expenses, we are full of hope, provided that trade improves,	217
or, at any rate, does not fall off. As you know, we are trying hard to	231
gain orders from abroad, and this will help. (S.I. 1.28)	240

39(29)

IMPRINT FOR MURDER

36(30)

(Notice use of all
capitals for names of
characters)

The SUPERINTENDENT is working at his desk. He looks up as,
following a knock, the door opens. Enter a gentleman of
some 50 years of age. He is wearing a full-skirted frock
coat and carries a top hat. The SUPERINTENDENT springs to
his feet.

SUPER.   Well, well, sir! Come in, come in! Delighted to see you
            after this long time. Take this chair, sir.

                        42(35)

GENTLEMAN   (Seats himself at end of Superintendent's desk)

            Nice to see you, Superintendent. I have been visiting an
            old servant who lives close by — and won't be living here
            or anywhere else very long, I fear. Couldn't miss the
            chance to have a word with you. I hope you are not too
            busy?

SUPER.   I'm very glad you did call, sir. I'm not all that busy.
            The only important matter at the moment is a local murder.
            All straightforward and cut-and-dried. Nothing to interest
            you, I'm afraid.

GENTLEMAN   I'm easily interested, Superintendent. Do tell me about it.

SUPER.   Very well. The murdered man was a rather unsavoury charac-
            ter, a money-lender by the name of Solly Isaacs. He was
            also strongly suspected of being a 'fence', and not above
            a spot of blackmail if opportunity offered.

GENTLEMAN   H'm! A very promising subject for murder.

SUPER.   Yes, indeed! He was found in his office by the cleaner
            first thing this morning with a bullet in his head, and
            the murder weapon, a revolver, on the floor near by. An
            anonymous communication put us on to a local lad named
            Harry Brant; so we picked him up, and, sure enough, his
            prints are all over the weapon, while his only alibi rests
            on the evidence of his wife.

GENTLEMAN   It sounds almost too cut-and-dried.

SUPER.   Well, the gun is his, and he can't explain its presence
            on the scene of the crime. I've sent it, with the bullet
            the surgeon recovered, to Scotland Yard for matching up.

GENTLEMAN   Of course, Superintendent, you won't need me to tell you
            that, if a man owns a gun, the fact of his finger-prints
            being on it is less remarkable than if they were not.
            And would any murderer today leave his gun behind com-
            plete with prints?

For formal meetings, such as General Meetings, Extraordinary General Meetings, and Committee Meetings, written notices are sent to those entitled to attend. The notice, which is prepared by the secretary, should contain details of the date, place, and time of meeting. The salutation and complimentary close may be omitted.

1. Practise typing Notice of Committee Meeting. Read the above explanation. Then type the following notice on A5 (210 × 148 mm) paper in single-line spacing. Left margin 25 mm, right margin 13 mm.

```
        THE CHAMPION LAWN TENNIS ASSOCIATION
                  73 High Street
             NORTHAMPTON   NN3 4NQ

      Chairman:                           Secretary:
      W. B. Sykes                       Miss P. Clarke

                                       12th February, 19..

        A meeting of the committee of The Champion Lawn Tennis
      Association will be held in the Committee Room at 73 High
      Street, on Friday, 27th February, at 7 p.m.


                                       Pauline Clarke
                                       SECRETARY.
```

2. Type the following in single-line spacing on A4 paper, and keep your typed copy in Folder No. 2 for future reference.

AGENDA

Typist: Set out numbered items under each other

When the notice of a meeting is to be sent out, it is normal practice to include the agenda, which is a list of items to be discussed at a meeting, those being listed in a certain order & numbered for easy reference as follows:

1. Apologies
2. Minutes of the last meeting
3. Matters arising out of the minutes. 4. Correspondence
6. Any special point for discussion
5. Reports 7. Any other business
8. Date of next meeting.

[As is the notice of a meeting, the agenda is sent to all who are entitled to attend. It is usually duplicated & care shd be taken to 'run off' additional copies for members who may forget to bring a copy to a meeting. [The word AGENDA is blocked at the left margin or centred on the writing line in spaced caps. The nos. may be blocked or if indented from the left margin, the longest line shd end the same no. of spaces from the right hand margin. Open or standard punctuation may be used.

Plays

Although the layout of plays may vary according to individual preference, the following points are generally acceptable and will be a guide to you. In a typewriting examination you should follow the general layout and instructions given.

1. Size of paper: A4.
2. Binding margin of 38 mm (1½").
3. INTRODUCTORY PAGES. These are not usually numbered. The arrangement is as follows:
   First page—TITLE PAGE: Title and type of play and author's name in capitals. Centre vertically and horizontally in typing line, taking into account the binding margin, i.e., Elite 18–94 (Centre point 56), Pica 15–77 (Centre point 46).
   Second page—SYNOPSIS OF ACTS AND SCENERY: Acts and numbers of Acts in capitals. Centre vertically and horizontally in typing line as in first page above.
   Third page—LIST OF CHARACTERS: Typed in capitals. If cast is included, characters are in lower case and cast in capitals. Type in double spacing and centre vertically and horizontally in typing line as in first page. Sometimes list of costumes is included in this page.
4. START OF PLAY. Page 1.
   (a) Dropped head for Act and Act number, i.e., leave 76 mm (3") at top of paper. Centre in typing line, i.e., margins Elite 18–94 (Centre point 56), Pica 15–77 (Centre point 46).
   (b) Turn up two single-line spaces and centre name of play etc., as in (a).
   (c) Margins for body of play: left 76 mm (3"), right 13 mm (½").
   (d) Names of characters: In capitals, starting 38 mm (1½") from left edge of paper; set tab. stop here and use margin release when typing names of characters.
   (e) Scene directions: Block at left margin.
   (f) Stage directions: Indent 13 mm (½") from left margin, i.e., start at scale point 42(35). Set tab. stop here.
   (g) Speeches: Block style at left margin, i.e., margins 36(30).
   (h) Unspoken words are typed in red in brackets or typed in black and underlined in red.
   (i) Numbering of pages: Pages numbered consecutively at top right-hand side, leaving 13 mm (½") at top of page. Turn up 2 single spaces after number before starting to type. Number may be just page, e.g., –2– OR 2. It may include the act and scene number, e.g., I–1–2 = Act I, Scene 1, page 2.

1. Practise typing play. Read and study the above explanation, and then type the following on A4 paper, using separate sheets for each of the first three introductory pages, and displaying these correctly. Keep your typed copy for future reference in Folder No. 2.

INTRODUCTORY PAGES
Centred on typing line Elite 18–94, Pica 15–77.

50(40)
TWO-ACT PLAY

48(38)
Period — ca. 1910

(First page) *39(29)* IMPRINT FOR MURDER

55(45)
by

51(41)
P. C. PRATT

(Second page) *54(44)*
ACT I

37(27)
SCENE: The Superintendent's Office at a
London Police Station

33(23)
The Superintendent's desk is sited right centre
with window behind, right. Door, left centre.
Chairs at both sides of desk, and at back.
Hatstand upper left. Bookcase back centre.

(Third page) *51(41)* CHARACTERS

(Double spacing) *40(30)*
SUPERINTENDENT
A GENTLEMAN
POLICE CONSTABLE
LUCY BRANT (wife of Harry Brant)
STAN LEWIS (a 'mobster')
MRS ALLEN (mother of Lucy)
HARRY BRANT (first suspect)

3. Practise typing Notice of Committee Meeting and Agenda. Type the following Notice and Notice of Meeting and Agenda on A4 paper, with margins of Elite 20–85, Pica 15–75. Use single-line spacing for the Notice, and double-line spacing between the numbered items in the Agenda. Use block style and open punctuation as in copy. Keep your typed copy in Folder No. 2 for future reference.

THE CHAMPION LAWN TENNIS ASSOCIATION
73 High Street
NORTHAMPTON   NN3 4NQ

Chairman   Secretary
W B Sykes   Miss P Clarke

12 February 1978

A meeting of the COMMITTEE of The Champion Lawn Tennis Association will be held in the Committee Room at the above address on Friday 24 February at 1900 hours.

A G E N D A

1   Apologies

2   Secretary to read the Minutes of last meeting

3   Matters arising out of Minutes

4   Correspondence

5   Additional cloakroom facilities.   Sub-Committee to submit 3 quotations for consideration

6   Any other business

7   Date and time of next meeting

PAULINE CLARKE
HONORARY SECRETARY

4. Type a copy of the following Notice of Annual General Meeting and Agenda. Use A4 paper, with margins of Elite 20–85, Pica 15–75. Notice to be in single-line spacing with double spacing between numbered items in the Agenda. Use the headings from exercise 3 above, insert suitable date, and type in block style with open punctuation.

The ANNUAL GENERAL MEETING of the Champion Lawn v.c. Tennis Association will be held in the Committee Room at the above address on Friday 31 March 1978 at 2000 hours.
AGENDA (spaced caps)
1. Apologies
2. Minutes of AGM held on 25 March 1977
3. Matters arising.
4. Correspondence
6. Treasurer's Report
5. Chairman's Report
7. Election of Officers & Committee
8. Any other business.

Pauline Clarke
Hon. Sec.

Skill building

Type each exercise (A and B) *once* for practice, *once* for speed, and finally *once* for accuracy. Margins: Elite 22–82, Pica 12–72.

A. Review alphabet keys

1.   The Fair was a blaze of light, and many youths and boys even queued to join in the exceptional fun on the cake-walk.

B. Improve control of figure keys

2. tie 583 row 492 you 697 eye 363 wit 285 your 6974 tire 5843.
3. Add 7,578, 4,600, 1,250, 8,543, 839, 795, 124, 120, 109, 99, 94, 83, 74, 62, 54, 37, 26, 9, and the total will be 24,496.
4. 1122, 2233, 3344, 4455, 5566, 6677, 7788, 8899, 9900, 01234.
5. 2345, 3456, 4567, 5678, 6789, 7890, 8901, 9012, 0123, 12345.

Accuracy/Speed Practice   Four-minute timing   Not more than 3 errors

words

AS.29   Which is better: to be an expert — a specialist — in some one | 12
direction, or to be a good all-rounder? | 20

In our modern world we need both. We could not do without the | 32
services of specialist physicians and surgeons, and in the sciences we | 46
owe much to specialists in research. It has been said that specialists | 61
are persons who know more and more about less and less, so that the time | 75
may come when they know everything about nothing. | 85

For beginners in business or those preparing for business, we feel | 98
that they should aim at good all-round knowledge, ability, and skill. | 112
Get the best accuracy and speed you can in typewriting and, at the same | 126
time, give proper attention to office practice, business arithmetic, and, | 141
above all, to that basic study without which all else is of little or no | 155
value — English. | 158

You may say that you have been 'doing' English for the past ten | 171
years or so, and this is no doubt true. However, as you have worked | 184
through the manuscript exercises in this book, you will have realized | 198
that, without a good knowledge of the use of words, you cannot expect to | 212
be an accurate and fast typist. By English we mean ordinary, practical | 226
English, which covers such matters as knowing when to write 'there' and | 240
'their', or 'here' and 'hear'; knowing with reasonable certainty where | 254
to put in commas, semicolons, and full stops; where to start a new para- | 269
graph, where to use a capital letter, whether to use words or figures. | 283
In brief, you should be sure of those simple conventions of written | 296
English which you must know when you are typing a letter which your | 310
employer will sign without feeling ashamed of it.   (S.I. 1.37) | 320

(a) Date ends at right margin.
(b) Paragraph(s) indented.
(c) The word AGENDA is centred on the typing line in spaced capitals and underscored.
(d) The Agenda items are indented
   i. If any of the items are going to take up more than one line, start the numbers five spaces from the left margin and stop five spaces short of the right margin, i.e., the longest line(s) are inset the same distance from both margins.
   ii. When none of the numbered items takes up the full width of the typing line, find the starting point for all the numbers by back-spacing (from the centre of the typing line) once for each two characters and spaces in the longest line, see example below.

Practise typing Notice of Meeting and Agenda in indented style.

5. Type a copy of the following exercise on A4 paper with margins of Elite 20–85, Pica 15–75. Use single spacing for the notice and double spacing between the numbered items in the Agenda. Follow layout shown. Keep your typed copy for future reference in Folder No. 2.

BROOKFIELD SPORTS AND SOCIAL CLUB
St. Nicholas Buildings
Newcastle-on-Tyne   NE2 3DJ

Chairman   Secretary
John L. Ashby   Sandra M. Green

                                          14th April, 1978

      A meeting of the Committee of the Brookfield Sports and Social Club will be held in the Staff Canteen on Friday, 12th May, at 7 p.m.

A G E N D A

   1. Apologies

   2. Minutes of last committee meeting

   3. Matters arising from Minutes

   4. Annual Summer Outing

   5. Suggestions for Winter Programme

   6. Any other business

   7. Date, time, and place of next meeting.

                                          Sandra M. Green
                                          Secretary

Further exercises on notice of meeting and agenda in indented style is given on page 15 of **Practical Typing Exercises, Book Two.**

The distribution of the Co's holding is as follows:—

Typist Tabulate these under headings Net Tangible Assets	No. of Co's.
Over £500,000 — 50	£200,001 to £500,000 — 40
£100,001 — £200,000 — 19	Under £100,000 — 7

trs.   The accounts and reports were adopted & the Board's proposal referred to above was approved.

'A' — thus continuing the unbroken run of increasing profits since the incorporation of the new Co.

'B' — that the directors recommended the payment of a final dividend

---

Job 77   Production Target—*20 minutes*

Display the following advertisement as effectively as possible. It is to fit on to a card measuring 178 mm × 229 mm.

FOR SALE BY PRIVATE TREATY

NEW FREEHOLD SEMI-DETACHED HOUSES

Now in the course of erection at

GROVE LANE, NEWCASTLE,

Staffordshire

by the

NEWCASTLE BUILDING CO. LTD.

Situated in the Borough of Newcastle, within walking distance of the centre of the town.

The Accommodation includes:

Entrance Hall, Through Lounge, Kitchen and Pantry Two Double Bedrooms, Single Bedroom, and Bathroom, Separate Toilet

Outside: Garage if required, Coal Bunker, and Garden to front and rear

All Main Services will be connected

For further details apply to:

WINTERTON & SONS

9 High Street, Newcastle.   'Phone: Newcastle 1563

The Chairman's Agenda may contain more information than the ordinary agenda. The right-hand side of a Chairman's Agenda is left blank, so that he can write in the decisions reached on the various points. The word AGENDA is centred (in closed capitals) in the left half of the writing line, and the word NOTES is centred (in closed capitals) in the right half of the writing line. The numbers start at the left-hand margin and are repeated at the centre of writing line. Open or standard punctuation may be used.

6. Practise typing Chairman's Agenda. Read the explanation above; then type the following on A4 paper in single spacing with double spacing between numbered items. Left margin 25 mm and right margin 13 mm. Keep your typed copy for future reference in Folder No. 2.

THE YORKSHIRE MOTOR RACING CLUB
105 Bradford Road
YORK   YO1 2DA

The ANNUAL GENERAL MEETING of THE YORKSHIRE MOTOR RACING CLUB will be held in the Green Room of the Grand Hotel, York, on Wednesday, 24 August, 1977, at 7.30 p.m.

AGENDA	NOTES
1. Ask the Secretary, Mr. Jones, to read apologies.	1.
2. Ask Mr. Jones to read Minutes of last Annual General Meeting.	2.
3. Matters arising. It is anticipated that questions will be asked about	3.
i. Cancellation of Rally last August.	i.
ii. The delay in amending the Regulations.	ii.
4. Chairman's Annual Report (copy attached).	4.
5. Ask Treasurer, Mr. Moss, to submit his annual report.	5.
6. Ask members if they have any questions.	6.
7. Election of	7.
i. Officers	i. (See attached list)
ii. Committee	ii.
iii. Honorary Auditor	iii.
8. Any other business	8.
9. Chairman to declare meeting closed.	9.

Further exercise on chairman's agenda is given on page 16 of **Practical Typing Exercises, Book Two**.

UNIT 8   47

Prepare a fair copy of the following Manuscript, ready for stencilling. Make all necessary corrections. It should be fitted on to one sheet of A4 paper.

caps → Estates Investment Trust Company Limited

Twelfth / The 12th Annual General Meeting of Estates
last / Investment Co. Ltd. was held on the 12th June, in London,
ACKLAND the Chairman, Sir Henry Ackland, presiding.
Run on The following is an extract from his circulated
statement :—

The steady progress of the Co's. business has
continued during the year under review resulting in a
nett increase of the investments by £327,623. Capital
Reserve shows an increase ~~of the investments~~ on the previous year's
figure despite the £200,000 scrip issue made from
this a/c.

caps ——→ Higher Income & Dividends

Turning to the statement of revenue, the Chairman
trs said that the income before tax, for the year, was
£358,153 as against £320,477 for the previous
Insert 'A' year. Allowing for tax, & adding the previous year's
carry forward, he said that there was an amt
of £504,048 available to cover the dividends of   Insert 'B'
dividend 6%, making with the 4% interim paid last Dec.
a total of 10% for the year on the issued and
paid-up Share Capital.

caps ——→ Proposed Scrip Issue
The Chairman also said in his report that a
u.c. resolution was to be put to the A.G.M, which
covered the proposal to capitalise the sums of
£400,000 by the issue of 400,000 new shares of £1 each,
& to distribute the same among the shareholders in
the proportion of 2 new shares for every 13 shares
held.

As you will see from the specimen in Exercise 7 below, there is a difference in the display of a notice of meeting and agenda for the Annual General Meeting of a limited company. The wording is also much more formal. This document is nearly always typed in block style with open or standard punctuation.

In addition to the notice and agenda, certain other information (where applicable) is given about: voting rights, proxy votes and forms, Directors' Service Contracts, Directors' Shares and Debenture Interests, etc.

7. Practise typing Notice of Annual General Meeting of Limited Company. Type the following exercise on A4 paper with margins of Elite 20–85, Pica 10–75. Use open punctuation and follow layout given in exercise. Leave 25 mm clear at top of page. Keep your typed copy for future reference in Folder No. 2.

THE BOLTON FURNISHING COMPANY LIMITED

NOTICE OF ANNUAL GENERAL MEETING

NOTICE IS HEREBY GIVEN that the Tenth Annual General Meeting of the Company will be held at the Queen's Hotel, Bolton, on Friday 28 April 1977, at 12 noon, to transact the following business:

1   To receive and consider the Directors' Report and Accounts for year ended 31 December 1976.

2   To confirm the recommendations of the Directors as to the payment of a final dividend.

3   To re-elect one Director.

4   To authorise the Directors to determine the Auditors' remuneration.

5   To transact any other business of an Ordinary General Meeting.

BY ORDER OF THE BOARD

A THOMPSON

SECRETARY

The Parade Works
Summer Hill
Bolton Lancashire BL2 3HN

6 April 1977

Any Member entitled to attend and vote at the Meeting whereof notice is hereby given may appoint one or more proxies to attend, and, on a poll, to vote instead of him; a proxy need not also be a Member.

Further exercise on Notice of Annual General Meeting and Agenda (Limited Company) is given on page 22 of **Practical Typing Exercises, Book Two**.

Type the following exercise on A4 and display as suggested below.

Books for Commerce Courses in Schools

Commerce for Schools
— Revised edition

Outhwaite   **£1.30**

A balanced course for CSE pupils of average ability which relates simple commercial examples to their daily lives. Comprehension and reinforcement of learning are achieved by the inclusion at the end of each chapter of sections such as 'Building your Vocabulary', 'Check your Reading' (questions to test comprehension), 'Question Time' (essay-type examination questions), and 'Learning by Doing'. Student projects are also included.

Communication in Retailing
Boggs   **£0.85**

An introduction to retailing that explains to young people at school, intending to enter retailing, the importance of communication in selling, and stresses the importance of what they say or do to their success in their jobs.

Study Notes on Commerce
Shafto   **£3.15**

A vital teacher's aid in looseleaf form.

A supplementary text designed to reinforce learning & aid revision.

Exploring Local Business
Watcham   **£0.95**

Provides a better understanding of the business community for pupils in their final year at school, and contains many practical activities.

Commerce Structure and Practice, 2/E
Shafto   **£2.25**

A broad review of all major aspects of modern commerce presented in an attractive and interesting style. Completely revised and up dated to cover recent developments, this new edition also includes many more illustrations, and meets the requirements of GCE 'O' level examinations.

Basic Business Arithmetic
Warson   **£1.95**

A basic textbook for students preparing for elementary level examinations which assumes little previous knowledge of the subject. Includes metric units, worked examples, and answers to all the carefully graded exercises.

— Revised edition

Set out as follows:

BOOKS FOR COMMERCE COURSES IN SCHOOLS

COMMERCE FOR SCHOOLS — Revised edition

Outhwaite — £1.30 — A balanced course for CSE pupils of average ability

Typist: Use single spacing for paras. Leave 2 clear spaces before starting the name of the next & subsequent titles.

175

11 April 1978

Please type the following notice & agenda
Use heading from exercise 3 on page 45.
A meeting of the COMMITTEE of / Champion
Lawn Tennis Assoc wl be held in / Committee
Rm at the above address on Fri 21 April
@ 2000 hrs.
AGENDA

I Apologies
II Minutes of the last Committee Meeting
III Matters arising out of Minutes IV Correspondence
VI New L.P. Records V Additional Cloakroom
facilities VII A.O.B VIII Date & time
of next meeting

Please display.

Typist- Please change Roman Numerals
to Arabic figures.

Please type the following notice & Chairman's
12 March 1978   Agenda
A meeting of / Directors wl be held in the
Board Rm on Thurs. 30 March @ 14 30 hrs.
AGENDA   NOTES

1 2 Ask Sec to read Mins   1
2 3 Matters arising   2   Please use
3 (I.) Appointment of Personnel   3 i   small
   (II) Branch office in Manager.   ii   Roman
                   Montreal   4 iii Numerals
4. Sales - Jan to March.   4
    Mr Chapman to report   5
5 Appointment of Agent in Cumbria
6 A.O.B.   6
1 Ask Sec to read apologies

Please type the following memo to PERSONNEL OFFICER from PURCHASING OFFICER. Ref. PO/TEN Today's date.

Further to yr Purchase Requisition (PO/PR/278) dated (last Wednesday) I have obtained the follow'g prices for electric typewriters:

13" (130 mm) carriage	~~£235~~	570
15" (381 mm) "	~~£250~~	590
17" (432 mm) "	~~£260~~	600

The type face can be either Pica or Elite.

N.P. [As you hv an allocation of £~~240~~ 500, presumably you wl wish to order the 13" carriage, but you did mention th yr typist does have to use A4 paper lengthwise on a number of occasions. Have a word w. the Financial Director & see if he is willing to increase yr allocation.

Please type the following letter ready for signature. Use suitable date. In addition to the file copy, make a copy for Miss J. Banks

J. White, 427 Pershore Road, Birmingham B5 2P0

Dear Mr. White, Yr letter of April 8 has done me a favour that I appreciate very much. Thank you for taking the trouble to write me. N.P. [Before yr letter was recvd one of these errors had bn discovered & was ~~amended~~ corrected in our first reprint. ←

N.P. [As I am sure I need not tell you, we make great effort to keep errors out of our publications. Yet an occasional error still slips through. N.P. [I hope you will continue to let us know abt any errors you may find in our books in future. I hope also, of course, that there wl not be any for you to find!

Yours very sincerely, John James, Commercial Editor

(The ti one wl be corrected in the next printing.)

(mentioning 2 errors th you hv found in one of our books.)

Type each line or sentence (A, B, and C) *three* times. If time permits, complete
your practice by typing each group once as it appears. Margins: Elite 22–82,
Pica 12–72.

A. Review alphabet keys

1. The lights of the oncoming bus quite dazzled this weary
driver, and the extra jerking probably caused this accident.

B. Build speed on common prefixes

2. convenience, confident, condition, consider, concern, confer
3. We are concerned about the condition of the conference hall.
4. I feel confident that you will confirm the present contract.

C. Build speed on common suffixes

5. settlement, equipment, agreement, shipment, payment, moment.
6. I am in agreement that payment for the shipments is now due.
7. At the moment we have yet to experiment with that equipment.

Accuracy/Speed Practice	Four-minute timing	Not more than 3 errors

words

AS.11   One chore which is an essential part of household routine, but which **14**
can be a burden if not tackled rightly, is the weekly wash. Badly washed **28**
clothes need more frequent replacements, and this means an enormous rise **43**
in household expenses. **47**

It may be found difficult to recognize the many new textiles on the **60**
market today and to know how these should be washed. So, when buying **74**
garments, always see that they have a label showing the washing instruc- **89**
tions — otherwise you should not buy them. Then again, there is the **102**
question of shrinking, which may happen with such materials as cotton or **117**
wool unless they bear a label to the effect that they have been pre- **130**
shrunk. **132**

Before washing coloured articles, it is advisable to cut off a small **146**
piece of the material from a seam or a belt and wash it in the normal way. **161**
Then place it between two pieces of white cloth, and press it with a hot **175**
iron. If you find that the colour has run into the white cloth, the **190**
garment should not be washed. **194**

You should not allow articles of clothing to become too dirty. If **207**
you do, drastic methods must be used to clean them, and these may help to **222**
destroy the fabric. The sorting of dirty laundry is of the utmost impor- **236**
tance. Lightly soiled articles should be passed through two lots of suds, **251**
so as to save rubbing. Very dirty garments should be left until last; **265**
then the dirt can be loosened in the first lot of suds and afterwards **279**
passed into the second suds. Woollen articles should be washed in luke- **293**
warm water. On most packets of soap powder or soap flakes the washing **307**
temperatures advised for the various types of fabric are shown. (S.I. 1.34) **320**

Typist — Mrs L M Robertson of 1231 Bristol Road South, Birmingham B31 12AJ wrote to us on Tuesday about our Save-As-You-Earn Scheme. Please type the following reply for despatch today.

Dear Madam

Save-As-You-Earn Scheme

Thank you for yr ltr dated ... abt our SAYE scheme , between £1 & £10,

N.P. SAYE is a 5-year contract btwn you & the Building Soc. You must agree to save a regular amt ea. month for 5 yrs. Provided you complete the contract, you are not paid interest but a equivalent bonus to one yr's savings, & on this bonus you do not pay any income tax. The bonus wl be equivalent to a compound rate of

N.P. interest of abt £50 p.a. If you leave all the money invested for a further two years, you wl at the end of 7 years hv a tax-free bonus

N.P. doubled. Unfortunately, there are penalties for stopping before the 5 years are up, altho' you always get back at least as much as

N.P. you hv pd. in. Please write to me again if you require further information.

Yrs ffy, EVERLASTING BUILDING SOCIETY LTD

J MILLS MANAGER 12;77

representing a gross rate of 12% p.a. to those paying income tax at the standard rate.

Here are examples of how yr savings wl accumulate:

Typist-plse display this before last para of letter

SAVINGS		REPAYMENTS			
Monthly	Total for 5 years	at 5 yrs		at 7 yrs	
		Bonus	Bonus plus savings	Double bonus	Double bonus plus savings
£1	£60	£12.4	£72.4	£24.8	£84.8
£2	£120	£28	£148	£56	£176
£3	£180	£42	£222	£84	£264
£4	£240	£56	£296	£112	£352
£5	£300	£70	£370	£140	£440
£10	£600	£140	£740	£280	£880

Technique development

For instructions on how to type a DRAFT copy, please see page 217.

For instructions on how to justify the right-hand margin, please see page 218.

1. (a) Type a draft copy, in double spacing, of the following two paragraphs. (b) Indicate on the DRAFT where extra spaces are needed in order to justify the right-hand margin. (c) Type a final copy with the right-hand margin justified. Use margins of Elite 20–85, Pica 10–75, and block paragraphs.

Most householders are now familiar with the 13-amp, 3-pin, electric plug. In fact the 5 amp and 15 amp seem quite antiquated to most of us. Never be complacent! Presumably in order to put us all to a great deal more expense, the International Electrotechnical Commission (IEC) has decided that the 13-amp plug is unsuitable and this body is suggesting that a new-type plug is essential.

Whether or not the 42 members of the Commission accept the recommendation remains to be seen.

Minutes

Details of any decisions or resolutions or business discussed at a meeting are recorded and preserved. These are known as Minutes. They are either written in a Minute Book or typed on loose sheets and kept in a Loose Leaf Minute Book. Each Minute is numbered, and a wide margin should be allowed for marginal headings. The Minutes should be written up as soon as possible after the meeting, and the third person and past tense are used. The numbering of the Minutes facilitates indexing.

Layout may be blocked or indented. Open or standard punctuation.

2. Type the following on A4 paper in single-line spacing with double spacing between numbered items. Keep your typed copy for future reference in Folder No. 2.

ORDER OF MINUTES

1. Description of meeting, including time, date and place.

2. Names of those present — Chairman's name appearing first, followed by the names of the officers.

3. Apologies received.

4. Reading of Minutes of last meeting.

5. Matters arising.

6. Correspondence.

7. Reports of Officers.

8. General business discussed — with details of any resolutions taken.

9. Any other business.

10. Place, date, and time of next meeting.

11. Place for Chairman's signature.

12. Date on which Minutes are signed.

Further exercise on justifying right margin is given on page 26 of **Practical Typing Exercises, Book Two.**

Type the following tabulation with diagonal column headings, and rule.

AVERAGE FAHRENHEIT TEMPERATURES

MONTH	ATHENS	BARCELONA	FLORENCE	GIBRALTAR	LISBON	MARSEILLES	MILAN	MOSCOW	NAPLES	ROME	SEVILLE
January	48	46	43	55	51	44	35	8	48	45	52
Feb.	49	48	44	56	52	46	38	9	49	47	56
March	52	50	49	57	54	50	46	18	52	51	60
April	59	52	56	61	58	55	55	30	57	57	64
May	66	58	63	65	60	61	63	41	64	64	70
June	74	69	72	70	67	68	70	53	70	71	78
July	80	74	77	73	70	72	75	66	76	75	86
Aug.	80	73	76	75	71	71	73	56	75	76	85
Sept.	73	69	70	72	68	66	66	46	70	70	78
Oct.	66	62	62	64	62	59	56	34	63	62	68
Nov.	57	58	52	60	64	51	46	22	53	53	60
Dec.	52	54	46	56	62	46	40	12	47	46	54

Typist - please type names of towns with initial caps & lower case.

Type the following abbreviations in alphabetical order, giving their meanings. Set out in 2 columns headed 'Abbreviation' and 'Meaning'.

e.g., viz, ad val, etc, PS, NB, MSS,

E & OE, OBE, Et seq, MOH, VC, BRS,

COD, RSVP, xd, NUT, TUC, NATO,

CBS, DEP, AEU, TGWU, PhD,

MA(cantab), c.i.f., NEDDY, NEB, TSA,

IMF, OPEC, IAB, ACAS, CAC, TOPS,

ESA, MSC, NALGO

3. Practise typing Minutes in block style—open punctuation. Type the following exercise on A4 paper, leaving 25 mm clear at top of page. Set tab stops for side headings at Elite 12, Pica 10; left margins at Elite 35, Pica 33; right margins Elite 90, Pica 75. Follow layout given. Note: If you are using Pica type face, the line endings will be different from copy. Keep your typed copy for future reference in Folder No. 2.

MINUTES of a Committee Meeting of the Brookfield Sports and Social Club held in the Staff Canteen on 12 May 1978 at 1800 hours.

PRESENT

Mr F L Ashby (Chairman)
Mr W Ferguson
Mrs J G Gregory
Mr W Keegan
Miss E K Ramsden
Miss S M Green (Honorary Secretary)

1	Apologies	Apologies were received from Mr M C Page and Miss J Whitecourt.
2	Minutes	The Secretary read the Minutes of the meeting held on 24 March. These were signed by the Chairman as being a correct record.
3	Matters arising	There were no matters arising from the Minutes.
4	Annual Summer Outing	It was unanimously agreed that the Secretary should arrange for an outing to Edinburgh on Saturday 24 June.
5	Winter Programme	It was agreed that the following suggestions be put to the Annual General Meeting

         a   Formation of Drama Group
         b   Visit to the theatre
         c   Annual Dinner/Dance

6	Date of next meeting	It was agreed that the next committee meeting should be held immediately after the Annual General Meeting on 8 September.

Chairman _____

Date _____

Job 69   Production Target—*15 minutes*

Display the following. All matter underscored to be typed in closed capitals—do not underscore.

REPRINTS AVAILABLE

(Typist – please put in order indicated by the nos. at the left-hand side. Do not type nos.)

① HOW TO MEET CHANGING NEEDS IN TYPEWRITING — A 9-part series by John L. Rowe covering such topics as correct touch, writing nos. & symbols, electric typing, development of speed and accuracy.

32 pages $1.00 per copy

⑤ DATA PROCESSING: AN INTRODUCTION
u.c. FOR STUDENTS — a four-part series by Merle W. Wood & Robert G. Espergen
u.c. th introduces data processing to High School students in language they can understand.

ESPERGEN

16 pages   50¢ per copy

② ELECTRIC TYPING — The columns written
caps. for Business Education by Marion Wood in wh she discusses skill

24 pages   75¢ " "
and production techniques in electric typing.

③ THE TYPING TEACHER AS A TECHNICIAN —
A series by Alan C. Lloyd on development, protection, & correction, & refinement of basic typing skill

16 pp.   50¢ per copy

④ HOW TO TEACH TRANSCRIPTION — A series of 4 articles th. constitute a detailed outline for a transcription course.

12 pp.   35¢ per copy

⑦ EFFECTIVE TEACHING TECHNIQUES FOR
H GENERAL BUSINESS — A nine-part series by Dr. S. David Satlow th offers suggestions for arousing student interest

SATLOW

20 pp.   75¢ per copy

⑥ SHORTHAND DICTATION LABORATORY —
A report on schools th hv installed electronic equipment for dictation.

L shorthand
16 pp.   75¢ per copy

⑧ GENERAL BUSINESS: Student projects th wl intensify learning —   caps
By Alan C. Lloyd

8 pp.   25¢ " "

⑨ HANDLING THE BUSINESS MANAGEMENT OF EXTRA-CURRICULAR ACTIVITIES — S. David Satlow's just-concluded 14-part series.

52 pp. $1.50 " "

through classroom discussion, group projects, etc.

4. Practise typing Minutes in indented style with standard punctuation. Type the following on A4 paper in single-line spacing, with double spacing between the numbered Minutes. Set margins and tab stops at points indicated. Keep your typed copy for future reference in Folder No. 2.

Left Margin
33(31)

Right
Margin
90(75)

Minutes of a Committee Meeting of THE CHAMPION LAWN
TENNIS ASSOCIATION held in the Committee Room at
73 High Street on 24th February, 1978, at 1900 hours.

PRESENT:

Mr. W. B. Sykes (Chairman)
Miss G. J. Brown
Miss P. Clarke (Secretary)
Miss J. Coley
Mrs. A. Rigby
Mr. R. C. Sadler

Tab-stop
12(10)

1. Apologies   Apologies were received from Miss H. Cook and
                       Mr. J. Crowe.

2. Minutes   The Secretary read the Minutes of the meeting held on
                       22nd November, 1977. These were signed by the Chairman
                       as being a correct record.

3. Correspondence   There was no correspondence.

4. Cloakroom   It was proposed by Miss Brown, seconded by Mrs. Rigby,
    facilities   and agreed nem. con., that the quotation from
                       E. Clements Ltd. for £1,250 should be accepted. The
                       Secretary was asked to see that the work was put in
                       hand as soon as possible.

5. Any other   Miss Coley raised the question of a revision of the
    business —   Standing Orders.
    Standing   RESOLVED: That a sub-committee consisting of
    Orders   Mr. W. B. Sykes, Mrs. A. Rigby, and the
                                 Secretary should examine the Standing Orders
                                 and submit a draft of any amendments.

6. Next meeting   It was agreed that the next meeting should be held on
                       20th April, 1978, at 1900 hours.

Chairman _____

Date _____

Further exercises on Minutes of Meeting (indented style) are given on page
17 of **Practical Typing Exercises, Book Two.**

Care of the typewriter

To aid you in the production of first-class work, it is essential that your typewriter is kept in good working order. To do this you need a cleaning kit comprising:

1. A hard type-brush.

2. A long-handled soft dusting brush.

3. A duster.

Every morning you should:

(a) Brush the type with the hard brush. Brush outwards from back to front—never from side to side.

(b) Clean mechanism inside frame with soft brush.

(c) Use the duster for the outer casing, the platen, and cleaning underneath the machine.

Always keep your typewriter covered when it is not in use, and, if you have to move it

(a) lock the margins;
(b) lift it by the base *from the back*.

Great care is necessary when oiling a typewriter, and it is preferable to leave oiling to an experienced mechanic.

Composing at machine

The following letter is written in abbreviated longhand. Type it on A5 paper, spelling all words in full.

```
We wr deltd to hv yr nws this a.m. and esp. to lrn that
all yr effts drg the 1st fw mnths hv bn rewd in sch a satis.
mnr.  We shl nw lk fwd to hrg yr vce on the Rdio Prog. on the
ausp. day in Jan.  It wll be a grt joy to the whl fam. & I nd
nt tell you hw prd we fl ovr hvg sch a tlntd reltv.  My own
princ. cse for plsre ls in the fct that it ws I who frst
sgstd yr tkg up brdcstg.  Ths gvs me a tny shr in yr scess.
```

Review Quiz No. 5

Type the following on A4 paper in single-line spacing, with double spacing between each item, filling in the correct word or words in the blank spaces. Do not write on your textbook.

1. When typing tabular work remember to mark . . . and . . . of vertical lines.

2. In tabular work with subdivided columns type the . . . headings first.

3. When typing accounts with 2 sides, the space allowed for both sides must be . . .

4. Leader dots should always be typed . . . each other.

5. Always leave . . . space before the start and after the end of leader dots.

6. No word or letter must extend . . . the last leader dot.

7. When ruling by underscore, turn up . . . before and . . . after horizontal lines.

8. When a printer's dash is inserted instead of a column heading, type . . .   . . .

9. A reference sign in the body of tabulation or manuscript has . . . space before it, but . . . space after it in the footnote.

10. Reference signs should be . . . slightly in the body of text.

11. In wide tabulation work space can be saved in the . . . or in the . . . column.

12. In marking scale-points for diagonal headings, mark the top of the diagonal line at the same point as the . . . vertical line.

13. When the Particulars Column of a tabulation is narrow, . . . leader dots should be used.

Turn to page 211 and check your answers. Score one point for each correct entry.
Total score: 18.

5. Type the following on A4 paper in single-line spacing, with double between the numbered items. All paragraphs, other than the first, should be hanging paragraphs where applicable. All numbers to be copied as written. Keep your typed copy for future reference in Folder No. 2.

LITERARY MATTER

For / typing of work such as short stories, books,
theses, etc., the follow will be a guide /-

1. Size of paper: A4 - one side only is used.

2. Spacing: Double - to leave room for corrections or additions

3. Margins: Left hand / wide, usually 38 mm so th sheets can be bound or fastened together - sometimes referred to as a stitching or binding margin.

Right / hand 13 mm to 25 mm. Top & bottom margins equal - first line of matter starting 25 mm from top & last line ending 25 mm from bottom. [To ensure uniform top & btm margins on ea sheet, adopt one of the follow methods:

(b) Rule a heavy line on backing sheet (wh is usually wider than the typing paper) across / complete width of sheet 25 mm from the top & at a point 25 mm from bottom.

4. Pagination (/ numbering of pages: First page is not numbered, second & subsequent pp are numbered 13 mm (turn up) from top in arabic figures & in / centre of / page; viz. - 2 - (dash, space, number, space, dash). After typing page no, turn up 3 single spaces before starting text. It is essential that Prefaces are usually numbered in small Roman numerals.

Throughout the whole work, the layout for chapter headings, use of capitals, numbering, etc., must be consistent.

5. Chapter headings & numbers: The 1st page of a chapter may be in the form of a "Dropped Head", i.e., the chapter no. is typed 51 mm to 76 mm from / top edge in Roman numerals or Arabic nos. The heading is typed on the 3rd single-line space below / chapter no. in capital letters & centred.

6. Catchwords: When a continuation sheet is necessary, the first word or 2 appearing on the contn sheet are sometimes typed at the foot of the preceding page below the last line and justified

Margin annotations: 1: · L 1-1 · L H · NP · Insert 'A' here · L i.e., · uc · L) · cont. sheet shd shd consistently the same distance at top of page · 10 · 5 ·

Type the following in tabulated form. Use vertical headings and rule.

Sales Meeting - caps
January - December 1977] *u/s headings*
Attendance Record

Salesmen	January	February	March	April	May	June	July	Aug.	Sept.	Oct.	Nov.	Dec.	Totals
G. A. LIGHT	X	X	X	X	—	X	X	X	—	X	X	X	10
D. O. WILLIS	X	—	X	X	X	X	X	X	X	X	X	X	11
H. COMPTON													
L. NICHOLSON													
C. HOBART, Jnr													
C. HOBART, Snr													
A. BOSWELL													
J. GILL-PARSONS													
M. LOMAX													
P. ELLSWORTH													
A. ST. JOHN BROWN													
F. SINCLAIR													
L. CHARTER													
K. KINGSTON													

Typist Please put names in alpha order, listing surnames first. I have not completed the attendances, but they were as follows: Kingston, Compton, Nicholson & Hobart Jnr. were absent in Jan. & Nov. Kingston was also absent in Aug. Charter, Boswell, Hobart Snr & Brown were absent in Feb. Lomax, Gill-Parsons, Ellsworth & Sinclair were absent July, Sept. & October. Lomax & Ellsworth were also absent in December.

at the right margin – this is known as a "catchword."

CONTINUED or PTO may be used in place of the catchword, but NOT the number of the page.

7 Footnotes: Typed as explained on p 24 in single-line spacing.

8 Correction of errors: The Typist is expected to correct errors in spelling, grammar, or punctuation.
Where a word can be spelt in 2 ways, the same spelling must be adopted throughout (in italics)

9 Words to be printed or already printed must be underscored.

'A' (a) Put a light pencil mark 25 mm from top bottom edge of sheet before this is inserted in machine.

---

6. Practise typing literary matter. Type the following chapter of a story in double-line spacing. Make all corrections indicated, and also correct any spelling, punctuation, etc.

OUR FARM
Chapter I
cap
Please type as dropped head

Winter had arrived at the farm. Conditions were same all over the country, but I fact was of little importance to Ethel & myself. We were for it, and it made us proud to think that we at least, were prepared for the worst. [We had always made plans for the winter wherever we had bn, but this yr. it was different.

We were not so concerned for ourselves. We had passed and suffered (together) many winters, but now our principle thoughts were centred on our little stock of cattle & we wondered how it wd be affected if the winter were a severe one. [Being responsible for a herd of cattle was something new &, although we had managed fairly well in the Summer & Autumn, we had no experience of safeguarding a heard through I cold winter days, &, especially, the cold nights.

I decided that I shd hv to hv a vehical of some

11. After horizontal line, turn up 2 and type sub headings at left margin and tab. stop.
12. The next group of sub-headings are centred on the word <u>Director</u>& the horizontal line is typed 2 spaces below the sub headings typed in 11 above.
13. To find the starting point for the word <u>Publicity</u> back-space from the centre of the word <u>Director</u> - one for each 2 in the longest word in ea column plus the spaces between the columns. This will bring you to scale point 28(19)
14. Set tab stops for the other 2 sub headings [42(33) and 56(47)].
15. Type or mark horizontal line fr center of <u>Advertising</u> to centre of <u>Despatch</u> [33(24) and 60(51)].
16. Turn up 2 spaces and type sub headings.
17. Calculate and type next group of sub headings which are centered on the word <u>Secretary</u>
16. When typing has been completed, insert vertical lines & horizontal lines if these hv not ben typed by underscore.

---

* If the chart were handwritten or not displayed, it wd be necessary to type a draft to find out how the sub headings balanced on ea other.
Ɨ The figures in "round" brackets are for Pica type face.

6. Display the following chart on a sheet of A4 paper.

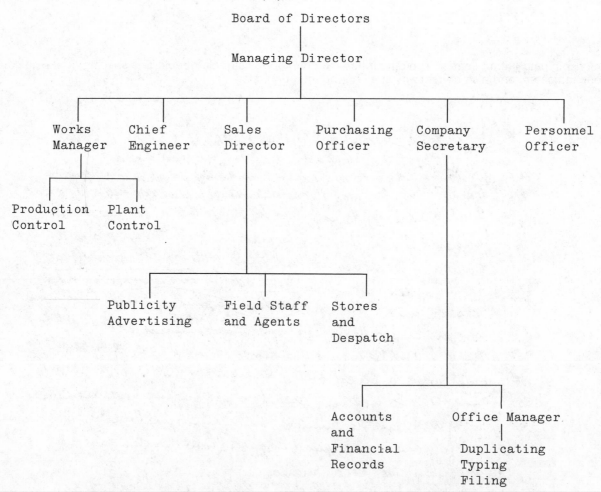

Further exercises on organisation charts are given on pages 56—57 of **Practical Typing Exercises, Book Two**.

^o kind, whether car or tractor I must decide ^, myself ^

stet I did not mention this to Ethel ~~particularly~~ ~~partly~~ because I did not want to worry her, but I must admit that ^ I was afraid she wd make up my mind for me.

N.P. ~~that was~~ (my principle reason was) [During one a friend of my jaunts to / village, I asked ^ for his advise. He tried to persuade me that a car was / only trs (thing) possible. I argued against it, but when he pointed out th we cd use it for going into / village to do our shopping, I almost agreed, but there still remained a doubt in my mind.

I almost wished I had confided in Ethel, asked ^ + ^ her for her advise, but / obstinacy of / male prevailed against it. How, I thought, wd a second-hand car, even w special tyres, cope w / mud + slush of / country-side in / winter time? Surely a tractor wd be a better proposition, but ^ how cd we, in / 1st flush of our (being landowners, go shopping in a tractor? — + this weighed heavily on my mind —)

It wd be better than a bicycle, wh I trs (at present,) used but did not seem to trs fit (very well) in w our ideas of a simple country life. Then again, I thought, what wd our new neighbours think ^ when we parked our (+ say) tractor at the market alongside their sometimes N.P. gleaming cars? [In the end Ethel solved the problem for me by suggesting th ^ we shd buy a tractor of / farm + a tricycle for shopping!

Further exercises on literary work are given on pages 27–28 of **Practical Typing Exercises, Book Two**.

56

5. Type the following exercise on A4 paper in single-line spacing with double between lettered and numbered items. Insert heading ʹORGANISATION CHARTSʹ. Correct any spelling mistakes or inconsistencies.

An organization chart shows the various departments in a business (in a large organization it could be details of the organization of one dept or even a section of a dept) and gives lines of communication, delegation, and authority. By studying an organisation chart, one can see for what a dept is responsible and to whom it is responsible. Usually, but not necessarily, top management is at the head of the chart & the connecting lines lead downwards to lower management.

The lines may be ruled by underscore, by ink, or by a combination of both, provided th the ink is the same color as the u/score lines.

When typing an organisation chart see th y leave equal margins at either side of the widest horizontal line(s). In the table on page 168 it wl be seen th the left margin starts at the begining of the word Production & theright margin ends w the word Personnel.*

When typing the organization chart on page 168, proceed as follows:

1. (a) Centre on paper and type first heading
    (b) Turn up 1 &, at centre point of heading just typed, put a pencil mark, or type an apostrophe, to tell y where to draw the vertical line. Turn up another single space.

2. Type second heading, turn up 1 & mark point for vertical line. Turn up another single space.

3. Fr the centre of the paper back-space once for ea 2 letters in th part of the word Production wh extends beyond the word Manager, & then continue back-spacing once for every 2 characters in the longest word in ea sub heading under the first horizontal line: i.e., Pr od uc tM an ag er, etc. Then backspace for the 3 spaces btwn ea group of subheadings. This will bring you to the left margin [14(5)‡] for the start of the word production.

4. As the first group of sub headings start to the right of the left margin
    (a) tap in once for ea letter extending to the left of the word Manager, i.e., Product and set tab stop at point reached [21(12)].
    (b) From 21(12) tap in and set tab. stop for beginning of ea sub-heading under the 1st horizontal line.

5. The first horisontal line runs from the centre of the word Manager to the center of the wordPersonnel. Find these 2 points [24(15) and 82/73] & mark or type horizontal line.

6. Turn up 2 spaces and type sub-headings at tab stops.

7. Mark, either in pensil or w the apostrophe, the centre point of the longest item in ea sub heading just typed to indicate the points at wh vertical lines must be drawn. Turn up 2 spaces.

8. It wl be seen fr the chart on page 168 th the group of sub-headings starting at the left margin is centred under the word Manager,

9. The word Production starts at the left margin; therefore, fr the left margin tap space bar once for each letter in the word Production plus three spaces and set tab stop for the word Plant: 27(18).

10. The horizontal line above Production & Plant starts from the centre of the word Production and ends at the centre of the word Control. Find these 2 points [19(10) and 30(21)] & mark or type horizontal line.

Type a copy of the following exercise on A4 paper.

BOARD MEETING No 364

Minutes of a meeting of / Board of Directors held at the registered office of the Co on [March] 14 1977 @ 1000 hrs.

~~Pres~~ PRESENT

Mr C H Fullard (Chairman)

Miss B J Round

Mr R Yeomans   Please put

Mr T. Chamberlain   in Alpha order

Mrs R Watkins

IN ATTENDANCE

Mrs A Randle (Auditor)

Mr C Sanders (Sec)

(MINUTES)

u.c./2 X The Sec read the minutes of the board meeting held on 14 Feb '77 ← (and after approval by the meeting the Chairman signed the Minutes)

1 APOLOGIES Mr F Rudge regretted th he was unable to attend.

3 MATTERS   Miss Round said th / new factory @ Barry,
ARISING   South Glam, wd be ready by June of next yr.

4. SUBSCRIPTIONS   It was decided to cease ~~meber~~ membership of the British Institute of Marketing, & the Sec shd give notice immediately.

5. SICK PAY   It was proposed by Mr Fullard, seconded by Mrs Watkins, & agreed unanimously th instructions u.c. abt deduction of National Health Sick pay fr salary pd during sickness (as outlined in Minute No 350/6) shd be circulated to all staff.

6. NEXT MEETING   As / date of the next meetg wd fall on Easter Monday, it was agreed th / Board shd meet on 18 April at 1000 hrs.

Chairman _____

Date _____

The headings of a table are sometimes typed diagonally, as in the table below. This can best be done if the figure columns are all made the same width, which will be the width of the longest line in any of the figure columns. To type such headings the paper will have to be inserted diagonally, and the headings must be typed parallel to the diagonal lines and centred between the two. It is advisable to rule the diagonal lines after the table has been completed, and, when the paper is reinserted to type the headings, the diagonal lines should be aligned with the alignment scale.

The scale-points for these lines must be marked in pencil, and the following procedure should be adopted:

1. Find in the usual way the horizontal spaces required for the column items and spaces between the columns (making all the figure columns the same width). Rule by underscore or ink the top horizontal line, or mark the beginning and end as usual.

2. Find the number of vertical line-spaces required for the headings in the same way as you did for vertical headings (see Page 164). Turn the paper up this number of spaces, and rule or mark the second horizontal line.

3. Along this second line mark in pencil the scale-points for the vertical lines between columns (which will also be the scale-points for the *bottom* of the diagonal lines) and set tab. stops for the start of each column as usual.

Mark the scale-points for the *top* of the diagonal lines as follows: The top of the first diagonal line should be marked at the same scale-point as the second vertical line, the top of the second diagonal line at the same scale-point as the third vertical line, and so on. For the top of the last diagonal line tap the space-bar once for the number of spaces required for the longest line of the column plus 3 extra spaces (to allow for spaces between columns) and mark the top of the last diagonal line at the point reached.

4. Practise typing diagonal headings. Type the following table in double spacing on A4 paper, lengthwise.

MILEAGE CHART

TOWN	Aberdeen	Birmingham	Bristol	Edinburgh	Exeter	Glasgow	London	Liverpool	Manchester	York
Aberdeen	—	403	480	115	555	142	488	326	326	299
Birmingham . .	403	—	88	288	163	289	110	90	80	127
Bristol	480	88	—	365	75	366	116	159	161	215
Edinburgh . . .	115	288	365	—	440	44	373	211	211	184
Exeter	555	163	75	440	—	441	170	235	236	290
Glasgow	142	289	366	44	441	—	394	212	212	207
London	488	110	116	373	170	394	—	197	184	145
Liverpool	326	90	159	211	235	212	197	—	35	97
Manchester . . .	326	80	161	211	236	212	184	35	—	64
York	299	127	215	184	290	207	145	97	64	—

Further exercise on diagonal headings is given on page 55 of **Practical Typing Exercises, Book Two**.

— 24 —

Typist: Please use a dropped head & double spacing.

CHAPTER II

l.c.   A <u>G</u>reenhouse will increase the scope & interest of

1-1 yr gardening activities/it can prove a profitable investment

at the present time indeed, especially/when we are encouraged to grow/vegetables. *our own*

You wl find a big saving from the rasing of plants

fr seeds and propagation fr cuttings for spring and sumer

displays in the open garden. This is far less expensive

& much more interesting than buying from nurseries. ~~For~~ *Further*

you could be picking tomatoes, not when they are a glut on

l.c. the <u>M</u>arket, but while/ *they are* still costing a fortune in the shops.

~~In the same way~~, *Similarly* in the depths of winter, when cut flowers

are so expensive, your home can be a blaze of colour ~~from~~

H with greenhouse/ raised blooms. You can also be gathering fresh green

salad crops. *ˣ.*   *Typist: I hv retyped page 24 - the 1st p. of Chapter II of my book on gardening Please type it again for me making all necessary corrections - both errors indicated & any others you may find.*

ˣ See Chapter III, pages 52–57

Type the following Menu on A5 (148 × 210 mm) paper, making corrections
as marked. Draw a frame round the menu leaving ½″ (13 mm) clear at top and
bottom and 1″ (25 mm) clear on either side.

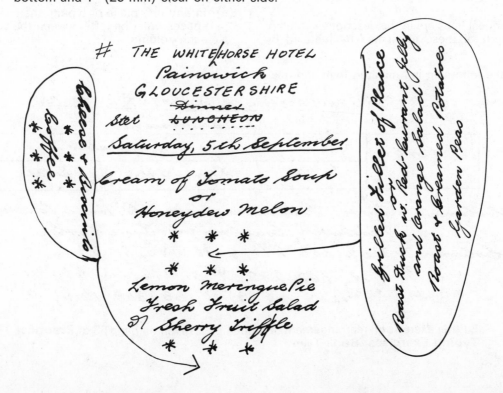

THE WHITE/HORSE HOTEL
Painswick
GLOUCESTERSHIRE
~~Dinner~~
Stet ~~LUNCHEON~~
Saturday, 5th September
Cream of Tomato Soup
or
Honeydew Melon
* * *
* * *
Lemon Meringue Pie
Fresh Fruit Salad
or Sherry Triffle
* * *

Grilled Fillet of Plaice
or
Roast Duck w. Red-currant Jelly
and Orange Salad
Roast & Creamed Potatoes
Garden Peas

Cheese & Biscuits
Coffee
* * *
* * *

2. Type the following on A5 paper. Use vertical headings for second and third columns and rule.

OFFICE DESKS

	Reference Number	Colour Number *	Height in	Height cm	Width in	Width cm	Depth in	Depth cm
Double Pedestal	350	218	28½	72.40	60	152.40	30	76.20
Single	352	110	28½	72.40	50	127.00	30	76.20
~~Typists~~ Typing	360	316	28½	72.40	55	139.70	30	76.20
Secretarial	361	319	28½	72.40	60	152.40	35	88.90
Executive	357	312	29	73.66	60	152.40	35	88.90

* See Colour Chart attached

Rearranging tabular matter

1. It is often necessary to rearrange the matter. Before starting to type it is essential that you make a rough plan of what has to be done.

2. When columns in tabulation are very wide, it is necessary to consider where space can be saved. The following hints will be of help to you in such cases.

(a) If the longest lines of the columns are in the headings, additional lines may be taken for these, so as to reduce the width required for the columns.

(b) If the longest lines are in the descriptive column, the length of these lines may be reduced by taking extra lines for lengthy items. If this is done, allowance must be made for these extra lines when calculating the number of vertical lines required.

(c) As a last resort, you may have to leave one space only between vertically ruled columns or a minimum of two spaces between unruled columns.

(d) To save vertical spaces, it may be necessary to omit spaces before and after horizontal lines, or to use half-spacing before and after these lines.

(e) In any one piece of typing, the same number of spaces must be left between the widest item of each column.

3. Display the following in tabulated form and rule.

SEA PASSENGER MOVEMENT BY PORTS

In thousands

Port	January to September		
	To U.K.	From U.K	Total

Column 1 – Dover, Folkestone, Harwich, Hull, London, Newhaven, Southampton, Tyne Ports.
Column 2 – 1132, 336, 271, 8, 32, 175, 58, 59
    " 3 – 1130, 362, 288, 7, 31, 174, 63, 61
    " 4 – 2262, 698, 559, 15, 63, 349, 121, 120

Further exercise on rearrangement of tabulation is given on page 53 of **Practical Typing Exercises, Book Two**.

Type the alphabetic review *once* for practice, *once* for speed, and finally *once* for accuracy. Margins: Elite 22–82, Pica 12–72.

Review alphabet keys

A junior executive of the firm was asked to explain the question raised by a young man who seems very hazy about it.

Accuracy/Speed Practice   Five-minute timing   Not more than 3 errors

words

AS.12   Science fiction is a term we link with weird creatures from outer   13
space or strange objects flying through the shadowy night.   Should we   27
not have more respect for science fiction?   I think we should, because   41
so many of the tools used in science and space travel are things that   55
I read about in science fiction.   61

I remember reading that strange story about a ship that could travel   75
beneath the oceans of the world and it was powered by energy from the   89
sea.   In my young days the author was laughed at for writing such fan-   103
tasy.   Today there are submarines that stay submerged for as long as a   117
year and they are powered by atomic energy.   Then there was that tall   130
tale about a visit to the moon — at a time when the only means of flight   144
was a balloon.   Now, today, man has landed on the moon on a number of   158
occasions and returned safely.   164

I also enjoyed reading that tale about a machine that could take a   177
person forward or backward in time.   As far as I know, such a machine   191
has not been made, but, at this very moment, some genius may be hard at   205
work on such an invention.   Would it be wise to look into the past?   Or,   220
what is more to the point, would it be a good thing to look ahead to the   234
year 2001 and see what is in store?   I often look back with joy, but the   248
thought of looking forward frightens me.   256

Of course, science fiction was not confined to story books.   There   270
have been many motion pictures that dealt with this subject and showed,   284
for the first time, the strange objects described in books.   The men   298
from outer space always had a ray gun as part of their standard equipment,   312
and what a useful weapon it was — to the space men at any rate.   Now earth   327
men have harnessed a ray called the laser beam.   It is used as a cutting   341
tool.   342

Which came first, fiction or fact?   Did scientists read the fiction   356
books and make up their minds to invent the things described in them?   370
Or were the writers of the books prophets who could predict what would   384
take place in the future?   Will the present fictitious flying submarine   398
become   fact?   (S.I. 1.28)   400

Vertical column headings

To find the number of line-spaces to be left between the first and second horizontal lines to allow for the vertical headings, count the number of characters and spaces in the longest line of the heading and add two extra spaces (i.e., one space before and one space after the heading). Then convert this number into single-line spaces as in the following example:

Assuming the longest line of all vertical headings takes up 16 horizontal spaces, the total number of horizontal spaces required is 16 plus 2 = 18. As there are 6 single-line spaces in 25 mm (1"), there are 9 single-line spaces in 38 mm (1½"). You should therefore turn up 9 single-line spaces after the first horizontal line, then turn up one more space and type the second horizontal line.

Another method of finding the amount of space required for vertical headings is to type the longest heading on a piece of paper and measure the space needed. When the paper is reinserted for the headings to be typed, see that the alignment scale is level with the vertical line already ruled (or marked) and arrange the heading in such a way that it is spaced equally between the 2 vertical lines. Also when typing the headings, remember to leave one clear space before and after.

NOTE: With vertical headings it is better for each heading to start at the point fixed for the longest line of the heading.

1. Practise tabulation with vertical headings. Type the following on A4 paper in double spacing. Rule in ink.

SHARE INDICES

Groups and Sub-Sections	Monday March 9	Friday March 6	Thursday March 5	Wednesday March 4	Tuesday March 3
Capital Goods					
Aircraft	106.08	106.00	106.53	106.90	106.62
Building Material ..	140.66	141.75	141.98	143.27	143.20
Engineering ..	109.70	109.91	110.16	110.33	110.62
Machine Tools ..	93.73	94.01	93.04	92.75	92.62
Miscellaneous ..	98.50	98.16	98.25	98.40	97.76
Consumer Goods					
Electrical	105.44	104.86	105.19	106.10	106.17
Household Goods ..	124.81	125.61	124.95	125.00	125.54
Rubber Goods ..	101.43	101.43	101.63	101.48	102.67
Other Groups					
Chemicals	115.42	115.41	115.61	115.41	115.93
Oil	151.63	152.25	152.89	152.77	153.17
Shipping	141.79	142.44	142.54	142.96	143.96

Further exercise on vertical column headings is given on page 50 of **Practical Typing Exercises, Book Two**.

Poetry

The following rules are a guide to the typing of poems:

1. *Positioning*: The longest line of the verse must be centred on the page horizontally, with uniform margins all round.
2. *Spacing*: Single-line spacing, double between verses.
3. (a) If alternate lines rhyme, these usually begin at the same scale-point (unless they are of irregular length, when they are centred). The first line and all lines rhyming with it are written at the margin, while the second and all lines rhyming with it are indented two spaces from the start of the first, third, etc., lines. (Short lines may be indented more than two spaces.)
   (b) In blank verse (i.e., where no lines rhyme), all lines also start at margin.
   (c) When lines are of approximately equal length, and when successive lines rhyme, these start at the margin, i.e., there is no indentation.
   (d) If all lines rhyme, these all start at the margin.
4. Each line starts with a capital letter.

1. Practise typing poems. Read and study the above explanation, and then type each of the following poems on A5 paper. Keep your typed copies for future reference in Folder No. 2.

(a) Alternate lines rhyme

The Brook

```
I chatter over stony ways,
  In little sharps and trebles,
I bubble into eddying bays,
  I babble on the pebbles.
```

Alfred Tennyson

(b) Blank verse

```
To be, or not to be — that is the question:
Whether 'tis nobler in the mind to suffer
The slings and arrows of outrageous fortune,
Or to take arms against a sea of troubles,
And by opposing end them?  To die — to sleep:
No more; and, by a sleep, to say we end
The heart-ache, and the thousand natural shocks
That flesh is heir to — 'tis a consummation
Devoutly to be wish'd.  To die — to sleep:
To sleep! perchance to dream: ay, there's the rub.
```

William Shakespeare

(c) Successive lines rhyme

To the Daisy

```
With little here to do or see
Of things that in the great world be,
Sweet Daisy! oft I talk to thee
    For thou art worthy,
Thou unassuming commonplace
Of Nature, with that homely face,
And yet with something of a grace
    Which love makes for thee!
```

W. Wordsworth

Skill building

Type each line or sentence (A, B, and C) *three* times. If time permits, complete your practice by typing each group once as it appears. Margins: Elite 22–82, Pica 12–72.

A. Review alphabet keys

1. The big garden adjoining a quaint cottage was kept very trim and the gaily-coloured azaleas were exceptionally fine.

B. Build speed on common word drill

2. please happy leave given paper money cause begin out say the

3. I am happy to say that he has given some money to the cause.

4. Before I begin to hand out the papers, ask her for her book.

5. Please tell her that I will leave here in about three hours.

C. Build speed on fluency drill

6. They said that they must plan each week what they must sell.

7. Last year that same call came when they were away from home.

8. Each must hear what that girl will talk over with Jill Wood.

9. This plan from some club made both boys very busy last week.

Accuracy/Speed Practice	Three-minute timing	Not more than 3 errors
		words

AS.28 We can well understand your concern over the increased rate for our insur- 15
ances. It is natural that you should want to know why this increase has come 30
about. We hope that the following information will be of help. 42

There are no longer any low-priced cars. As a result, we are now insuring 57
greater values, and a person who is insured wants to be compensated for the 73
financial loss that he has sustained. 80

All costs today are far above those which we have been accustomed to pay. 95
Repair costs on cars used by our policy-holders average over one hundred per 110
cent more for each claim than in 1950. Similar increases which have occurred 125
in all other items must be included in the cost of insurance. The costs of 140
labour have increased in proportion to the cost of living. The prices of 154
everyday necessities have increased. In comparison with these prices, we 169
still believe that the cost of your protection is very reasonable. 182

There is no doubt that car insurance rates could be much less if only we 197
would be more careful. We have it within our power to reduce the rate of 211
insurance to any point we see fit if we would reduce accidents to a minimum. 227
If we all work together, we shall again bring insurance rates down. (S.I. 1.40) 240

UNIT 23

2. Type the following exercise on A4 paper in single spacing with double between numbered items. Make any corrections necessary. Keep your typed copy for future reference in Folder No. 2.

Setting out diagram, etc.   (Centre in caps and
u/s)

You may be asked to leave blank spaces for the insertion of photographs, etc., or you may hv to draw geometrical figures. The diagram or blank space left must be the exact size indicated. For instance, if y were asked to leave a BLANK space of 2" (51 mm) y shd turn up 13 (THIRTEEN) single-line spaces. However, if y hv to INSERT LINES and use the UNDERSCORE for the horizontals, y wd turn up the exact number of lines. For example, if you had to draw a square 2" (51 mm) deep, & you were using the u/s for the horizontal lines, type the first horizontal line, turn up 12 (TWELVE) & type the second horizontal line.

Horizontal & vertical lines may be drawn in ink or by means of the u/s. Alternatively, the horisontal lines may be typed by the underscore & the vertical lines drawn in ink, provided the ink is the same colour as the lines typed by the u/s.

When typing from complicated copy, it is a good plan to quickly type a draft to see how much space the typing, drawing, etc., is likely to take up.

It is essential, when a diagram has typing beforeand after it, th there is a blank space before the first line and after the last line. The same spacing wd apply if you were leaving a given space for a photograph or picture — there shd be a clear space above and below.

When typing theexercise on p 62 proceed as follows:

1. Use margins of 20—85 Elite, 10—75 Pica.
2. Centre main heading on typing line.
3. Type first paragraph & turn up 2 single spaces.
4. Fr left margin type underscore for 1st horizontal line - 2" (51mm) = 24 Elite or 20 Pica spaces. The square is 2" (51 mm) deep; there- fore, turn up 12 and type second horisontal line from left margin.
5. Re-set left margin at 47(33)*. This point is arrived at by taping space bar once for every space in thewidth of the square [24(20)] plus 3 spaces to seperate the diagram from the typing.
6. Type matter on right of diagram.
7. Turn up twice, reset left margin at 20(10), and type next para. Turn up twice.
8. The diagram on the right-hand side will take up 1½" (38 mm) horizontally which is 18 Elite or 15 Pica spaces. You will need to leave 3 spaces clear btwn last typed character & start of diagram: this gives a total of 21 Elite, 18 Pica spaces. There- fore, before typing the matter on the left of the diagram, re-set right margin at 64 (85 — 21) Elite, 57 (75 — 18) Pica.

can be typed, set on a machine like a Varityper (VARITYPER)
(wh prints letters of different sizes & types) or even
be printed. The finished copy is then photographed
and / image either transferred to a sensitized plate
th wl be used as a master or transferred indirectly
to a copying m/c. This process is suitable for large
quantities.

Photo-copying ← All caps

By this method of duplicating an exact copy
of an original document can be ~~produced~~ reproduced. The
basic principle is / action of light on paper wh has
ʒ/ bn chemically treated. It is becoming v. popular
trs/ in many offices, because of the accuracy & speed w
wh / copies can be obtained. This process is not
economical for / production of a large no. of copies.
This process

Bibliography

A Bibliography is a list of books or magazine or newspaper articles included in footnotes or at the end of a chapter or book to show the source from which information has been taken. It includes the author, the title of the work, place and date of publication, and sometimes the pages to which reference is made. The items are listed alphabetically. If any item takes more than one line, the extra lines are indented ten spaces. The author's name is written first, followed by his Christian name or initials. Titles are usually underscored, or may be typed in capitals. The following specimen will give you an idea of the most common method of typing a Bibliography.

4. Practise typing a bibliography. Read the above explanation. Then type a copy of the following on A5 paper in single-line spacing, with double spacing between each item. List authors alphabetically.

```
Shafto, T A C: STUDY NOTES ON COMMERCE
        McGraw-Hill Book Company (UK) Limited, 1973

    Holt, G: TYPING FLUENCY AND ACCURACY PRACTICE
    McGraw-Hill Book Company (UK) Limited, 1977

Drummond, A M, and Scattergood, I E: TYPING FIRST COURSE
        McGraw-Hill Book Company (UK) Limited, 1977

Outhwaite, W: COMMERCE FOR SCHOOLS, pp 28-35
        McGraw-Hill Book Company (UK) Limited, 1977

Gavin, R E, and Sabin, W A:
        REFERENCE MANUAL FOR STENOGRAPHERS AND TYPISTS
        McGraw-Hill International Book Company
```

9. Type paragraph on left of diagram, taking care not to type beyond scale point 64(57).
10. Diagram: type first horizontal line from scale point 68(61).
11. Turn up 6 single line spaces and type second horizontal line.
12. Remove paper from machine and insert vertical lines.

---

* Figures in brackets are for Pica type face.

3. Type the following exercise on A4 paper using margins of Elite 20—85, Pica 10—75.

FILING EQUIPMENT

STAX ON STEEL FILES are a deluxe series of reinforced transfer drawer files with mosonite reinforced panels back and front, and extra strength at the sides.

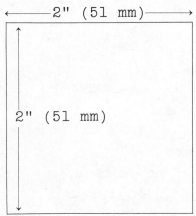

These files represent the best in storage efficiency, the most in economy. STAX on Steel Files will give years of good active service. Our clients are more than satisfied with the smooth drawer action and the superb engineering which means that one drawer takes only its own weight no matter how high they are stacked.

Size: A4 — 13" x 10½" x 24"
           (331 x 267 x 610 mm)

All filing systems are procedures for retrieving information with optimum speed and at minimum cost.

The use of ACCO Fasteners requires personnel to observe orderly arrangement of input, and secures the information in proper sequence until retrieved. As a consequence, wasteful search time is eliminated and time and money are saved.

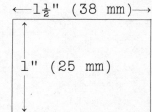

NOTE TO TYPIST: Do not type measurements on diagrams

Indent→   <u>Spirit Duplicating</u>   All caps

This is another kind of duplicating process, somewhat similar to stencilling, & for up to two hundred copies this method is cheaper than stencilling.

A copy [master] is prepared by means of a sheet of hectographic carbon (i.e. a sheet coated w an aniline dye). The matter is typed through an ordinary typewriter ribbon on to the sheet of hectographic carbon being placed @ / back of the paper w/ coated side upwards.→ [a special paper having a glossy surface,]

Run on (This hectographic carbon can be obtained in different colours, so th spirit duplicating can be used when colour work is required.→

(an ordinary pen or pencil being used.)

Handwritten copies may also be produced on a spirit duplicator, & When / master is completed, the carbon sheet is discarded. The master is then fitted to / duplicating m/c, & as the ~~duplicating~~ paper on wh copies are being made passes through / m/c, it is moistened by spirit & / print is transferred to / sheet of paper.

All th is necessary is to insert a sheet of hectographic carbon of / particular colour req'd, so th / part of / master sheet may be typed through blue, anor through purple, anor through red, etc., & when / copies are run off these appear in / different colours, unlike the stencilling process / wh requires a separate stencil to be used for whatever part of / matter is to be in a different colour.

        Offset Litho Process ← All caps

This method of duplicating requires a thin

sheet / metal or paper / on wh / matter is typed. A special typewriter ribbon is also necessary, or / matter

NP / can be written by hand w special pencils. [Where fine quality is needed, masters are usually re-produced by a photographic process. The writer copy

Job 24

Type the following exercise on A5 landscape paper. Draw the diagrams but do not insert measurements. Type the words in the diagrams, centring them vertically and horizontally.

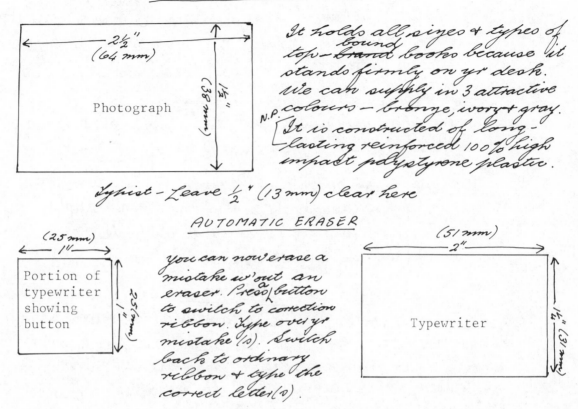

CLEAR-VIEW COPY HOLDER

2½" (64 mm) — 1½" (38 mm) — Photograph

It holds all sizes & types of top-bound books because it stands firmly on yr desk. We can supply in 3 attractive colours — bronze, ivory & gray. N.P. It is constructed of long-lasting reinforced 100% high impact polystyrene plastic.

Typist - Leave ½" (13 mm) clear here

AUTOMATIC ERASER

(25 mm) 1" — 1" (25 mm) — Portion of typewriter showing button

You can now erase a mistake w'out an eraser. Press a button to switch to correction ribbon. Type over yr mistake (s). Switch back to ordinary ribbon & type the correct letter(s).

(51 mm) 2" — 1½" (38 mm) — Typewriter

Job 25

Display the following exercise on a card measuring 148 × 210 mm. Centre vertically and horizontally.

MODERN SECRETARIAL PROCEDURE

by

KATHLEEN M TROTMAN

Because one of the most important features of a good secretarial course should be to explain why the procedure is necessary— not only how it is done—and to enable students to see their future jobs in the context of the organization of their firms, this book provides a useful introduction to the structure of business.

Published by McGraw-Hill Book Co. (UK) Ltd.

Further exercises on diagrams are given on pages 23, 29, 30 and 72 of **Practical Typing Exercises, Book Two**.

f(e) Replace m/c cover.

L.c./ e(f) Leave Cylinder in correct position.

After (3) Holding / bottom of / stencil & backing (sheet) in one hand attach / head portion* of stencil to / cylinder of / duplicating m/c by placing / perforations, or slots, over / stubs.

---

* The face or readable side of / stencil shld fit against / drum & back of / backing-sheet upper most.

‡ Check copies carefully. If there are any unwanted spots of ink caused by cracks in / stencil, apply correcting fluid. If necessary, a slight tear can be repaired by use of paper. (gummed)

'A' INTERLEAVING

Stencil copies are usually run off on paper having a soft, absorbent surface. Because this kind / paper dries up / wet ink / especially if good quality quick-drying ink is used / copies can be run off one after / or w'out danger of smearing. However, Sometimes it is necessary to / l.c. use bond paper. (or or non-absorbent paper) in order to lend prestige to / copy.

Most / manfrs. can supply an automatic inter-leaver or drying mechanism; otherwise, / process must be performed by hand & so time / wasting. H

When such paper is used, it is necessary to insert blotting sheets between ea. stencilled copy to prevent smearing. This process is known as interleaving.

Stationery

The job you are doing will determine what kind of paper you use, so that you must choose the quality which is suitable. You should ask yourself: How much handling will the paper receive? How long will it have to last? How many carbon copies are wanted? The process by which paper is made results in the fibres running in one direction—called grain. The longer the fibres, the stronger the paper in the direction they run. When the grain is horizontal the paper bends more easily round the platen and is less likely to slip. When the grains run vertically, it is easier to make neat erasures. In any case, erasing strokes should always be made in the same direction as the grain.

The most commonly used paper in business for original copies is bond. The appearance of bond paper is a bright non-fading white, combined with an opaque and uniform finish.

Some paper has a watermark, i.e. a sketch or wording which can be seen when the sheet is held to the light. Its chief value is that it identifies the right side of the paper. When you can read the watermark, you are looking at the side of the paper on which you should type.

Composing at machine

Type the following on A5 paper, replacing the words underscored by another word without appreciably altering the meaning.

We must <u>endeavour</u> to <u>comfort</u> that <u>small</u> child who, I <u>hear</u>, has lost some <u>coins</u> with which she <u>intended</u> to <u>purchase</u> a <u>present</u> in the <u>city</u> for a <u>person living near her home</u>. She is very much <u>troubled</u> as she fears her mother will be <u>angry</u>.

Review Quiz No. 2

Type the following on A4 paper in single-line spacing, with double spacing between each item, filling in the correct word or words in the blank spaces. Do not write on your textbook.

1. Paragraph headings which are typed with initial capital and lower case characters must be . . .

2. Side headings are typed inside the . . . margin and usually in . . .   . . . with or without . . .

3. When letters or figures are used in enumerations either in brackets or followed by a full stop, . . . spaces should be left after final bracket or full stop.

4. Roman numerals in enumerations may be blocked to . . . or to . . .

5. Footnotes are typed in . . . . . . spacing preceded by . . . . . . and . . . space is left after the reference symbol in the footnote. The reference symbol in the body of the text is typed . . . to word.

6. A notice of a meeting is generally accompanied by an . . .

7. Records of business discussed at a meeting are called . . . and are entered in a . . . . . .

8. The first page of manuscript is . . . numbered but subsequent pages are numbered and usually at . . .

9. When the first page of a chapter starts lower than the remaining pages, this is called a . . .   . . .

10. Prefaces are usually numbered in . . .   . . . numerals.

11. Minutes of a meeting are written in . . . person and in . . . tense.

12. When open punctuation is used, full stops are omitted after numbered items, . . . clear spaces being left after numbers.

Turn to page 211 and check your answers. Score one point for each correct entry. Total score: 26.

On occasions it may be necessary to cut out a word, phrase, sentence, or even a paragraph and replace it with a new piece of stencil—this is known as 'grafting', and the following steps should be taken:

1. Place stencil, face upwards, on a piece of cardboard.

2. Cut out the incorrect piece with a sharp knife (or a razor blade) and ruler, cutting as closely as possible to the typed characters.

3. On a spare stencil type the matter, taking particular care not to type beyond the size of the piece cut out.

4. Cut out the piece typed in No. 3—it should be slightly larger all round than the piece cut out from the original stencil in No. 2.

5. Place in position and check.

6. If accurate, spread adhesive lightly round edges.

7. Place graft in position immediately, ensuring that the newly typed matter is in correct alignment.

8. Strengthen edges of graft at back and front by applying correcting fluid.

9. Leave to dry for a few minutes.

2. Type a copy of the following on A4 paper in single-line spacing, with double spacing between paragraphs. Keep your typed copy for future reference in Folder No. 2.

When yr stencil is ready for running off, take the following steps:

1. Remove carbon paper.

2. Rotate ~~cylinder~~ drum by means of handle to force a little ink thro'. 3 4. Turn the handle slowly until the stencil falls into position. 4 6. Inspect stencil, & smooth out any creases by gently pushing stencil to outside & bottom edges.

4 5. Remove backing sheet.

7 6. Prepare duplicating paper by fanning it. Then place in feed tray. 7 8 Adjust feed & receiving tray to suit size of paper being used.

8 9. Raise feed tray. 9 10. Run off a few trial copies.

10 11. Adjust position of paper & density of inking as required.

12 11 Set counting device for desired no. of copies.

13 12 Switch on electricity ( ) if an electric machine.

When req'd no. of copies has bn run off:

(a) Drop feed tray & remove unused paper.

c (b) Remove stencil by detaching @ heading.

d (c) If y expect to use stencil again:

Insert 'A' here

i. Remove all excess ink by means of blotting paper or an old newspaper.

ii. When stencil is clean & dry store in an old stencil box.

b (d) Remove copies from receiving tray.

Cont'd.

Insert 3 → on the drum

TYPIST – Better put in a heading – RUNNING OFF A STENCIL. Also, pl. use hanging para. for no. items.

Job 26   Production Target—*10 minutes*
Type the following on A4 paper using appropriate display. Use double-line spacing for the main text.

The following 2 verses are from "A Red, Red Rose" written by the great scottish poet Robert Burns. u.c.

O, my luve's like a red, red rose   LUVE'S
That's newly sprung in June;
O, my luve's like a melodie
That's sweetly play'd in tune.

Typist. Please insert a heading: ROBERT BURNS—1759—1796

As fair art thou, my bonnie lass,
So deep in luve am I;
And I will love thee still, my dear,
Till a' the seas gang dry.

Robert was born in Alloway, Ayrshire, in th yr 1759. His father was a peasant farmer.

Run on Education in Alloway was of a high standard & in his youth he eagerly read every book

N.P. on wh he cd lay his hands. He began writing poetry in his early teens & by the age of 25 his genius as a poet was beginning to show in / mass of poetry wh he had written.

One of the most famous poems depicts an Ayrshire peasant's household. The scene is similar to th of / home into wh he was born & he vividly describes / end of the week's labours & the gathering of / family on a Sat

N.P. evening. All his works give a clear picture of the beauty of nature; tender sentiments; & his spontaneous & inborn genius.

His poems so appealed to people / th many of his long poems were repeated by them &, even today, if every printed copy of his works were lost, the majority of his poems cd be written down from memory by many people all over the world.

, although they might not have read poetry,

& 'even in those days, H part /th days,
"the Cotter's Saturday night" —

COTTER'S

65

l.c. 9.¶ You will be able to see if there are any characters either
¥ ¥ (overcut or h undercut h, & this w. enable you to adjust yr. touch f.
u.c. future stencils. (by holding up the finished stencil to the light

)h 3.¶ A sheet of this carbon paper, coated side upwards, is placed
between / stencil & / backing sheet wh. is attached to the stencil.
Also place anoī sheet of carbon paper w./ coated side
towards / backing sheet. This wl give a carbon copy on / backing
sheet & wl simplify checking.

JOINING A STENCIL

If, near the bottom of a pr., y. hv. omitted a few words or a
sentence, it is not necessary to type / whole stencil again.
Cut the stencil after the last complete para. & join anoī
¶ portion of stencil. Reinforce / join by applying correcting
N.P. fluid. [If y. do not hv. a brief carriage typewriter, this process is
helpful when stencilling a balance sheet or similar document
Cut the stencil in half & type ea half separately.
Join them together as suggested above. (which has to be duplicated
on A4 paper lengthwise.

by using a special adhesive
supplied by / stencil manf.

'A' Special stylus pens can also be obtained for drawing lines
or for handwriting.
'B' & this necessitates 'care being taken to see that ea colour
comes precisely in / required position on / completed document.
'C' The figures shown down ea. side of the stencil correspond
H to / vertical line spacing of the typewriter. ⇐

E It is advisable to leave at least 13 mm clear space
(inside the frame) at the top & sides of the stencil.

F If the fluid in / bottle has become thick, it shd
not be used.

H (The horizontal nos. represent pica
& elite letter spacing.

Type the following as a folded leaflet. Display as effectively as possible.

Page 1 – Front   Dawson & Co Ltd (closed caps)

Annual Dinner ← (spaced caps and underscore)
&
Social Evening ←

SATURDAY 2 DECEMBER 1978
Social Club Dining Room (closed caps and underscore)

1830   Dress Informal

Page 2   PROGRAMME (spaced caps)
1900 Dinner

⊙ Chairman: MR F LONGMORE
1945 TOASTS l.c.
2030 SOCIAL EVENING l.c.
2250 Auld Lang Syne

Dancing To
KEN SANDWELL AND HIS BAND

TOASTS (spaced caps and underscore)
"HER MAJESTY THE QUEEN"
Proposed by: The Chairman

OUR GUESTS
Proposed by: The Chairman
Reply on behalf of Guests: Miss W. Warner (caps)
* * * *
EXPANSION PROGRAMME
MR L RUTHERFORD
(Managing Director)

(Cont'd on next page)

2 ☆. Carbon paper is supplied w./ stencils, the object of wh. is two-fold: In the first place it helps to avoid / chipping out of certain characters, &, secondly, it makes the stencil easier to read f. checking purposes.

1. ꜰ First, thoroughly clean / type faces, so th. no character is clogged. With
ʟᴄ Elite type .... brush the type face frequently during / cutting of the stencil.

4 ꜰ/stet When you ~~insert~~ the stencil into / typewriter, see that the line or scale at the top of the stencil is level w. the alignment scale. If necessary, adjust it in the ordinary way by means of the paper release lever.

5 ☆ u.c. note the frame ⟨Insert 'c' here⟩ of / stencil & be careful not to type outside this. ꜰ [ᵃ ⟨No. 6⟩ firm, sharp & even touch is required f. striking the keys, but

⊙ᴧ Certain letters need to be struck more heavily than others / letters such as m, w and, particularly, upper-case letters. More open

E letters such as o, c, e, underscore & punctuation marks need a lighter stroke, as otherwise / centres may fall out. If this does happen, type the letter on a piece of spare stencil, & with a pin & a speck of correcting fluid insert the letter in the space.

7 ¶ After ᵗʰᵉ ᵃ stencil has been typed, ⌊³carefully⌋ ⌈check⌉¹ it² before you take it out of the m/c.

8 ¶ Although you shd. avoid making mistakes, an error can be rectified by / use of correcting fluid. The procedure is as follows :-
    (a) ᵇ Flatten the letters to be corrected.
  a (b) Turn the platen up a few lines.
    (c) Put a pencil or flat ruler underneath the stencil ⸍ so as to separate it from the carbon.
    (d) Paint out the error with a very small quantity of correcting fluid. Leave for a few seconds to dry, then remove pencil or ruler, & type in / correct letter(s) or word(s). ꜰ

Typist — Omit the brackets before & after the lettered items above & leave 4 clean spaces after each letter.

⟨(just above or below the word to be corrected)⟩

PAGE 3   MENU   (spaced caps)
Prawn Cocktail
cream of asparagus Soup

Baked york Ham   Double
Pineapple – Californian Style   spacing
New Boiled Potatoes
      Braised Celery
           Peas

[CHOU] l.c. Chou À L'orange
              cheese & Biscuits   → Insert accent
                 coffee   in ink
               *   *   *

Job 28   Production Target—*25 minutes*

Type the following 2-page exercise in double spacing with indented paragraphs except for (a) lettered items which should be in single spacing with double between items; these should also be inset from left and right margins and in block style; (b) the 2 paragraphs quoting Mr. Booth's statement should be in single spacing with double between the paragraphs and inset with hanging paragraphs.

Reminder: Footnote must be typed on the same page as that in which the reference appears in the text.

Notice No. 1743/9/76 (Leave 25 mm (1") clear at Top of page and Type at left margin.)

Centre   STATUTORY HOLIDAYS (England & Wales) caps
both   Christmas Day 1976 and New Year's Day 1977 *
lines   The Secretary of State for Employment, Mr. A. Booth,
recently announced that:

,1976,^ (a) Tuesday, 28th December, wl be designated as a
Day^   holiday in substitution for Christmas, wh falls
              on a Sat; and

,1977,^ (b) Monday, 3rd January, wl be designated as a
u.c.^ Yh   holiday in substitution for new years day.

        The following 2 paras are taken f/ statement
made by Mr Booth:

"^   ^ The designation of/ substitute Bank Holiday in
  ,^   any part of / U.K. does not over ride, & is
,^ ^holiday   not intended to interfere w/ alternative^ arrange-
              ments made btwn employers ↓ (for example, in
              those sectors w. special needs, & those in wh
              employees normally work on Saturdays).
              & employers wh are consistent w. pay
              policy.

Manifolding

It is often necessary to make more than one copy of typed material, and there are various processes which may be used, the choice being dependent on the number of copies required. When only a few copies of a letter or document are wanted, these can be produced by Manifolding, i.e. by the use of carbon paper. However, even with light-weight paper and feather-weight carbons, the number of copies which can be obtained is limited—usually five or six can be made on a manual machine and up to fifteen on an electric typewriter. Also a great deal will depend on the hardness of the platen and the clarity of the type face.

If a larger number of copies is required than can be produced satisfactorily by the manifolding method, one of the following processes may be used:

(a) Stencil duplicating.
(b) Spirit duplicating.
(c) Offset litho.
(d) Photo-copying.

These various processes are described briefly in the following notes.

1. Type a copy of the following on A4 paper in double spacing. Keep your typed copy for future reference in Folder No. 2.

STENCIL DUPLICATING (Spaced caps + underscored)

l.c. By this process ∧ A master copy of stencil is prepared, the required matter being H ∧ typed on a stencil sheet wh is made of special wax ∧ like paper. l.c. is fed through the Rotary duplicator

stet When / stencil has bn prepared, it is attached to a drum on a rotary m/c, of which there are many different types makes, but all of these work on more or less / same principle. The paper used for the copies, which is called duplicating paper, presses against the drum, + ink is thru H the cut ∧ out forms of the characters. [When a stencil is 'cut' by typewriter, the ribbon is switched out of action, so th / type face strikes on to the stencil w'out passing thru the ribbon, thus H producing a clear ∧ cut character.

Insert 'A' here

Colour work can be produced on rotary duplicators. This entails having a different drum for each colour. In this , ∧ case ∧ however ∧ a separate stencil must has to be prepared f. ea. colour instead of / whole of / matter being typed on one stencil,

but the drum containing the ink can be changed in a few seconds.

Insert 'B' here

When a stencil is to be cut, the follows. points shd be noted:

"The Gov. wl make ∧ provisions, ... to cover the future arrangements wh wl be made for a holiday taken in lieu whenever a∧ holiday or public holiday falls on a Sat. or Sun. where it is not already provided for under the 1941 act."

In 1942 gp. union reached an agreement w employers on the basis that:

(a) Where Christmas Day, Boxing Day, or new year's day falls on a Sat, staff shd be given a whole day's pd holiday on 24th, 31st or 28th Dec. as may be appropriate & according to / needs of employers.

(b) Where Chris. Day, Box. Day, or New year's Day falls on a Sun., an alternative day was to be regarded as a public holiday & given as a whole day's ∧ holiday.

Insert 'A'

N.P [although it wl be seen fr / Gov. statement th there is no ~~necessity~~ ~~requirement~~ to alter any holiday plans ~~who may~~ already arranged, employers after consultation w. staff organisations, ✓to adopt the dates suggested by the Sec. of State, i.e., 28th Dec & 3rd Jan, rather than dates previously agreed btwn the Union & employers.

(may consider it desirable,)

any queries shd be referred ~~immediately~~ to the Gen. Secretary of the Union.

* Under the Banking & Financial Dealings act, 1971, monday, ~~23rd~~ 27th Dec, wl ~~not~~ be taken as a holiday in place of Boxing Day.

"A" (c) Staff required to work on Sundays to be pd the appropriate rate for Sun. work.

legislative

∧ Bank ∧ n.c.

u.f is

u.ch ∧h

ths

paid∧

s.tet

Skill building

Type each exercise (A, B, C, and D) *once* for practice, *once* for speed, and finally *once* for accuracy. Margins: Elite 22–82, Pica 12–72.

A. Review alphabet keys

1.   It was a hazardous task that the steeplejack performed, but owing to his vast experience he could now do it quickly.

B. Build accuracy on shift key drill

2. You Must Always Check All Work Before Removing From Machine.

3. The Forty-Second Annual General Meeting of Johnson & Wilkins Ltd. was held on Friday, 14th April, the Chairman presiding.

4. Tours to Belgium, France, Holland, Italy, Majorca and Spain.

C. Build accuracy on shift lock drill

5. OUR ORDER No. 8681/116.10/EX/2, of 16th AUGUST, is EXTREMELY URGENT. Delivery MUST be made by 31st OCTOBER without fail.

6. EXETER (Devon): LONDON 170; BODMIN 64; PLYMOUTH 42; BUDE 50.

7. NEWCASTLE-UPON-TYNE; OGMORE-BY-SEA; SOUTHEND-ON-SEA; LANARK.

D. Build accuracy on concentration drills

8. U.S.S.R.: Novo-Nazyvayevskoye; Dnepropetrovsk; Ilovlinskaya.

9. Thailand: Nakhon Ratchasima; Ukraine; Mezhizichi-Koretskiye.

10. Wales: Crib-y-Ddysgyl; Bwlch-cum-Orthin; Nant Ffrancon Pass. Llanfairpwllgwyngyllgogerychwyrndrobwllllandysiliogogogoch.

Accuracy/Speed Practice	Two-minute timing	Not more than 2 errors
		words

AS.27   The Thames Valley is a district well known to thousands of people, 13
not only from this country but from every part of the world. The 26
scenery is lovely, while the winding river is frequented by fishing and 40
sailing enthusiasts. However, it is the history of the district which 54
chiefly appeals to visitors. There is Runnymede, where King John signed 69
the Magna Carta in 1215. Kingston still has the "king's stone", on 80
which were crowned seven Anglo-Saxon monarchs. The town, granted a 95
first charter by King John in 1199, is a busy market town in these days. 110
Richmond, in early times called Shene, meaning brightness, is also popu- 124
lar. It was Charles I who enclosed the Great Park and stocked it with 138
deer, but it was not until the reign of Charles II that the public were 153
allowed to go into the royal park.   (S.I. 1.33) 160

Type a copy of the following Notice and Agenda.

THE BOLTON FURNISHING COMPANY LIMITED

ELEVENTH

Notice is hereby given that the /ANNUAL GENERAL MEETING of this Co will be held at the Merchants House, High Street, Bolton, on Friday at 12 noon, for the following purposes: *(31 March 1978)*

Block

1 ~~To declare~~ To receive and, if approved, adopt the accounts of

v.c. the Company and the reports of the directors and auditors for the year ended *31 December 1977*.

3 To elect Directors.
The following Directors will be proposed in accordance with Article 114:
Miss U Martyn-Davis   *MARTYN*
Mrs M L Pugh

2 To declare dividends.

To authorise

e.c. 4 The Directors to fix the remuneration of the auditors.

5 To transact any other business which may be transacted/ *at the AGM.*

BY ORDER OF THE BOARD

A THOMPSON

SECRETARY

The Parade Works
Summer Hill
Bolton Lancashire

1st March 1978

Notes

, who may be unable to attend the meeting,

, on a poll, to vote instead of him, +

a A Member entitled to attend/ at the above meeting is entitled to appoint a proxy to attend and/ such proxy need not also be a Member. For the convenience of shareholders/ a form of proxy is enclosed, and this shd be completed and returned so as to reach the Registered Office of the Co not less than 48 hours before the time fixed for the meeting.

b In accordance with the provisions of Section 29, Companies Act 1967, Directors' Service Contracts + dealings in shares + debentures wl be available for inspection fr the date of this notice @ the Registered Office + during the meeting.

Typist: Please type dates consistently. Lettered items under Notes — put letter at left margin, leave 3 clear spaces and block paragraphs.

Type the following table on A4 paper in single spacing. Rule all lines in ink.

TURNOVER OF WORLD TRADE

	World Trade Turnover* ‡				
	1938	1950	1962	1963	1964
	in milliards of U.S. dollars				
Industrial Countries:					
Western Europe –					
E.E.C.	10.5	20.5	47.4	45.7	49.5
E.F.T.A.	10.5	21.7	36.7	35.1	37.1
Other Countries	1.4	4.1	6.7	6.4	6.8
Total for Western Europe	22.4	46.3	90.8	87.2	93.4
United States ‡ and Canada	7.3	26.2	47.0	43.1	46.1
Japan	1.5	1.8	7.1	5.9	7.1
Total for industrial countries	31.2	74.3	144.9	136.2	146.6
Non-industrial countries					
Latin America	3.2	12.4	18.0	16.7	16.5
Other countries	10.0	30.4	46.6	44.1	44.7
Total for non-industrial countries . . .	13.2	42.8	64.6	60.8	61.2
World Trade Turnover ..	44.4	117.1	209.5	197.0	207.8

* Excluding trade between the USSR, eastern European countries & mainland China.

‡ Preliminary

‡ Including military aid shipments

Type a copy of the following Minutes.

THE BOLTON FURNISHING COMPANY LIMITED

MINUTES of the ~~Thirty-first~~ *Eleventh* Annual General Meeting held at *the Merchants House, High Street, Bolton, on Fri 31 March 1978 at 12 noon*.

PRESENT

Mr. F Nelson Fraser (Chairman)
Mr. A M Todd
Mr. P W Hamilton
Mrs M L ~~Pubh~~ *Pugh* ⎤
Mr ~~M~~ Bradley *LB.* ⎟ Directors
Miss U Martyn-Davis ⎦

Typist - please put Directors in alpha. order.

IN ATTENDANCE

Mr A. THOMPSON (Sec) *l.c.*
Mr L. Broadfield (Auditor)

1	Notice of Meeting	The Sec read the Notice convening the meetg
2	Apologies	Apologies were received from the following Members

Please put names in alpha order

Miss R Arnott Mrs J Blood
Messrs E Pugh W Hamilton R Grey F Lamb

3. Reports and a~~c~~counts   It was unanimously RESOLVED
"Th the Report of the Directors and the a/cs for the yr ended *31 Dec '77* be & are hereby approved and adopted."

4 Dividends   ←It was unanimously RESOLVED
"That the following dividends be paid to all persons *whose names appear as shareholders* of the Co. on *28/2/78* and th such dividends be paid forthwith:
Preference Shares 7½%
Ordinary Shares 10%."

6 Auditors   It was RESOLVED
"~~That Messrs. Walker & Broadfield, Chartered Accountants, having agreed to continue in office as auditors for a further year~~
Th authority is hereby given to the Directors to fix the remuneration of the auditors Messrs Walker & Broadfield.

5 *Election of Directors*   *It was unanimously ~~agreed~~ RESOLVED)*
"Th Miss U Martyn-Davis & Mrs M L Pugh be & are hereby re-elected Directors of the Co."

7 *Vote of thanks*   *A vote of thanks to the Chairman & the ~~o~~ Members of the board concluded the meetg.*

Chairman _____

Date _____

Type a copy of the following table in single-line spacing on A4 paper (210 × 297 mm). All underscored headings in the first column should have a clear line-space above and below them. Rule all lines in ink and insert leader dots.

Analysis of Vacancies notified & Filled ← Closed caps & underscore

| Group | All districts | | | |
| | Notified | | Filled | |
	Boys	Girls	Boys	Girls
Practical/Constructional				
Indoor				
Designing, making or repairing in metal	4,968	2,165	2,709	685
Wood ——————	288	7	196	2
Other materials ————	1,357	2,060	679	920
Outdoor				
Building & Civil Engineering	1,203	---	751	---
Agriculture ————	86	6	55	4
Scientific & Medical				
Laboratory & Scientific Jobs	188	60	38	8
Medical, Nursing, etc. ———	33	108	---	80
Personal Service				
Hotel & Catering ————	1,395	2,084	639	833
Sales Work	110	205	57	59
Clerical/Administrative				
General Office	1,200	2,655	433	1,053
Office Machines	152	750	64	236
Shorthand-Typists	---	356	136	136
TOTAL	10,980	10,456	5,621	4,016

Type each line or sentence (A, B, and C) *three* times. If time permits, complete your practice by typing each group once as it appears. Margins: Elite 22–82, Pica 12–72.

A. Review alphabet keys

1.   Dick was extremely delighted to be requested to play in the Junior Festival Concert, held at the Zoological Gardens.

B. Build speed on fluency drill

2. Next week they will have some more pens from that nice shop.
3. Some boys whom they know must have gone home late last week.
4. This girl says they will soon have read that book once more.
5. They will come past that road when they walk home from work.

C. Build speed on common letter combinations

6. although discount thought amount should about doubt your our
7. I thought the amount of discount you allow us is not enough.
8. I am anxious that you should quote for this particular work.
9. We thought we should like to open an account with your firm.

Accuracy/Speed Practice

Note: You should now aim at increasing your speed by 5 words a minute.

One-minute timings   Not more than 1 error

		words
AS.13	We thank you for your note, and regret to inform you that we do	13
	not stock the particular type of case for which you are now asking,	26
	but we can make these up for you if you would like us to do so. Unfor-	40
	tunately, at this stage we are unable to quote you a definite price,	54
	but we will look into our costs and let you know by the end of the	67
	present week the price we are able to quote and the delivery date.	80
	(S.I. 1.25)	
AS.14	When you have to type envelopes from cards or lists, it is a good idea	14
	to turn each card or list, with the envelopes you have already completed,	29
	face downwards on the desk, so that, after you have finished all of them	43
	and turned them back again, you will find that they are in the right order	58
	ready for checking. This method will greatly simplify your work and save	73
	time. Why not try it for yourself? (S.I. 1.27)	80

5. Type the following table in blocked style on A5 portrait paper.

FIXED TERM INVESTMENTS

Account	Interest Rate	Equivalent gross yield – tax at 35%
Fixed Term Bonds Minimum £5,000 – Maximum £10,000		
1 year 2 year 3 year	8.15% 9.10% 9.55%	12.54% 14.00% 14.69%
Monthly Income Bonds Minimum £1,000 – Maximum £10,000		
2 year 3 year	8.75% 9.30%	13.62% 14.31%

6. Type the following exercise in blocked style on A5 paper.

W A FOSTER & CO LTD – spaced caps

THREE-YEAR SUMMARY

u.c. Year ended 31 December	1975	1976	1977
Sales	37,202,000	48,097,000	56,963,000
LESS			
Goods and Services ...	24,210,000	32,345,000	39,652,000
Wages & Salaries ...	10,259,000	11,733,000	13,426,000
Debenture Interest ...	148,000	145,000	142,000
Depreciation	852,000	852,000	1,041,000
TOTAL COSTS	£35,469,000	£45,075,000	£54,261,000

Further exercises on tabulation (blocked style) are given on page 54 of **Practical Typing Exercises, Book Two**.

Typing decimals

1. Always use full stop for decimal point.
2. Leave NO space before or after decimal point.

3. No punctuation is required at end of figures, except at the end of a sentence.

1. Practise typing decimals. Read the above explanation, then type a copy of the following in double spacing.

For your guidance, we give you below, as requested, the
measurements in the metric system (to three decimal places).
0.990 x 1.371 x 1.219 metres.   3.353 x 3.048 x 2.743 metres.
3.657 x 2.590 x 1.524 metres.   2.108 x 5.100 x 1.890 metres.

Typing sums of money in context

1. If the sum comprises only pounds, type as follows: £5, £10, or £5.00, £10.00.
2. If only pence, type: 10p 7p
   NOTE: *no* space between figures and letter p, and no full stop after p (unless, of course, it ends a sentence).
3. With mixed amounts, i.e., sums comprising pounds and pence, the decimal point and the £ symbol should always be used, but *not* the abbreviation p.
   Example: £7.05. The £ sign and p should *never* appear together.
4. If the sum contains a decimal point but no whole pounds, a nought should be typed after the £ symbol and before the point. *Example:* £0.97.

2. Practise typing sums of money in context. Read the above explanation and then type a copy of the following in double spacing.

Our invoice of the 6th May was for a total sum of £10.55, whereas
the cheque we have received is made out for £10.00 only, so there is
a balance due of £0.55 (55p), which please remit by return.

Typing decimals in columns

1. When typing decimal figures in columns see that the decimal points come under one another.
2. There must be the same number of decimal places in each line of the column, so that where necessary the figure 0 is used to make up the required number of decimal places. For example, if there are two decimal places, type 6.00, 6.60, 6.66. If three decimal places, type 6.000, 6.600, 6.660, etc. If there is no whole number, type 0 before the decimal point, e.g. 0.66.

3. If pounds and pence are typed in columns, the £ sign is typed over the unit figure of the pounds. No sign appears over the pence or decimals of a pound.
4. If the column contains whole pounds only, the £ sign is typed over the longest item, e.g.,

$$\begin{matrix} £ & & £ \\ 200.55 & \text{but} & 240 \end{matrix}$$

3. Practise typing columns of decimals. Type the following on A5 paper (148 × 210 mm), using a left margin of 20 and setting tab stops for the second, third and fourth columns at 35, 51 and 64 respectively.

		£	£
1,240.52	1,505.125		
4,668.24	3,242.150	101.45	101
3,101.50 ←Do not turn up	4,925.500	25.50	25
←Turn up 2			
9,010.26	9,672.775	126.95	126
←Turn up 1			

Tabular work frequently has footnotes to explain some reference to the figures or details in the table. The same rules apply to these footnotes and their corresponding reference signs in the body of the table as those already explained for manuscript work, i.e., the footnotes are typed underneath the table in single-line spacing, with double spacing between each. The reference sign in the body is typed immediately after the item to which it refers without a space being left. In the footnote the reference sign is typed (usually as a superior character) and one space is left after it.

4. Type a copy of the following table in double-line spacing, and rule in ink on the typewriter. Insert leader dots.

DEVELOPMENT AREAS

The following table gives the numbers of persons registered as unemployed and the percentage rates of unemployment in each of the Development Areas at 16th November, 19 . .

Development Area	Number of unemployed persons on registers at 16th November, 19 . .			Percentage rate of unemployment*	
	Males	Females	Total	Males	Females
North-Eastern	28,653	9,125	37,778	3.8	3.0
Western	1,540	591	2,131	3.7	3.7
Scottish	40,796	15,117	55,913	5.3	3.6
South Wales and Avon	14,946	6,606	21,552	2.9	3.5
Clwyd	947	529	1,476	3.3	5.2
South Lancashire	2,337	1,726	4,063	2.3	3.3
Merseyside	672	682	1,354	1.3	1.8
North-East Lancashire	19,329	5,793	25,122	3.0	3.2
Total, all Areas	109,220	40,169	149,389	4.1	3.2

* Number registered as unemployed expressed as percentage of the estimated total number of employees (employed and unemployed).

Tabulation—blocked style

To save the typist's time, most organisations prefer block style tabulation and most examining bodies accept this layout unless, of course, the examiner asks for a particular style. Blocked style means that the main and sub-headings are blocked at the left margin; column headings and column items are blocked at the tab. stop set for the start of the longest line except the first column heading which is blocked at the left margin. Even with the blocked style, figures in columns must have units under units and tens under tens, etc. The £ sign is blocked above the first figure in the longest line or over the £ sign in the total. *Vertical centring of column headings.* All headings start on the same horizontal line which will be the starting point for the deepest heading.

Where fractions are not provided on the typewriter, these should be typed as follows:

(a) By using ordinary figures with the solidus, e.g., 1/12 5/16
Where whole numbers are included, a space is left, or a full stop inserted, after the whole number, e.g., 2 1/12, or 2.1/12.

(b) Fractions may also be typed with the enumerator above and denominator below the typing line, e.g., $3\frac{5}{12}$. This method is used particularly in equations or arithmetical formulae.

(c) Method (a) or (b) may be used *in combination with fractions provided on the typewriter*, but a combination of

$$2\frac{5}{16} \text{ and } 3.9/16$$

may not be used in the same exercise.

(d) Whichever method is adopted, it is important to use the same consistently throughout one piece of work.

Note the spacing in the following:

$$\frac{\frac{5}{12} + \frac{3}{5}}{2\frac{1}{12} - \frac{1}{5}}$$

←Do not turn up
←Turn up 2 spaces before the whole number
Turn back half a space to insert numerator

4. Practise typing fractions. Read the above explanation, then type a copy of the following on A5 landscape paper in double spacing. Margins: Elite 20–85, Pica 10–75.

We thank you for your letter, and are pleased to inform you that we can supply from stock various dies with bores of $\frac{1}{2}$", 5/32", 3/16", 9/32", 11/32", as well as larger sizes of 1.1/12", 1.5/12", 1.5/16", 1.7/16", up to 1.13/16".

5. Type the following on A5 landscape paper.

$$\frac{3.125 \times 2.592}{1.561} - \frac{30.25}{17.65} \qquad \frac{14.78 \times 1.665 - 3.42}{11.86} \qquad C + \frac{41.6 + \frac{1.811}{n} + \frac{0.00281}{i}}{1 + 41.6 + \frac{0.00281)}{i} \quad \frac{n}{)\sqrt{m}}}$$

Reflection formula: $\dfrac{\sin^2(i-r)}{\sin^2(i+r)} + \dfrac{\tan^2(i-r)}{\tan^2(i+r)}$ in which i and r are the angles of incidence and refraction respectively.

Business letters

Open punctuation. When typing a letter with open punctuation, no punctuation is inserted in the reference, date, name and address of addressee, salutation, complimentary close, and any wording below. In the body of the letter, follow the instructions given on page 40.

Printed heading. If you are using paper with a printed heading, turn up three single-line spaces after the last line of the printed heading before starting to type. If you are using plain A5 portrait paper, turn up 9 single-line spaces before typing the reference. With A4 plain paper turn up 12 single-line spaces before typing the reference.

For further exercises on fractions, see page 31 of **Practical Typing Exercises, Book Two**.

Apart from the use of the underscore, on most modern typewriters provision is made for the speedy ruling of both horizontal and vertical lines. On the alignment scale you will find two small notches or round holes. Place the point of a pencil or suitable ball pen in one of these notches or holes and hold it in position against the paper with the right hand. With the left hand on the carriage release, by running the carriage along you will obtain a continuous horizontal line. To avoid running the carriage too far, it is advisable to stop about two spaces before the scale-point at which the horizontal line is to end, and then tap the space-bar until the scale-point is reached.

To make a vertical line, instead of running the carriage along you release the platen ratchet by means of the interliner and turn the platen up with the left-hand knob. If the vertical lines extend almost to the bottom of the page, it is better to rule these by hand after the paper has been removed from the machine, to avoid the paper slipping when the platen is turned down for the start of the next line. After you have had some practice in ruling in this way, you will find that it saves a great deal of time, particularly if carbon copies are being taken.

3. Practise ruling on the typewriter. Read the above explanation, and then type the following in double-line spacing on A5 paper. Rule all lines as explained above.

FINANCIAL MANAGEMENT

Average Salaries according to age group

| Age Group | Average Emoluments £ | Range | | Recent Annual Percentage Increase % |
		Lowest £	Highest £	
25-29	2000	1700	2300	21
30-34	2500	2000	2800	13
35-39	3000	2300	3500	14
40-44	3500	2700	4000	11

Tabulation notes

1. Where the 'Particulars' or 'Description' column has no heading, but has a long dash to represent the printer's dash, five consecutive hyphens should be typed centrally. One hyphen only is not sufficient. The underscore may also be used to represent the dash, but, as this necessitates the use of the interliner to ensure that the underscore is centrally typed, it is better to use hyphens instead of the underscore.

2. In figure columns, where the figures run into thousands, three consecutive hyphens should be typed to represent a blank; one hyphen is not sufficient in this case.

3. No abbreviations, apart from those words which are always abbreviated, should appear in tabulation work. An exception is made in column headings when it is necessary to save horizontal spaces.

Further exercises on tabulation with leader dots are given on pages 53–54 of **Practical Typing Exercises, Book One.**

Letters can be displayed in various ways, the styles most commonly used being illustrated below. In deciding which to use, you should follow the method adopted by your employer. For information concerning the typing of business letters, see 'Parts of a business letter' and 'Steps in typing a letter' on pages 214 and 215.

Fully-blocked (sometimes called 'blocked').

Begin every line at the left margin.

Semi-blocked (sometimes called 'indented').

Date and complimentary close as shown, with first line of each paragraph indented.

6. Study the layout of the following fully-blocked letter, then type a copy on A5 portrait paper with margins of Elite 12–62, Pica 5–55. Keep your typed copy for future reference in Folder No. 2.

Turn up

3 spaces ⟶

Our Ref RHC/LY

4 September 1978

3 spaces ⟶

R L Dodds & Co Ltd
14 Queen Street
Bury St Edmunds
Suffolk   IP33 2AA

Leave 6 spaces between county and postcode, and one space between 2 halves of code

3 spaces ⟶

Dear Sirs

2 spaces ⟶

Thank you for your order No 112/78, dated 31 August, which will be delivered on 11 September.

2 spaces ⟶

We regret that, because of rising costs, it has been necessary to increase prices, and we suggest that you be good enough to ask us to quote you our up-to-date prices before placing an order in future.

2 spaces ⟶

We hope that these arrangements will be acceptable to you.

2 spaces ⟶

1 space ⟶

Yours faithfully
W A FOSTER & CO LTD

5 spaces ⟶

1 space ⟶

ROGER H CAMPBELL
SALES DIRECTOR

Leader dots (full stops) are used to guide the eye along lines of figures from one column to another. There are four methods of grouping which can be used, viz.

1. One dot three spaces .   .   .   .

2. Two dots three spaces ..   ..   ..

3. Three dots two spaces ...   .

4. Continuous dots ....

Continuous dots (No. 4) are the simplest and are recommended unless you receive instruction to the contrary.

Type leader dots lightly and evenly.
If any item in the column takes more than one line, the leader dots should be typed only on the last line of the item.

When using grouped dots (No. 2 for example) care must be taken to see that the groups of dots come underneath one another in all lines. To ensure this, you should adopt the following procedure: Bring the carriage to the first tab. stop set for the first column of figures; back-space once for every space between first and second columns plus an extra two spaces. At this point set tab. stop. Back-space 5 from the tab. stop just set, and set another tab. stop. Continue in this way until you have approximately reached the last word of the shortest line in particulars column. Bring carriage back to margin and type first line, using tab. bar to insert leader dots if and when required.

NOTE: There must always be at least one space between the last word and first dot or the last dot and the vertical line, i.e. leader dots must never be typed right up to preceding or following word or line, and no word or letter must be allowed to extend beyond the last leader dot on the line although leader dots may extend beyond the last word.

2. Practise typing table with leader dots. Read the above explanation, and then type a copy of the following table in single spacing on A5 paper.

PRESCRIPTIONS BY MEDICAMENT CLASS

Medicament Class	Estimated Total		Average Net Ingredient Cost per Prescription in pence
	Number of Prescriptions in millions	Net Ingredient Cost £ millions	
Tablets, capsules, lozenges...	109.9	42.3	93
Mixtures, linctuses, etc.	53.4	8.3	38
Eye, ear, nasal drops, etc.....	5.7	0.8	36
Injections, etc.	2.6	2.1	193
Other liquid preparations	8.5	2.2	62
Ointments, pastes, etc.......	15.5	4.4	67
Other solids, etc...........	3.4	1.2	87
Trusses and hosiery	0.8	1.1	325
Total..................	199.8	62.4	—

It is the custom with some firms to have all correspondence addressed to the firm and not to individuals. If, therefore, the writer of a letter wishes it to reach a particular person or department, the words 'For the attention of Mr. . . .' are typed at the left margin on the second single-line space after the address and before the salutation. This wording is also typed on the envelope two single-line spaces above the name. If typed in lower case letters it must be underscored. (Note: The salutation will, of course, be in the plural, i.e., Dear Sirs.)

Enclosures

When any enclosure is to be inserted in a letter, this should be indicated in one of the following ways:

(a) By typing: Enc., Encs., Encl., or Encls. at left margin at bottom of letter (at least 2 single-line spaces below signature), or the word 'Enclosure' may be typed in full. In both cases lower case letters (with an initial capital) or upper case letters may be used, with or without underscore.

(b) A printed and/or numbered label may be affixed at foot of letter. Some firms also state what the enclosure is. Example: Enc. Invoice.

7. Practise typing letter with 'Attention' line and enclosure. Type the following letter on A4 paper, using margins of Elite 20—85, Pica 10—75. Keep your typed copy for future reference in Folder No. 2.

Turn up

3 spaces ———→

3 spaces ———→

2 spaces ———→

2 spaces ———→

```
      Your Ref RHC/LY      Our Ref FJL/BB


      8 September 1978


      W A Foster & Co Ltd
      12 Chester Road
      Carlisle      CA2 3HP

      FOR THE ATTENTION OF MR R H CAMPBELL

      Dear Sirs

      Thank you for your letter dated 4 September in which you informed
      us about price increases.

      We should be pleased to have a quotation for the goods listed on
      the attached sheet.

      At the same time, please let us know whether you would be prepared
      to accept orders for larger quantities with deliveries split over
      a certain period, eg, every 3 or 4 months.  We understand from
      your representative, Mr J. Frost, that if we order in larger quan-
      tities you would give us a larger discount.

      We look forward to hearing from you.

      Yours faithfully
      R L DODDS & CO LTD



      F J LOWE
      PURCHASING OFFICER
```

Minimum of
2 spaces ———→

```
      ENC
```

Further exercises on fully blocked letter with standard punctuation are given on pages 5 and 6 of **Practical Typing Exercises, Book One.**

Tabular statements sometimes have columns with subdivisions, each of which has a main heading which has to be centred right across the subdivided columns, and also separate headings for each subdivision. In such cases, it is advisable to type the deepest column headings first. The specimen below is an example of such a table, and the steps explained under the table will give you an idea of how to proceed.

1. Practise typing table with subdivided columns. Type the following table on A5 paper (210 × 148 mm) in double spacing. Keep your typed copy for future reference in folder No. 2.

<u>SINGLE-SUBJECT EXAMINATIONS</u>

Subject	Number of Papers Worked	Results		
		1st Class	2nd Class	Failed
Arithmetic	5,400	900	1,800	2,700
Commerce	1,456	35	485	936
Economics	1,858	22	619	1,217
English Language	14,120	706	6,956	6,458
Office Practice	132	11	63	58
Typewriting	28,760	2,771	9,586	16,403

1. Proceed as usual as far as marking the beginning and end of first horizontal line.

2. Along this line mark as usual the scale-points for the vertical lines which extend to the top, and set the tab. stops for the start of each column including the subdivided columns.

3. As the deepest heading is the last group bring carriage to tab. stop for start of column with subdivisions, and centre the heading above the subdivided columns.

4. Mark in the beginning and end of the horizontal line underneath this heading, and along this line mark scale-points for the vertical lines of subdivided columns.

5. Type the headings of each of these columns, starting at the tab. stop already set for each, as these headings are the longest lines.

6. Turn up one single-line space and mark beginning and end of second horizontal line.

7. Then proceed to type heading above column 2, bearing in mind that this must be centred vertically on the headings already typed. To do this, count the number of lines and spaces in the headings typed—in this case 4—and from this number take the number of lines to be typed in the heading of column 2, and divide the result by 2, i.e., $4 - 3 = 1 \div 2 = \frac{1}{2}$. With the alignment scale on the first line of heading already typed (the word 'Results') turn up half a space for starting point of first line in heading of second column.

8. Calculate and type heading over first column.

9. When ruling the vertical lines for the subdivided columns, see that you do not extend them right up to the top.

Further exercises on tabulation with subdivided headings (indented style) are given on pages 55–56 of **Practical Typing Exercises, Book One.**

In a fully blocked letter the subject heading (if any) is typed at the left margin and underscored if in lower case. The subject heading may be typed in closed capitals without the underscore.

Displayed matter in fully blocked letters

When matter is to be displayed in a fully blocked letter, all lines start at the left margin, one clear space being left above and below the displayed matter. If the displayed matter is in columns, leave 3 spaces between each column.

NOTE: If definite instructions are given for the matter to be 'inset', then it must be 'inset' even in a fully blocked letter. For method of display see page 86.

8. Practise typing fully blocked letter with subject heading and displayed matter. Type the following letter on A4 paper with margins of Elite 20–85, Pica 10–75. Display portion should have 3 spaces between each column.

```
Your Ref FJL/BB      Our Ref RHC/LY              12 September 1978
```

(Note: in fully blocked letters date may be typed so that it ends at the right margin.)

```
R L Dodds & Co Ltd
14 Queen Street
Bury St Edmunds
Suffolk        IP33 2AA

FOR THE ATTENTION OF MR F J LOWE   PURCHASING OFFICER

Dear Sirs

BUYING IN QUANTITY

In reply to your letter of 8 September, we have pleasure in quot-
ing you for part of your order as follows:

10    Executive Cases    No EC 283    £23.14 each
20    Concertina Files   No CF 74     £12.75 each
25    Pocket Diaries      No PD 69      £1.10 each

John Frost, our representative in your area, tells us that he saw
you on Friday last, and, as you are not in urgent need of the
other items on your list, we suggest that we call and see you on
Tuesday 26 September at 10 am to discuss your future require-
ments and the question of discount for larger quantities.

Please let us know if 26 September is convenient to you.

Yours faithfully
W A FOSTER & CO LTD


ROGER H CAMPBELL
SALES DIRECTOR
```

Further exercises on fully blocked letter with standard punctuation are given on pages 7, 8, 9, 11, 38, 52, 57 and 58 of **Practical Typing Exercises, Book One**.

Skill building

Type each line or sentence (A, B, and C) *three* times. If time permits, complete your practice by typing each group once as it appears. Margins: Elite 22–82, Pica 12–72.

A. Review alphabet keys

1.   The calves grazing in the field jerked their heads with fright when alarmed by the explosions at the near-by quarry.

B. Build speed on common letter combinations

2. very here over cover refer other there better orders service

3. I refer to our order which must be delivered here next week.

4. We must give credit for the very good service on all orders.

5. Her other insurance policy is much overdue and must be paid.

C. Build speed on common phrases

6. for the, for these, for them, for their, for that, for this.

7. But for them, we would have no excuse for this visit to you.

8. For the time being, we are happy for that to remain dormant.

9. Thank them for their good wishes and for all these presents.

Accuracy/Speed Practice

Note: You should now aim at increasing your speed by 5 words a minute.

One-minute timings   Not more than 1 error

words

AS.25   Everyone should have a hobby. It is healthy and can lead to a 12
longer and happier life. The choice of the hobby is not so important 26
as how you make use of it. If your job is one that necessitates your 40
sitting down at a desk for hours at a time, you should choose a hobby 54
that will enable you to unwind your muscles or one that will help you 68
to relax. It will also bring added interest into your life. (S.I. 1.30) 80

AS.26   In these modern times, scarcely a month goes by without some 12
well-known and well-loved building being demolished and replaced 25
by concrete and steel. This is the case all over the country, and 38
if we are to have new towns and cities, it must, we know, be done, 51
but how sad it is to see some renowned building disappearing before 64
our eyes, and another, often of less architectural beauty, put up 78
in its place.   (S.I. 1.32) 80

Production typing

Job 31   Production Target—*10 minutes*

Type the following letter on A4 paper. Mark it for the attention of D. F. Grant, Esq.

lc JARRETT, GRANT & Sons Ltd
27 Durham Way
STOCKTON ON TEES   Suitable date
Teeside   TS19 7LE

Dear Sirs,

Advertisement in the Agricultural Journal

We have recd. yr. ltr. of 16 March w. regard to above adverts, & thank y. for yr. offer of services for our products. [We are quite ready to take yr. offer into consideration, but we would like to hv. a reply to / following points in order to give us some idea of yr. selling capacity.

a) The extent of / territory y. feel capable of covering satisfactorily.

b) The display facilities at your disposal.

d) The approx. min. turnover y. anticipate for the first 12 months of / agency.

For yr. guidance we encl. a catalogue of our main products. [When we hv. had an opportunity of considering / above inform, we shall be pleased to arrange an interview to suit yr. convenience / when / question of commission & terms of payment can be discussed.

Yrs ffy

W B A Thompson Ltd   R L Moss   Man. Dir.

Typist — sorry I omitted (c) it should read :
How you propose to introduce our products on yr. market.

before fixing an appointment to discuss this matter

N.P.

N.P. u.c

UNIT 11   77

Typist: Please send a memo to Mr K Brownhill, Man. Director. From: Co. Secretary. Ref. EF/MHB. Subject: KINGSLEY & LEITH LTD. Please mark the memo CONFIDENTIAL, & type an envelope for Mr. Brownhill.

Further to our conversation prior to the Board meeting on Tuesday last, the year-end figures for Kingsley & Leith Ltd are as follows:

	1977	1978
	£000	£000
Turnover	10,557	14,772
Pre-tax Profit	1,302	1,565
Earnings per Ordinary Share	16.01P	18.49P
Total Net Dividend per Ordinary Share	3.9130P	4.3042P

The year 1978 will be their 10th successive yr w. an increase in turnover of over 40%.

Type the following letter on A4 paper, taking two carbon copies: one for file and one for Despatch Manager. Use shoulder headings for sub-headings.

Paines & Byron Ltd., North Bridge Rd., BERKHAMSTED, Herts. HP4 1BL Your ref. AL/Buying. Our ref. GJP/HOS

Dear Sirs,   Order No. A430

We thank you f yr order received w yr ltr this morning & , as requested, we wl arrange f the gds to be ready by the end of the mnth.

DESPATCH
We sh await the instructions of yr forwarding agents, w. whom we wl communicate as soon as the gds are ready for despatch.

PAYMENT. At 30 days fr date of despatch – less 2½% discount, or in cash @ time of despatch w. 3% discount.

PACKING. The gds wl be packed in four cases.

N.P. [Please let us know wh method of payment you decide to accept, so th we may make out our invoice accordingly.

Yrs ffy, W. LAMBERT & CO. LTD   Sales Dept.

Typist: Please insert the section abt PACKING before the para. headed PAYMENT

Type the following letter on A4 paper. Insert suitable date and subject heading
'Agency'.

R L Moss Esq
Man. Dir.
W. B. A. Thompson Ltd
7 Birmingham Rd
Wolverhampton WV2 4DB

Dear Mr Moss

Thank you for yr ltr of ... abt my firm acting as agents f yr products.

The following are the answers to the points I raised in yr ltr letter:

(a) We wd be prepared to cover the following counties: Tyne & Wear, Cumbria, North Humberside, North, South & West Yorkshire.

(b) Our display facilities at the above address are limited, but we cd set aside one room for this purpose. *measuring 5 m x 6 m*

(c) At present we hv 2 field reps covering the counties mentioned in (a) & if we were appointed yr agents, we wd consider engaging another 2 reps.

(d) Anticipated turnover is difficult to assess; however, as yr products are ~~natural in demand~~, we estimate orders in the region of £12,000 per annum

I wd be available to discuss these points w. you any day next week. Perhaps you wd like to visit us & meet my two Directors * & myself as well as our 2 reps mentioned in (c). If not, I shl be pleased to call on you. Kindly let me know wh will be convenient to you.

Yours sincerely D F Grant

Typist - please use block paras for (a) - (d)
      also at * please insert:
      (John E Jarrett & Michael J Williams)

Typist: Please type a fully-blocked letter with open punctuation.

Job 62   Production Target—*15 minutes*

Type the following table in double spacing, centring it both horizontally and vertically. Rule all lines by underscore.

STATISTICAL RECORDS

Choice of Employment Conferences

Type of School or College	Number of Schools	Number of Conferences	Number of First School Reports Received	No. of First Vocational Guidance Interviews
Grammar, Technical & Commercial	36	45	3,784	3,673
Comprehensive & Bilateral	5	14	1,267	1,157
Other Secondary Schools	110	345	13,481	12,478
Independent and Private Schools	10	4	179	161
Approved Schools	2	9	85	33
TOTALS	91. 247163	423	18,796	17,502

Job 63   Production Target—*15 minutes*

Type the following table in double spacing, centring it both horizontally and vertically. Rule all lines in ink. List trades alphabetically.

NUMBER OF EMPLOYEES AT 31ST DECEMBER, 1977

Trade	Males	Females	Total
Rubber goods & Materials	78000	35 800	113,800
Cardboard Boxes, Cartons, etc	23,000	31,400	54,400
Wood Containers & Baskets	18,600	5,600	24,200
Brushes & Brooms, etc.	13,300	8,300	16,500
Linoleum, Leather Cloth, etc	8,200	4,200	17,500
Furniture & Upholstery	95 000	35,200	130 200
Games & Sports Requisites	11 400	19,000	30 400
TOTALS	247 500	139 500	387,000

Skill building

Type each exercise (A, B, C, and D) *once* for practice, *once* for speed, and finally *once* for accuracy. Margins: Elite 22–82, Pica 12–72.

A. Review alphabet keys

1.   Through an involuntary error on your part, the question of the Zenith Club Dinner must be adjourned until next week.

B. Improve control of figure keys

2. tour 5974 tore 5943 your 6974 wore 2943 tier 5834 were 2343.
3. Add together 123, 234, 345, 456, 567, 678, 789, 890, and 91.
4. Sales: £20,846,000; Profit: £1,735,889; Assets: £12,451,469.
5. Dividends: 1959 — £293,617; 1960 — £485,732; 1961 — £86,247.

C. Build accuracy on shift key drill

6. Miss J. Levy, Mr. K. Yates, Mrs. D. Tate, Messrs. Rowe Bros.
7. Dear Sir, The Misses C. & E. A. Levy, Messrs. H. F. Gittins, I. Norton, P. St. John Clark, and O. Watson-Viney will visit the Mass X-ray Unit at Zephyr Street on Monday, 3rd October.

D. Improve concentration

8. Schon lange ist es mein Wunsch, in Deutschland eine dauernde Stellung zu erhalten, um den dortigen Handel kennenzulernen.

Accuracy/Speed Practice   Two-minute timing   Not more than 2 errors

words

AS.15   There is a tendency for our lives to become fuller as time goes on, 13
and the problem is how to find time for all the things we want to do. 27
The best way is to decide what is the most important, and to use up as 41
far as possible the periods which have hitherto been idle. Those of us 55
who travel by train or bus can use this time if the train or bus is not 69
too crowded. Then again, there is always the week-end, part of which 83
should be set aside for the reading that we may not have had time to do 98
during the week. For though it is vital that the student should not 111
miss her daily study, we must not make cast-iron rules for any one thing 126
without bearing in mind all the other claims we may have on our time. 139

    Our plans must always be flexible, and we must see that we have 152
time for relaxation as well as for study.   (S.I. 1.24) 160

UNIT 12   79

Ruling in ink

If horizontal and vertical lines are to be ruled in ink, follow the same procedure as for ruling by underscore, but in this case the beginning and end of each horizontal line must be marked in pencil, as well as the vertical lines. When table has been completed, remove paper from machine and, with a fine nib, rule lines carefully and neatly to scale-points marked, using red or black ink. Always wipe edge of ruler after ruling each line to prevent smudging. It is essential that vertical and horizontal lines meet exactly.

Column headings in tabulation

Column headings in tabulation are usually typed in lower case with initial capitals. They may be centred horizontally and vertically as in the example below.

Column headings should not be underscored.
NOTE: If column headings take more than one line, they must be typed in single spacing.

2. Practise centring column headings. Type the following table in double spacing on A4 paper. Rule all lines in ink. List industries in alphabetical order. Centre column headings vertically and horizontally.

TREND OF INDUSTRIAL PROFITS Monthly Table of Company Profits (£000's)				
Industry	Number of Companies	Profits	Depreciation	Tax
Aircraft & Components	7	31,550	8,876	8,423
Paper & Packaging	43	67,193	20,693	22,809
Building Materials	100	97,825	25,292	33,619
Iron & Steel	23	144,699	54,071	38,524
Electricals (Light)	60	86,750	27,150	26,627
Motors, cycles & components	31	70,979	25,582	21,025
Electricals (Heavy)	13	69,854	19,959	21,613
Breweries, Distilleries & Soft Drinks	49	115,622	47,554	13,695
Clothing & Footwear	417	32,215	7,032	11,245
Machine Tools	20	12,870	1,720	5,252
Engineering & Metal	262	194,388	44,400	66,543
Chemicals & Allied	73	315,282	89,581	101,588
Rubber Manufacturing	13	33,665	11,292	11,920
Construction	41	29,496	9,423	8,660

Further exercises in centring of column headings are given on pages 53–54 of
Practical Typing Exercises, Book One.

Technique development

1. Display the following on A4 paper. The rectangle should measure 203 mm × 70 mm. Keep your typed copy for future reference in Folder No. 2.

Sizes of Envelopes

C5   229 × 162 mm (9" × 6⅜")
takes A5 paper unfolded
and A4 paper folded once

C6   162 × 114 mm (6⅜" × 4½")
takes A4 paper folded twice
and A5 paper folded once

D11   220 × 110 mm (8⅝" × 4¼")
takes A4 paper folded equally into three

Post Office Regulations

1. Post Office regulations require address to be parallel to the length and not to the breadth of the envelope.

2. Postal town should be typed in capitals.

3. The *postcode* should be typed as follows:

   (a) It is always the last item in the address and should have a line to itself.

   (b) If it is impossible, because of lack of space, to put the code on a separate line, type it *six* spaces to the right of the last line.

   (c) Always type code in block capitals.

   (d) Do not use full stops or any punctuation marks between or after the characters in the code.

   (e) Leave *one* clear space between the two halves of the code.

   (f) NEVER underline the code.

Example:

Messrs W H Ramsay & Co
Mortimer Street
LONDON
W1N 8BA

Ruling of tabulated statements

Tabulated statements are sometimes made more effective and clearer by ruling horizontal and/or vertical lines. Although it is assumed that you have already learnt how to rule up tabulated work, the following notes will serve as a reminder.

1. If horizontal lines only are ruled, use the underscore and let the lines project two spaces beyond the margins on either side.

2. Always turn up one single-line space before a horizontal underscore and two single-line spaces after.

3. If both horizontal and vertical lines are required, rule these (a) either by underscore, in which case the paper has to be removed from the machine after the table has been typed, and reinserted sideways for the ruling of the vertical lines; (b) or by ink; (c) or a combination of the two, e.g., horizontals by underscore, verticals by ink. See that the ink ruling is the same colour as the underscore line.

4. The vertical lines between the columns must be ruled exactly in the middle of each blank space. It is therefore advisable to leave an odd number of spaces between the columns—one for the vertical ruling, and an equal number on either side of the ruling.
The points on the scale at which the vertical lines are to be ruled should be marked by light pencil marks at the top and bottom of the columns.

5. To find the point at which to mark the vertical line, proceed as follows: (a) Move to tab. stop following vertical line. (b) Divide number of spaces between columns by 2 and take next highest figure, e.g., 3 spaces between columns—divide by $2 = 1\frac{1}{2}$, call it 2; 5 spaces between columns = $2\frac{1}{2}$, call it 3. (c) From tab. stop back space 2 (or whatever the figure is), and put a pencil mark.

NOTE: Do not extend the vertical lines above or below the horizontals—see that they meet exactly.

1. Practise ruling. Read the above explanation, and then type a copy of the following table in double spacing on A5 paper (210 × 148 mm). Rule horizontal lines by underscore and vertical lines in ink.

ROBINSON & CO. LTD.

Report of Tenth Record Year

Year to 31st December	1977	1976	1975
	£	£	£
Group profit before tax	308,146	356,601	404,581
Taxation	159,905	157,643	179,693
Group net profit	148,241	198,958	224,888
Ordinary dividend			
(Less tax)	55,125	55,125	60,637
Revenue reserves and			
unappropriated profit	801,289	923,438	1,069,247

Further exercises on tabulation are given on pages 32–34 of **Practical Typing Exercises, Book One.**

Tabulation with columns of figures

When columns in a table contain figures, care must be taken to see that units come under units, tens under tens, etc.
If you do not use the comma to separate thousands from hundreds, etc., figures must be set out as explained on page 140. However, if any number in any column of a table contains six or more figures, all groups must be in threes even though the column may contain items of less than six figures.

2. Type a copy of the following on A4 paper in single-line spacing with double spacing between the items. Keep your typed copy for future reference in Folder No. 2.

ADDRESSING ENVELOPES, POSTCARDS, ETC. *Please use hanging paras*

(1) Always be sure to use an envelope sufficiently large to take / letter.

(2) Many firms hv their name, printed in / top left *address* corner. This ensures / safe & speedy return of / ltr if ↑ for any reason ↑ it cannot be delvd.

(3) Always type / envelope f ea ltr immediately after typing the ltr.

(4) Single / line spacing & block style are preferable on a small envelope. With larger envelopes / address may be better displayed & more easily read by being typed in double / line spacing

(5) On most envelopes the address shd be started about 50 mm from the / edge & | 1st line shd be approx ½ way down. *such as Personal, Confidential, Private,*

(9/8) Remember to type the envelopes f any extra carbon copies to or offices or persons f their inform̃. *wh may be sent*

(6) Special instructions, shd be typed, in caps & underscored, 2 spaces above / name of the addressee.

(7) "Recorded delivery", "Registered mail" and "Special Delivery" are typed in top left-hand corner in capitals and underscored.

(8) "By hand" is typed in the top right-hand corner in capitals & underscored.

3. Cut slips of paper size 229 × 102 mm and type the following addresses in block style.

```
Richard Daniel Ltd  11 Canal Street  Manchester  M4 6HD
Miss A Blackie  15 Hall Lane  Upminster  Essex  RM14 1AP Private
Wilson & Mansfield Ltd  Market Street  Leicester  LEI 6DF  For the
                                        attention of Mr A J Wilson
International Co Ltd  101 Hempstead Road  Watford  Herts  WD1 3EY
Mrs A M Little  10 Sealand Road  Bristol  BS1 3BQ
Mr M Jones  4 Clitton Road,  Northampton  NN1 5BQ
Dunn Bros Ltd  320 High Street  Huddersfield  HD1 2NE Recorded delivery
F Ferguson Ltd  St Giles Street  Edinburgh  EH1 1YW
Everitt Ltd  20 Thomas Street  Liverpool  L1 6BJ (Confidential)
B France & Co Ltd  439 Oxford Street  London  W1A 1BH
```

Type the alphabetic review *once* for practice, *once* for speed, and *once* for accuracy. Margins: Elite 22—82, Pica 12—72.

A. Review alphabet keys

Amongst the junk she bought from the auction sale was a unique glazed pottery case which was in excellent condition.

Accuracy/Speed Practice	Five-minute timing	Not more than 3 errors

words

AS.24

A remarkable young Roman slave earned his own freedom by invent- 13
ing a system of shorthand in the last century before the Christian era. 27
His name was Tiro, and he was born south of Rome in the year 103 B.C. 40

In 96 B.C. this bright young slave was sent to Rome to study with 54
his master's two sons, who were called Marcus and Quintus. They were 68
about the same age as Tiro, and treated him like a friend rather than a 82
slave. As the boys advanced in their studies their friendship grew 95
stronger, and when the master died, Marcus became Tiro's legal owner. 109
He made Tiro his secretary. 114

It is not quite clear just when Tiro invented his system, and some 127
people go as far as to say that he stole a system already in use in 140
Greece. Others say that he merely perfected abbreviating devices used 154
by the Greeks. However, most agree that Tiro's "notes" were the first 168
organized system that enabled a writer to take down the spoken words as 182
fast as they were said. In those days the notes were written on clay 196
tablets. According to some sources, Marcus himself picked up a short- 210
hand system during one of his trips to Greece and taught it to Tiro, who 225
adapted it to Latin. Whether this is true or not we do not know, but it 239
was Tiro who wrote the shorthand treatise that was soon distributed 252
throughout the Roman Empire under his name. 261

The system was taught in schools to children of all classes, and 274
the Romans were quick to realize the value of it. 284

Tiro was a great help to Marcus, and, as a result, he was made a 297
free man. He showed his gratefulness by remaining Marcus's friend as 310
well as his devoted secretary. 316

Tiro wrote several books on the Latin language, but his greatest 329
contribution to the advancement of civilization lies in the widespread 343
use made of the Tironian shorthand. Not only was the system taught in 357
the Roman Empire, but with the advent of Christianity, it was adopted 371
by the early Christian churchmen as a practical means of spreading the 385
new religious doctrine and recording the deeds of the saints and martyrs. 400

(S.I. 1.38)

4. Type a copy of the following on A4 paper in single-line spacing with double spacing between the numbered items. Keep your typed copy for future reference in Folder No. 2.

FORMS OF ADDRESS

Standard Punctuation

1. Courtesy titles must always be used when writing to individuals.

2. Use Mr. OR Esq. (NEVER both) if writing to a male person.

6 3. Address a married lady & a single lady as follows: Mrs. L. Brown and Miss J. Clark (if names are different)

Mrs L & Miss C. Brown (if names are / same).

10 If the word 'Sen.' (Senior) or 'Jun.' (Junior) is used, *immediately* this comes after / name & before Esq.; & is preceded & followed by a comma. Always leave one clear space after the comma.

12 Letters after a person's name must be arranged in order of importance, as follows: (a) Military Decorations, (b) Civil Decorations, e.g., O.B.E., (c) University Degrees, e.g., M.A., (d) M.P., (e) J.P.;

3 Rev. or Dr. or Sir replaces (Esq. Mr. or)

5 Use The Misses . . . when writing to more than one single lady w / same name.

4 Use Messrs. when addressing more than one male person.

not 11 Letters after a person's name do not require a space between them, but a space must be left between ea. group of letters.

9 Use no courtesy title for limited companies, even if the name includes a personal name.

7 Address 2 married ladies of / same name as mesdames

8 *impersonal* Use no courtesy title with names or those beginning w 'The.'

5. Cut slips of paper size 229 × 102 mm and type the following addresses in block style. Use open punctuation and insert any courtesy titles that have been omitted. For instructions on addressing overseas mail, please see page 215.

Holt & Marsden 14 Main Street, Aberdovey, Gwynedd LL35 OEA

Rev R N Rose The Presbytery St Anthony's Rd Limerick Irish Republic

Valerie Ryan-Miller 2917 Coconut Grove, MIAMI, Fla., USA AIR MAIL

The New Dry Cleaning Co. 36 Doncaster Rd Scunthorpe Sth Humberside DI6 2TA

Juan Garcia 6A Bloque L'Ancora Flats JAVEA, Alicante Spain

Jas. L. Marlow Senior OBE The Gables Alfreton Derby DE5 7TA

Mc Intosh & Co Ltd 171 Abbey St Dunfermline Fife KY12 7AA Confidential

For the attention of Martin J Mc Intosh

Joan & Betty Haywood Halifax St Brighouse West Yorks HD6 1AY

Further exercises on envelope addressing are given on pages 18 and 38 of **Practical Typing Exercises, Book One,** and on page 8 of **Book Two.**

Type the following Monthly Sales Analysis on A4 paper in double spacing, leaving 3 spaces between columns. Centre vertically and horizontally.

Monthly Sales Analysis caps & u/s

(in £'s)   Typist - please put commas in figures

Month	Credit	Cash	Hire Purchase
January	2510	100466	25627
Feb.	1445	129865	20446	tr↓
March	1565	146400	23263
Apl	3626	70121	10414
May	4324	85320	9648
June	6210	65812	8040	tr↓
July	6384	74697	8762
Sept.	7123	73297	9142
Oct	8354	78501	10092
Nov.	9364	102454	9555	tr↓
Dec.	10450	94136	12456
August	4234	64110	7322

Display the following on A4 paper.

EASTFIELD POLYTECHNIC - spaced caps

Staff Vacancies - closed caps

Dept.	Subject & Grade	Salary £
(3) Mathematics and Statistics	Mathematics	
	Senior Lecturer	3,300
(2) Industrial Engineering	Lecturer II	3,000
	Management	
	Senior Lecturer	3,300
(Please put in numbered order - do not type nos.)	Manufacturing Technology	
	Senior Lecturer	3,300
	Metallurgy	
(1) Computer	Lecturer II	3,000
	Computers	
	Principal Lecturer	3,700
	Sen. Lecturer	£ 3,300

The words PRIVATE, CONFIDENTIAL, and PERSONAL are typed 2/3 single-line spaces above the name of the addressee at the left margin, in capitals and underscored.

The words URGENT, RECORDED DELIVERY, REGISTERED, SPECIAL DELIVERY, BY HAND, are typed at the left margin 2/3 single-line spaces after YOUR/OUR REF., in capitals and underscored.

6. Type the following letter on A4 paper, using suitable margins. Type an envelope.

Our Ref VB/JLM

URGENT

3 October 1978

R L Dodds & Co Ltd 14 Queen St Bury St Edmunds Suffolk IP33 2AA

For the attention of Mr F J Lowe Pur Officer

F J LOWE

Dear Sirs

QUOTATION

Our Sales Director, Mr Roger Campbell, has asked us to send y a quotation f the following:

Item	Quantity	Unit Price	Discount
Open-plan Screens	50 or over	£6&5	10%
Computer Media Cabinets	20 or over	£1,500	15%

N.P. [Samples of the tweeds used for the open-plan screens are enclosed.

We look forward to receiving your order.

Yrs ffy

W A FOSTER & Co LTD

N.P. [the Unit Prices quoted are valid until end of Oct 1978.

Valerie Beaufort (MISS)

Sales department

Enc

Further exercises on typing fully-blocked letters with open punctuation, Private, Confidential, etc., are given on pages 33, 38, and 40 of **Practical Typing Exercises, Book Two.**

4. Practise typing columnar work with heading. Type the following table on A5 paper (210 × 148 mm), centring vertically and horizontally. Leave three spaces between columns.

<u>PRICE REDUCTIONS</u>

<u>Gift No.</u>	<u>Description</u>	<u>Old Vouchers</u>	<u>New Vouchers</u>
215	Transistor Radio	5,800	5,500
218	Record Player	4,900	4,300
902	"Convertible" Compact	460	400
903	"Convertible" Compact	530	470
1005	Dressing Case	1,350	1,350

5. Type the following financial statement on A5 paper (210 × 148 mm), centring vertically and horizontally. Leave three spaces between columns.

NORTHERN CONSTRUCTION CO. LTD. ⎰—centre + underscore

Financial Statement

Trading Results	1976	1977
	£	£
Trading Profit before taxation	1,917,204	1,649,482
Profit after/before taxation	864,361	733,143
nett dividend to shareholders	6fl.686	493,797
nett profit retained in business	259,675	239,346
Group turnover (approx.)	9,250,000	8,250,000

Further exercise on tabulation is given on page 31 of **Practical Typing Exercises, Book One**.

Numbers

Many offices do not insert a comma to separate millions from thousands, and thousands from hundreds. In this case the figures are typed as follows:

(a) Numbers comprising *five* figures or less are blocked together, e.g., 1723, 26785.

(b) Numbers comprising *six* or more figures are grouped in threes (starting from the unit figure) with one space between the groups instead of commas, e.g., 9 687 253.

NOTE: If commas are used to separate millions from thousands, and thousands from hundreds, leave no space before or after comma, e.g. 9,687,253.

Production Typing
Job 33

Production Target—*8 minutes*

Type the following letter on A4 paper, using suitable margins. Type an envelope.

Our Ref AS/AM

J A Corbett Esq

P M Peters & Co Ltd

Whitecross

LINLITHGOW

West Lothian EH49 6JQ

Typist — Please use today's date & mark the letter & envelope 'Confidential'

Dr Sir

Miss Jane A S Tongue

The above named gave us yr name as a referee when she applied for the position as

u.c. Shthand-Typist in our sales dept.

We shd be glad if you wd be kind enough to let us know whether y consider the applicant to be honest & reliable & generally suitable.

I hve encl a valuation paper wh I hve shd be grateful if you wd complete & return on the

stamped

& encl self-addressed envelope.

Yrs ffy

W A Foster & Co Ltd

Alan Suffran

Personnel Officer

2. Practise typing column work. Display the following table in double-line spacing on A5 paper (210 × 148 mm), leaving 5 spaces between columns.

<u>LIST OF SCHOOL OFFICERS' BADGES AVAILABLE</u>

Captain	Monitor	Physical Education
Vice-Captain	Monitress	Birthday
House Captain	Leader	Merit
Form Captain	Sports	Good Conduct
Head Boy	Swimming	Department
Head Girl	Netball	Punctuality
Prefect	Football	Courtesy

3. Type a copy of the following on A4 paper in double-line spacing. Keep your typed copy for future reference in Folder No. 2.

COLUMN HEADINGS — CENTRED STYLE

In addition to main headings, ea. column usually has its own heading wh must be taken into a/c when deciding on longest line in a column.

1. If heading is shorter than longest item in the column it must be centred over the longest item.

2. To do this, find the centre point of column by tapping space bar once for every 2 letters & spaces in the longest item. Begin from the scale point set f the start of the column.

3. From centre point thus reached backspace once f every 2 ltrs & spaces in the heading. Start to type heading from this point.

If heading is longest line in column, column items must be centred under it as follows:

(a) Type the heading @ scale point set for start of the column + spaces in heading.

(b) Find centre point of column by tapping space bar once f every 2 letters, beginning fr 1st ltr of the heading.

(c) Fr centre point thus reached, back-space once f every 2 letters & spaces in longest column item under heading.

(d) Re-set tab stop (or margin stop if in first column) at this scale point for start of column items.

Before typing column headings, therefore, type following steps: Type 1st & black parts please for numbered items.

Skill building

Type each line or sentence (A, B, and C) *three* times, and, if time permits, complete your practice by typing each group once as it appears. Margins: Elite 22–82, Pica 12–72.

A. Review alphabet keys

1.   The take-over bid made was entirely unexpected, but was judged to be inadequate in view of the size of the business.

B. Build speed on common phrases

2. to go, to me, to do, to be, to say, to ask, to pay, to come.
3. It seems to me that you should be able to go home this year.
4. We hope to be in a position to ask you to come and visit us.
5. We do not know whether to pay or to return the damaged toys.

C. Build speed on common prefixes

6. complete, commerce, compare, combine, comply, commit, common
7. Compare the completed contract with the one now recommended.
8. She will be compelled to comply with the complete programme.
9. To avoid complicating the issue, he will not commit himself.

Accuracy/Speed Practice	Three-minute timing	Not more than 3 errors

words

AS.16   The interview is a 2-way process. The interviewer should find out   13
if you have the desired qualifications and suitable personality. You   27
must try to size up the job to see if it is what you are looking for.   41

    Before the interview, the interviewer will have studied your   53
Application Form and Job Sheet to find out what the job is about — what   67
has to be done, how it has to be done, and where it has to be done. He   81
will then be ready to ask you a number of questions designed to confirm   95
statements made on your Application Form and to find out other facts   109
about you.   111

    When the most suitable person has been chosen, her references are   124
checked. This may be done by mail or by telephone. If they are in   137
order, the chosen person will be offered the job.   147

    When you receive a letter offering you a post, see that you write   160
back straight away, thanking the writer for the offer and giving your   174
decision.   176

    In a new job there are many things to learn. No matter how well   188
you have been trained, your new employer is sure to ask you to do one   202
or two tasks in a different way. When he does so, carry out all instruc-   217
tions he gives. If, later on, you feel your way is better, there is   231
usually no harm in saying that you think it is.   (S.I. 1.33)   240

UNIT 13

1. Type a copy of the following on A4 paper in single-line spacing with double between paragraphs. Keep your typed copy for future reference in Folder No. 2. Type ordinal numbers as in manuscript.

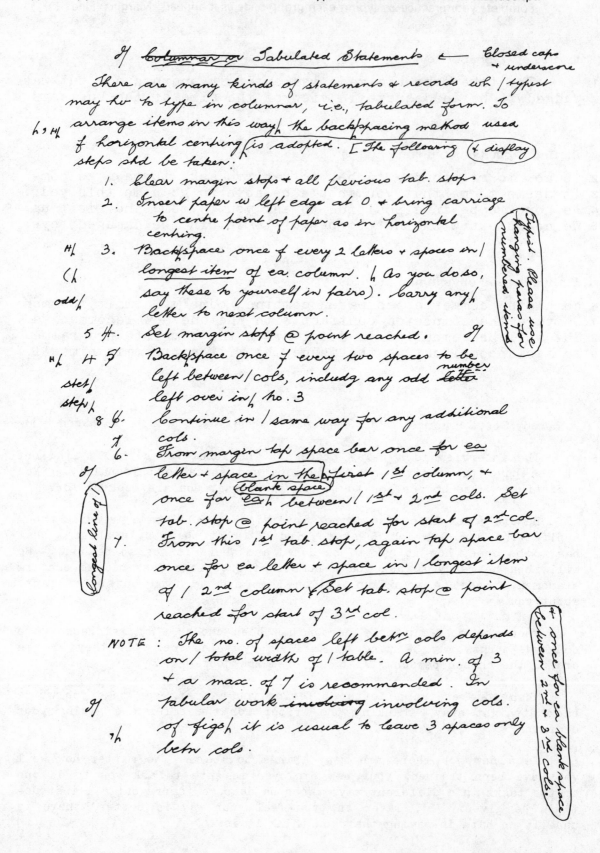

Columnar or Tabulated Statements — Closed caps + underscore

There are many kinds of statements & records wh / typist may hv to type in columnar, i.e., tabulated form. To arrange items in this way / the backspacing method used f horizontal centring is adopted. [The following + display steps shd be taken:

1. Clear margin stops + all previous tab. stops

2. Insert paper w left edge at 0 + bring carriage to centre point of paper as in horizontal centring.

3. Backspace once f every 2 letters + spaces in / longest item of ea. column. (As you do so, say these to yourself in pairs). Carry any / letter to next column.

5 4. Set margin stops @ point reached.

4 5. Backspace once f every two spaces to be left between / cols, includg any odd number left over in / no. 3

8 6. Continue in / same way for any additional cols.

6. From margin tap space bar once for ea letter + space in the first 1st column, + once for ea blank space between / 1st + 2nd cols. Set tab. stop @ point reached for start of 2nd col.

7. From this 1st tab. stop, again tap space bar once for ea letter + space in / longest item of / 2nd column. Set tab. stop @ point reached for start of 3rd col.

NOTE : The no. of spaces left betn cols depends on / total width of / table. A min. of 3 + a max. of 7 is recommended. In tabular work involving cols. of figs / it is usual to leave 3 spaces only betn cols.

Typist. Please use hanging numbers for numbered items

longest line of /

+ once for ea blank space between 2nd + 3rd cols.

Semi-blocked letter

The semi-blocked style differs from the fully blocked as follows:
(1) Paragraphs are indented (at least five spaces) from left margin.
(2) Subject-heading is centred on typing line, one clear line-space being left above and below the heading.
(3) Displayed matter is sometimes arranged in such a way that the longest line is centred on the typing line. To do this, find the centre point of the body of the letter by adding together the points at which the left and right margins are set, and divide by 2. Bring writing point to this scale-point and back-space once for every two letters and spaces in the longest line. Leave one clear line-space above and below the displayed matter. Most organisations will accept an inset portion inset only from left margin where continuous matter is being typed. The inset must be at least five spaces from the margin.
(4) The complimentary close starts at approximately the centre of the typing line (or slightly to the right) and the name of the company is typed on the next line. There should be a minimum of 4 clear line-spaces between the name of the company and the signatory. If there is any designation, this should be typed on the next single-line space.

1. Practise typing semi-blocked letter. Type the following letter on A4 paper (210 × 297 mm) with margins 22/82 (Elite), 12/72 (Pica). Keep your typed copy for future reference in Folder No. 2. Type an envelope.

JS/AKL   1st September, 1978

The National Bank Ltd.,
Davies Street,
LONDON.   W1Y 2AA

For the attention of Mr. H. Harper, Manager

Dear Sirs,

                    Appointment of Bankers

     We have to advise you that it was resolved at the Board Meeting held today that you should be appointed bankers to the Company.

          The following documents are therefore enclosed:

               1.   Copy of the Directors' Resolution.

               2.   Copy of the Company's Memorandum and
                    Articles of Association.

               3.   Specimen signatures of those who are
                    to operate on the account.

               4.   Certificate of Incorporation.

     Will you please return the last document at your earliest convenience.

                         Yours faithfully,
                         W. J. BUSH & CO. LTD.

                         John Scrivens
                         Secretary.

Encs.

Further exercises on semi-blocked letters are given on pages 13–17 of **Practical Typing Exercises, Book One**.

Type each line or sentence (A, B, and C) *three* times. If time permits, complete
your practice by typing each group once as it appears. Margins: Elite 22–82,
Pica 12–72.

A. Review alphabet keys

1.   An exceedingly smart native boy operated the punka with
zeal, by jerking a quite frail rope attached to his big toe.

B. Build speed on common letter combinations

2. anything anxious change answer annual thank than can and an.
3. Thank them. Anything they can do will be more than welcome.
4. We are anxious to have your answer about the annual meeting.

C. Build speed on fluency drill

5. That boy said the baby was very ill when the lady went away.
6. The four men went off down the road when that shop was shut.
7. They said that the tour was good but that the food was poor.

Accuracy/Speed Practice	Four-minute timing	Not more than 4 errors
		words

AS.23   You may not find shopping much fun if you can only buy absolute   12
necessities on a shoe-string, but at any rate you can spend a most   26
interesting morning looking around some of the curious shops to be   39
found in London. The Old Curiosity Shop, which dates back to the   52
sixteenth century, is well worth a visit. Or, if you like books, you   66
could pass a whole morning browsing in certain bookshops in Charing   79
Cross Road. The large stores, too, will be found of interest. Some,   93
we are told, sell everything from an elephant to a pin. Youngsters   106
will be thrilled with the animals and birds which are on sale in the   120
pet store, whilst you can wander around at your leisure in the fashion   134
department.   136

Visitors to London should not fail to see Kew Gardens — a favour-   149
ite spot, particularly in lilac time. These gardens were originally   163
the grounds of Kew Palace, which goes back to the Hanoverian period;   176
these are now botanical gardens, which contain some thousands of rare   190
plants, and there is never a time when they are quite bare.   202

Another place of interest is Kenwood House, standing in its own   215
grounds in the middle of Hampstead Heath. There you could think you   228
were in open country. The park, designed in the eighteenth century,   242
has a lovely view from the house; and in the spring there are daffodils   256
in profusion, followed by a wonderful display of azaleas and other   269
flowers. A fine collection of old furniture and pictures in the house   283
also makes Kenwood House a place which is well worth a visit, and one   297
which could not fail to please. Next time you are in London, why not   311
make a special point of visiting these places?   (S.I. 1.37)   320

Ditto marks

When the same word is repeated in consecutive lines of display matter, quotation marks may be used under the repeated word. If there is more than one word repeated, the quotation marks must be typed under each word. The abbreviation 'do.' (without the full stop in open punctuation) may be used under a group of words. When used with blocked style, the ditto marks should be blocked at the beginning of each word; with centred style the ditto marks should be centred under the word(s).

Postscripts

Sometimes a postscript has to be typed at the foot of a letter, either because the writer has omitted something he wished to say in the body of the letter, or because he wishes to draw special attention to a certain point. The postscript should be started two single-line spaces below the last line of signatory, and should be in single-line spacing.

2. Practise typing letter with postscript. Read the above explanation, and then type the following letter on A4 (210 × 297 mm) paper, with margins 22/82 (Elite), 12/72 (Pica). Keep your typed copy for future reference in Folder No. 2. Type an envelope.

GAS/MBB   (Insert today's date)

Stewart & Goodall Ltd.,
Norton Road,
IPSWICH.   IP4 1LU

For the attention of the Purchasing Officer

Dear Sirs,

                        Enquiry

     We thank you for your enquiry for details and prices of our Shaped Covers for all makes of cars, and we enclose our catalogue of these covers which, we may say, are a remarkably quick-selling line.

     As you are in the trade, we are quoting below our wholesale prices, but would point out that these apply only to minimum orders of 10 covers in sizes of any assortment.

          Length 366 cm for small cars ... £6.45 each
            "   396 cm " medium "   ... £6.75   "
            "   427 cm " large   "   ... £8.15   "

We look forward to receiving a trial order from you.

                    Yours faithfully,
                  for J. APPLETON & CO. LTD.

                    G. A. Sanders
                    Sales Department

PS.   Prices for smaller quantities will be quoted on request.

Enc.

Production typing

Job 58
Production Target—*20 minutes*
Type in correct form on A5 paper an Income and Expenditure Account for the Stockfield Social Club for the twelve months ended 31st July, 1978.

Expenditure

Donations to Charities	£2.35
Printing, Postage and Stationery	24.77
Heating + Lighting	30.50
Dance Band	15.25
Sundry Expenses	7.22
Excess of Income over Expenditure	
	£

Income

Sale of Badges	£5.25
Proceeds fr. Dances	10.77
Subscriptions	123.00
Arrears of Subscriptions	10.50
Conference Fees	21.00
(Typist – please calculate, and put in totals)	£

Job 59
Production Target—*20 minutes*
Type the following Balance Sheet in correct form on two separate sheets of A5 paper.

BALANCE SHEET OF ROBINSON & SONS LTD
AT 31ST DECEMBER 1978

LIABILITIES

	£	£
Capital		
1,000 Shares of £1 fully paid		1,000
General Reserve		1,095
Current Liabilities		
Trade Creditors	975	
Inland Revenue (Staff Income Tax)	30	1,005
Balance for Distribution		277
		£3,377

ASSETS

	£	£
Fixed		
Fixtures	869	
Less Depreciation	122	747
Investment (Lloyds Bank)	500	
Accrued Interest	55	555
Current		
Stock-in-Trade		1,487
Trade Debtors		498
Cash at Bank and in hand		90
		£3,377

Production typing

Job 34   Production Target—*10 minutes*

Type the following letter on A4 paper. Type an envelope.

yr. ref (Ref. from previous letter)
Our ref. JH/LP

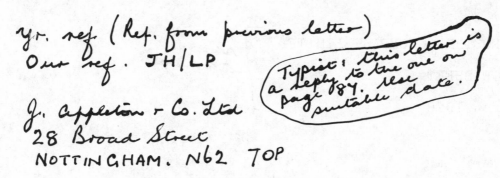
Typist: this letter is a reply to the one on page 84. Use suitable date.

J. Appleton + Co. Ltd
28 Broad Street
NOTTINGHAM. N62 7OP

         Thank you for yr. ltr. dated

N.P.   and f. yr. catalogue of car covers. [Attached
V.C.   please find our Order No. 218/70 for 10 of
If possibly la. size   [We shd. like dely of these by
1.c.   Wednesday of next week *   Should this
       be impossible, please let us know immediately

line/   If this/ sells well, we will certainly
      order in larger quantities and we wonder
of   what further what further additional discount y. wd.
      allow on an order such as

       200 - 366 cm. @ £6·45 (Small cars)   1.c.
       150 - 427 cm. @ £8·15 (Large cars)   1.c.

"/" We note that all orders are /carriage fwd/;
O/ 1.c however However, in /case of a large
(/)/ order /as above/ wd. y. be prepared to
N.P. pay the carriage? [The next occasion
      yr. rep. is in this area, please ask
      him to call.

        Yrs. ffy Stewart + Goodall Ltd
          J. Haddleton M.P.O.A.
          Pur. Officer

Please mark letter for attn. of G.A. Sanders + for more salutation.

150 -396 cm/ @
£6·45 (medium cars)

       * Typist - please insert date

W.A. FOSTER & COMPANY LIMITED

BALANCE SHEET

31 March 1978

Block at left margin

	1977	1976
	£	£
Fixed assets	2,849,984	2,550,674
Quoted investments	144,255	90,838
Interests in subsidiaries	12,190,767	11,033,120
	15,185,006	see 13,644,632
Current assets	602,878	1,954,636
Current liabilities	(4,980,568)	(4,851,004)
Net current assets (liabilities)	(4,377,690)	(2,896,368)
	10,807,316	10,684,266
Issued capital	1,888,406	1,888,406
Reserves	8,438,432	8,453,244
	10,326,838	10,341,650
Borrowings	328,406	342,301
Deferred taxation	152,072	315
	10,807,316	10,684,266

Further exercise on Balance Sheets (vertical presentation) is given on page 25 of **Practical Typing Exercises, Book Two**.

Type the following on A4 paper in single-line spacing with double between
numbered items.

(circled note, with arrow) NOTICE TO ALL OFFICE STAFF

Closed caps + underscore

DECIMAL CURRENCY ← *spaced caps + underscore*

← To ensure consistency in all office documents, please follow very carefully the instructions given below:

1. Cheques

(a) When handwritten

Figures	Words
£140·05*	One hundred + forty pounds 05
£70·00	Seventy pounds
£0·75 £	Seventy-five pence
£60·23	Sixty pounds 23

* note use of hyphen instead of decimal point

(b) When typed

Figures	Words
£80·00	Eighty pounds
£73·42	Seventy-three pounds 42

(circled note) £ Always have at least one figure (a nought if necessary between the pound sign + / hyphen (or decimal point).

2. p is / abbreviation for new pence. It is placed after the amt + there is no full stop unless it ends a sentence.

3. Any amt over 99½ new pence must be expressed as pound(s), e.g., 80p + 50p = £1.30 (one pound thirty), and NOT as 130 pence

4. Amounts in whole pounds shd be written: £5, £324,000, OR £5·00, £324,000·00   *(circled note)* Typist: in this case raise these 2 points

5. When typing column work:

(a) w. pounds + pence the £ sign always goes over the unit figure of the pounds column.

(b) w pounds only — centre the £ sign over / longest line in / column.

A. C. BANKS
OFFICE MANAGER

3. Practise typing single-page Balance Sheet. Type a copy of the following on A5 paper (210 × 148 mm). Use blocked or indented style.

WILLIAM WOODHOUSE

BALANCE SHEET
as at 30th June, 1978

LIABILITIES	£	ASSETS	£
Sundry Creditors	700.62	Leasehold premises	1,000.00
Expenses out-		Fixtures and	
standing	52.00	Fittings	456.50
Reserve Account	500.00	Stock-in-Trade	550.62
Capital Account	2,300.90	Sundry Debtors	845.88
		Cash in hand	50.00
		Cash at bank	650.52
	£3,553.52		£3,553.52

4. Type a copy of the following Balance Sheet on two separate sheets of A5 paper (148 × 210 mm). Note that two money columns are needed on both sides. After completion of the typing, join the sheets together.

W. J. BRIDGWATER & CO.

BALANCE SHEET AS AT 31 MARCH, 1978

	£			£	
Capital as at 1 April	3,000		Fixed Assets		
Add Profit for the yr	1,085		Freehold building	2,500	
	4,085		Plant + machinery	1,000	
Less Drawings	1,000		Motor Vehicle	500	
	3,085			4,000	
Current Liabilities			Current Assets	£	
Bank Overdraft	£525		Stock	750	
Creditors	1,800	2,325	Debtors	500	
		£5,410	Cash	160	1,410
					£5,410

Skill building

Type each exercise (A, B, and C) *once* for practice, *once* for speed, and finally *once* for accuracy. Margins: Elite 22–82, Pica 12–72.

A. Review alphabet keys

1. Jack was quite delighted when they visited the tropical zone and was impressed by the exotic colours of the flowers.

B. Build accuracy on shift lock drill

2. WHAT'S-HIS-NAME, GO-AS-YOU-PLEASE, EIGHTY-TWO, MOTHER-IN-LAW

3. WHAT'S-HIS-NAME should call and see his MOTHER-IN-LAW today.

4. I do not like your GO-AS-YOU-PLEASE attitude one little bit.

C. Build accuracy on concentration drill

5. As a teacher of pharmaceutics, pharmacognosy, pharmaceutical chemistry and forensic pharmacy, I use an old PHARMACOPOEIA.

Accuracy/Speed Practice	Four-minute timing	Not more than 3 errors

words

AS.17　　What a grand place Majorca is for a holiday. In fact, it seems to me 14
that nature designed it as a holiday playground. The climate is pleasant 28
at any season, with cool sea breezes on the hottest day. Along the coast 43
line there are fine sandy beaches and you can swim all the year round. 57

Palma, the capital, is a fine city with its port and old town all in 71
one. To the east of Palma is Pastilla where there is a perfect stretch of 85
golden sand running along the bay to Arenal. Also, there are 2 or 3 smaller 100
beaches where the soft sand and shallow waters make bathing safe for chil- 114
dren, and there is plenty to do — water ski-ing, horse riding, bathing, 128
boating, etc., and, by night, a variety of bars and night clubs where you 143
can enjoy music and dancing. 151

Arenal has the finest beach on the island. Here you will find a 3-mile 165
long sweep of golden sand, gay night life in clubs, and restaurants, etc., 178
and yet only some 20 minutes from Palma. A short distance beyond Arenal, 193
among the rocks, there are ideal conditions for snorkel and skin-diving. 207

Palma Nova has superb sandy beaches with safe bathing for all ages, 220
and rocky coves for the more daring. There are excellent shops, bars and 235
cafes and plenty of evening entertainment. Palma Nova is set in some of 249
Majorca's most delightful countryside with warm-scented pine woods and 263
hills, yet with the delights of Palma only some 8 miles away. 276

If you prefer a quieter holiday, you will like the fishing village of 290
Porto Cristo, which is 40 miles east of Palma. Here there are fascinat- 305
ing hill walks which reward you with wonderful views of the island's coast. 319

(S.I. 1.37)

There are two other accounts which you may have to type, both of which have two sides like the Receipts and Payments Account.

1. *Income and Expenditure Account.* This is used by a non-trading concern or non-profit-making institution, such as a club, society or other charitable institution.

The right-hand side contains details of income received during a given period, and the left-hand side shows the expenses incurred. The difference between the two sides represents either a deficit (if expenses exceed income) or a surplus (if income exceeds expenses).

2. *Profit and Loss Account.* This is used by a trading or profit-making concern. The right-hand side contains details of profit, and the left side details of expenses.

The layout used when typing an Income and Expenditure Account and a Profit and Loss Account are the same as those applying to a Receipts and Payments Account.

2. Practise typing Income and Expenditure Account. Type the following on A5 paper (210 × 148 mm). Follow layout which is in block style.

FAIRHURST SPORTS AND SOCIAL CLUB

Income and Expenditure Account
for the year ended 31 December 1977

Expenditure	£	Income	£
Rent	70.00	Subscriptions	320.00
Cleaning	105.00	Dances	217.25
Heating and Lighting	83.24		
Stationery	41.35		
Postages	26.64		
Printing (due)	15.83		
Excess of Income over Expenditure	195.19		
	£537.25		£537.25

Balance sheets

A Balance Sheet is a statement of the Liabilities and Assets of a firm or company, and shows the financial position at a given time. A few small organisations still type their Balance Sheet with the Liabilities on the left-hand side and the Assets on the right-hand. If a Balance Sheet is set out in this way, a long-carriage machine should be used so that the Balance Sheet can be typed across the width of the paper. If a long-carriage typewriter is not available, the Balance Sheet usually has to be typed on two separate sheets of A4 paper, one sheet being used for Liabilities, and the other sheet for Assets.

The rules applying to the typing of Balance Sheets are the same as those already explained for Receipts and Payments Accounts. To ensure sufficient space being left for money columns (a Balance Sheet usually has at least two money columns on both sides), it may be necessary for the wording of an item to be taken on to more than one line.

If two separate sheets are used, the heading of the Balance Sheet should run right across the two sheets without a break, half being typed on the Liabilities side, and ending close to the right-hand edge of the sheet. The other half is typed on the Assets side, starting close to the left edge of the sheet.

The side containing the larger number of items should be typed first, and, before starting to type the second sheet, you should make a light pencil mark to show the precise point at which the heading is to be continued, to ensure that the two parts of the heading are in line with each other. Also mark lightly in pencil on the second sheet the line on which the £ sign appears, the line on which the first item is to be typed, and the exact position for the total, so that the two sides may coincide exactly.

When typing is completed, the two sides may be joined together by a strip of Sellotape or other adhesive affixed to the back, care being taken to see that the edges just meet.

Today's Balance Sheet is usually presented vertically. A simple example is given on page 135.

Carbon copies

It is necessary to keep, for filing purposes, at least one carbon copy of each letter or document typed. To take a carbon copy, take the following steps:

1. Place face downwards on a flat surface the sheet on which the typing is to be done.

2. On top of this place a sheet of carbon paper with the coated surface upwards.
3. On top of these place the sheet of paper on which the carbon copy is to be made. Pick up all sheets together and insert in machine with coated surface of carbon paper facing the platen.

Headings

Main headings, paragraph headings, and shoulder headings are used in letters in the same way as in manuscript work, see instructions on pages 3, 4, 5, and 6.

1. Practise typing letter with headings. Type the following letter, taking a carbon copy for filing. Use paragraph headings for sub-headings. Type an envelope.

> John Gasnell — 60, Upper Duke St, Liverpool L15 3BL
> We have pleasure in enclosing our new illustrated Price-List wh gives full details of the attractive range of gifts we have available for Christmas. Selection of Gifts. You wl notice th, on the back page we hv illustrated in full colour a representative selection of the gifts we can supply. Display of Christmas gifts The full range of Christmas Gift packs is permanently on view in our London Showrooms & also in the main provincial cities. Order Form. We hv also included an order form for the convenience of those wishing to
> NP! place their orders direct [May we ask you to keep this letter for ref. purposes?
> Yrs ffy W A FOSTER & Co. LTD Roger H. Campbell Sales Director

Additional carbon copies

In addition to the carbon copy required for filing, many business letters are typed with extra carbon copies, which are sent to any persons who may be concerned. If a copy of a letter is sent to someone other than the addressee, the letters cc. (= carbon copy) are typed at the left margin (usually at foot) followed by the name of the recipient. Where a copy is being sent to more than one person, the names are typed after cc. one underneath the other, and the name of the person for whom the copy is intended is either ticked at the side or underlined, e.g.,

(First copy)	(Second copy)	(Third copy)
cc. Mr. Jones✓	cc. Mr. Jones	cc. Mr. Jones
Mrs. Stone	Mrs. Stone✓	Mrs. Stone
Mr. French	Mr. French	Mr. French✓

Receipts and payments account

There are certain accounts which you may be asked to type for your employer, such as Receipts and Payments Account, which is used by clubs and societies. The purpose of this account is simply to show in summarised form the cash received and the cash paid out during a given period, and the amount of cash in hand. There are two sides to the account. The left-hand side shows the amount of cash in hand at the beginning of the period and the money received during the period, while the right-hand side shows the payments made. The difference between the two sides is the balance in hand at the end of a given period.

Guide to typing Receipts and Payments Account

1. Allow equal space for the Receipts and Payments sides.

2. The left and right margins must be equal.

3. Leave at least 5 spaces between the end of the money column on the left side and the start of the items on the right-hand side, so that, after completion of the typing, a thin red ink line may be drawn down the centre to divide the two sides, with equal spaces on both sides of the ink line.

4. Type the longer side first.

5. Use double spacing between each item. If any item requires more than one line, type the item in single-line spacing, indenting two spaces the second and subsequent lines.

6. The totals on both sides must be typed opposite each other. This may mean leaving a blank space on the shorter side before inserting the total.

7. The horizontal lines above and below the total and the total itself are typed as explained on page 72.

1. Practise typing Receipts and Payments Account in indented style. Type the following on A5 paper (210 × 148 mm). Rule red line down the middle.

FAIRHURST SPORTS AND SOCIAL CLUB

Receipts and Payments Account
for the year ended 31st December, 1978

Receipts	£		Payments	£
Cash in hand	9.33		Rent	30.00
Cash at bank	30.50		Cleaning	13.50
Subscriptions	105.00		Heating and	
			Lighting	39.12
Profit from			Stationery	5.25
Dances	8.37		Postages	13.31
Refreshments	5.13		Cash in hand	7.15
			Cash at bank	50.00
	£158.33			£158.33

Blocked layout

In the above type of document it is now common practice to block the headings. For an example please see the Income and Expenditure Account on page 133. You will notice that in the example on page 133 the £ sign is placed over the first figure of the longest line. It could also be placed over the £ sign in the total.

For information about letters starting Dear Mr, Miss, John, Mary, etc., and ending yours sincerely, please see page 214.

2. **Practise letter with cc.** Type the following letter with a carbon copy for filing and extra copies for Office Manager and Supplies Dept. Insert date. Use A5 paper. Mark letter and envelope CONFIDENTIAL and RECORDED DELIVERY.

> John Wilkes, Man. Director J. Wilkes & Sons Ltd
> High. St St Neots Huntingdon Cambs PE 19 2AA
> Dear Mr Wilkes
> Further to our meeting of Wed. last (Please put in date)
> when we discussed the question of yr acting as an
> Agent f our goods, I now hv pleasure in enclsg
> uc/ NP 2 draft copies of our agency agreement. [As soon as
> convenient, perhaps y wl let me know whether the
> agreement in its present form is acceptable. Yrs sincerely

Blind carbon copies

It sometimes happens that the writer does not want the addressee to know that copies have been distributed, in which case the typist types a bcc. (blind carbon copy) note. When the letter is finished the carbon copies are reinserted into the machine. At the foot of these copies the typist then types the bcc. note at the left margin, as follows:

bcc. Mr. Jones
<u>Mrs. Stone</u>
Mr. French

marking the name of the recipient as before. The bottom copy on which all the bcc. notes appear is the one kept for filing.

3. **Practise typing letter with blind carbon copies.** Take one file carbon and one bcc. copy for Mr. J Overton. Keep your typed copy for future reference in Folder No. 2. Use A5 paper. Type an envelope.

> Ref FNG/GED   Today's date
> Walter Jameson [JAMESON] Ltd., 24 Milton St., Bury, Lancs. B19 0SW
> For the attention of the Mr. J G Brown, Chief Buyer
> Dear Sirs,
> <u>Office Supplies</u> Although we hv serviced yr type-
> writers for several yrs, you may not hv realised th we are
> specialists in or office machinery & stationery. In any case,
> we shd appreciate the opportunity of submitting our quotations
> f any of yr office requirements the next time you are in
> NP/ need of supplies. [In particular, we hv an exceptionally
> attractive line in "Everclean" Carbon Paper, of wh we
> enclose a specimen sheet, & we sh be pleased to quote for
> N/P either standard or special sizes in this carbon. [We look
> forward to hearing from you whenever you are
> interested in renewing yr equipment. Yrs ffy, Sales Manager
> H. A. FOSTER + CO. LTD.

Skill building

Type each exercise (A, B, and C) *once* for practice, *once* for speed, and finally *once* for accuracy. Margins: Elite 22–82, Pica 12–72.

A. Review alphabet keys

1.   The physical fitness of the walkers was really amazing, and at the request of the judge extra big prizes were given.

B. Build accuracy on shift lock drill

2. SEVENTY-FIVE, NO-MAN'S-LAND, NINETY-SIX, DO-OR-DIE, Cardiff.

3. SEVENTY-FIVE men were lost in NO-MAN'S-LAND and they all had to make a DO-OR-DIE effort to escape their WOULD-BE captors.

4. NINETY-SIX members of the party would like to stop at Largs.

C. Build accuracy on common prefix drill

5. per, permit, person, perfect, perhaps, permanent, personnel.

6. Perhaps you would see that all permanent staff report to the Personnel Officer. It would be perfect if you could give us permission to question all persons who perused the document.

Accuracy/Speed Practice	Three-minute timing	Not more than 3 errors

words

AS.22   Not only does the Private Secretary or the Personal Assistant have to   14
attend meetings and take down Minutes, but she also has to see that the   28
agenda is sent out and that the conference room is ready for the meeting   42
at the proper time.   46

The first thing to do, as in any job, is to avoid last-minute snags.   60
It could happen that you have had to deal with a most important telephone   74
call, and when you do at last reach the meeting you find all the chairs   88
round the table taken, and there just isn't room for you to squeeze in. 103
The result of this is that you will find yourself in a corner of the room, 118
unable to hear either the main speaker or any of the others. On another 132
occasion you may find that you are seated next to a member who really needs 147
a table to himself, because he always tends to spread his papers over the 161
place just where you want your shorthand book to rest. 172

To avoid these snags, see that the room and the table are adequate and 186
that there is plenty of seating — have a chair or two more in case extra 201
people arrive. Keep for yourself a seat near the chairman. 213

One secret of a successful meeting is to start your plans early. See 227
that all those who are entitled to attend have a copy of the agenda. 240

(S.I. 1.32)

For guidance on typing the name and address of addressee at bottom of first page of a letter, please see page 214.

Continuation sheets for letters

A long letter may require a second sheet. This is called a Continuation Sheet, and sometimes the name or initials of the sender are printed in the top left-hand corner. Otherwise, always use a plain sheet the same size and colour as the previous page.

The only details which you should type are the following: Name of addressee, page number, and date, starting on 4th single space from top.
In fully-blocked letters, all these details are typed at the left margin in double spacing, in the following order: Page number, Date, Name of addressee.
In semi-blocked letters the name of the addressee is typed at the left margin, the page number is centred in typing line and typed as follows: - 2 - and the date ends at the right margin. The letter is continued on the third single-line space below the continuation sheet details.

When a continuation sheet is needed, the letter must be so arranged that at least three or four lines are carried to the second page. On no account must the continuation sheet contain only the complimentary close and name of writer. Also at least two lines of a paragraph must be left at the bottom of the first page.

NOTE: The word 'Continued' or 'P.T.O.' is not normally used in letters. A catchword, i.e., the typing of the first word appearing on a continuation sheet at the foot of the preceding page, is sometimes used. Number of next page *must not* be used as a catchword.

4. Practise letter with continuation sheet. Type the following letter on A4 (210 × 297 mm) paper, with a continuation sheet. Use margins of 12/72 (Pica) and 22/82 (Elite), and single-line spacing. Type an envelope.

```
Our ref FLK/MKJ                                              (Insert date)


Dear Miss Johnson

        Thank you for your letter dated        about a book suitable for
Secretarial Students taking the shorthand-typist's and audio-typist's
examination.   SECRETARIAL TYPING by D M Sharp and H M Crozier is
an integrated course of dictation, typewriting, English usage, and
secretarial duties for shorthand-typists, audio-typists, and personal
or private secretaries.   The correlation of general office and duties
is an essential part of the text.   The inclusion of comprehension,
written and spoken communication and basic English usage provides
continuing and ample training in accurate & speedy transcription.

        The following are the outstanding features of the book —

Planned Text
        Each of the units deals with some aspect of applied office or
secretarial typing.   With few exceptions, the units may be taken in
any order, thus enabling the work of the typing room to be linked with
that being done in Office Practice and Clerical or secretarial duties.
Correlation of Shorthand and Typing

        The accompanying Secretarial Dictation text contains, unit
for unit, ample informative and office-style dictation practice.   This
Dictation practice requires the application of typing skills to real-
istic office problems.



Miss L M Johnson
29 New Road
Birkenhead        L41 6NH
```

(Typist: This exercise is continued on the next page. The amount you type on the first page will depend on the size of type face on your machine, and need not necessarily be as above.)

Type the following Programme on A4 paper as a folded leaflet, displaying it as effectively as possible.

FRONT
PAGE   BIRMCHESTER CIVIC HALL

LONDON PHILHARMONIC SYMPHONY ORCHESTRA

C O N C E R T

8th May, 19 , 7 p.m.

Programme: 40p

THE LONDON PHILHARMONIC SYMPHONY ORCHESTRA

Leader: Leonard White

Conductor: Hans Wassermann

P R O G R A M M E

Centre these lines across pages 2 + 3

Page 2

Overture 'Russian Easter Festival'   Rimsky-Korsakov

Pavane pour une infante défunte   Ravel

Piano Concerto No. 3 in C Minor   Beethoven

Soloist: ALEXEI PUSHKOV

I N T E R V A L

(Refreshments on sale)

* * *

Page 3

Prelude and Liebestod   Wagner
(Tristan and Isolde)

Fantasia on a Theme of Thomas Tallis   Vaughan Williams

Symphony No. 1 in F Minor   Shostakovitch

* * *

Centre as a blocked para. As this concert is being broadcast, the audience are requested to be in their seats 5 mins. prior to the commencement of the Programme.

Please send the following note to MISS A M BROWN of 28 CRESCENT RD, BRIGHTON, Sussex. BN2 3RP. Use plain A5 portrait paper and date for today. My address is 4 ST JAMES'S ROAD, CROYDON. CH3 6YU

Dear Miss Brown, As y were unable to come to the concert last week, I thought you might like to hv a copy of the programme, wh I am sending you herewith. I wl advise you well in advance when the next concert wl be held. Sincerely yours,

Secretarial Duties

The *acquisition* ~~acquiring~~ of secretarial skills and knowledge, in addition to the ability to apply typing skill, is treated as essential. Much of the text and many of the exercises cover the office practice and secretarial duties examination requirements. As the teacher of type-writing often teaches office practice or secretarial duties, the text brings flexibility to the planning of courses and classroom teaching.

Audio Typing

The additional practice of the Secretarial Dictation Text meets *l.c.* the requirements for examinations for audio-typists.

English Usage Teachers recognize the importance of correct English usage in transcription, but many find it difficult to ensure that their students use in transcription and in the typing room the skills learned in the English lessons. The text contains ample exercises for punctu-ation, spelling, meaning and use of words, and correct sentence con-struction.

Exercises

An outstanding *immediately* feature is the wide range of practical exercises. These are included after the teaching and learning situation to which they relate. All the exercises can be typed, thus encouraging the use of the typewriter as a machine for communication. If this is not practicable, many exercises can be handwritten either in class or as *H H* out of class preparation. In addition to a wide range of office typing jobs, English usage exercises comprising spelling and correct use of words, punctuation and styling, clear and concise expression, provide excellent transcription training for the shorthand-typist and audio-typist. The composition of letters, reports and memos, and summaries, ensures that original work is not overlooked. *& correction of errors*

Knowledge of secretarial duties and aptitude for secretarial skills are ensured by the inclusion of a *wide* range of exercises, many of which have been taken or adapted from past examination papers.

Secretarial Typing is a follow-on text for full-time, part-time and evening students who have completed the basic keyboard training and are preparing for office jobs, and shorthand-typist's or audio-typist's examinations.

I am sure you would find this book ideal for the students you have in mind.

(A) In addition to Applied l.c. typing practice, each Unit contains simple practice exercises to develop secretarial skills, correct English usage & comprehension.

Closed caps for words underscored

Yours sincerely

SALES MANAGER
McGRAW-HILL BOOK CO. (UK) LTD

Further exercise on two-page letter is given on pages 36–37 of **Practical Typing Exercises, Book Two**.

Typist - I would like this in draft form. Mark it
"DRAFT". Use treble spacing and wide margins -
say left margin of 38 mm.

BACK FEEDING

consisting It sometimes happens that an addition or
alteration has to be made to a p. of a document/
of sev. sheets/ stapled together (wh. hv. bn.) This
can be done/ by what is known as/ backward
feed/, ie., inserting the paper into the m/c from/
front of/ platen instead of in/ normal manner. To
do this the following steps shd be taken:—

1. Erase neatly any letter(s) th. hv. to be
   altered.

single/ 2. Insert a/ sheet of paper in the m/c in
   /usual way.

4. 3. Turn the platen backwards so th/ two
   sheets are fed together sufficiently/ far
   f. the loose sheet to be removed. The
   typewritten sheet on which/ alteration is
   to be made is held/by/ feed mechanism
   (firmly) & (by means of the/ paper release lever)
   it can be adjusted to the correct position
   for/ addition /or alteration/ & / necessary
   correction then made.

(without having
to unfasten
sheets)

& just 3. 4. Between /sheet of paper/
inserted and/ platen, insert/ ∧
   bottom of / page and note
   alteration to be made. To
   be altered.

5. If/ letters next to/ alteration's are light
   (when rubbing out) may h. also
   rubbed over/ adjacent letters/ type
   over these so that all letters are /
   same shade.

Typist -
please use
hanging
paragraphs
for numbered
paras.

Job 36   Production Target—*20 minutes*

Type the following 2-page letter on A4 paper and take one carbon copy. Mark the letter PERSONAL and type an envelope.

Block at left margin in single spacing

LEIGHTON LESTER AND LEVITT
Chartered Architects
14 High Street
UPPER GATEHOUSE
NO5 6BT

Block at right margin

T R Leighton FRIBA
H Levitt ARIVA

Telephone: 8976 44332

Your Ref   Our Ref

Today's date

Peter R Howard
Chairman of the Managers
Lodge Comprehensive   UPPER GATEHOUSE   NO5 6BT

Dear Sir

Following the recent request made by Mr A St G Granger, Headmaster of the abve school, we have carried out an examination of the school building

ROOF
One location was found where the asphalt was craked and immediate repair has bn put in hand. There are one or 2 other places where *we* suspect but ~~I~~ hope that it will give (trouble) after the current work has been completed. (the asphalt is) (no further)

CEILING — CLASSROOM 9
We noted a crack in the ceiling of classroom 9. This is a continuance of an earlier problem of differential deflection in the concrete units/ *& could be adequately dealt w. as part of the routine internal decoration.*

EXTERNAL TIMBER
It is most important that this transom is repaired & ~~I am~~ *we are* arranging to have this done. It is also essential th external redecoration of all timber work shd be subject to professional supervision if it is going to give a guarantee of satisfactory performance for a reasonable no. of yrs.*

urgently/ *The external windows are/ in need of redecoration. At the moment they are under serious risk of decay, &, indeed, one transom already shows signs of decay. (Typist — then run on — It is ...)*

* *run on/* *We find by experience th firms of decorators who the lowest/ gain contracts on the basis of/ prices frequently do a sub-standard job, wh is useless fr the point of view of protection of external timbers Perhaps you wd be kind enough to let me*

with smart ideas unless they also sell the product.

3. A research dept. wh includes a housewives' panel, field workers & a modern kitchen, supported by a completely mechanized dept. for statistical obtaining reactions to food products & their sales & advertg methods.

6 4. Complete photographic & film unit

4 5 A display unit for designing & manfg point-of-sale displays.

A good chess player never forgets th he is in the game for the thing: he wants to checkmate his opponent's king. He may be able to do it in 2 moves, or he may take a hundred moves. But th is the thing wh he is after. He may be moving the pawn of general publicity, he may making any one of a 1,000 advertg moves, but ultimately he expects be his advertg by its effect on sales to make his business bigger, or steadier or all these together. he may be protecting a castle of fixed prices,

, or more permanent, or more profitable,

Quality Advertising is at the service of all go-ahead organizations for home and export publicity.

We shd like to meet yr executives to discuss informally how we can help to put yr products on the housewife's shopping list.

Yrs ffy QUALITY ADVERTISING LTD

J L LEE DIRECTOR

And so the good advertiser never loses sight of the fact th he is aiming finally at sales.

'A' It can, in time, make the name of yr product an automatic reaction in every housewife's mind when she enters a food store.

5. A series of 6 shop windows for constructing experimental display work.

know what you think about it in due course.

HEATING SYSTEM

With regard to the long list of breakdowns th Mr Granger has supplied us with, I understand fr him th these are all associated w. the underfeed stokers.

Run on / All th we can add (is th solid fuel operated to what is known already) by underfeed stokers is a notorious maintenance of this size / problem in schools, due either to wear on the mechanical parts, impurities in the fuel, or inadequate routine maintenance. The initial installation of the solid fuel system was made as a result of intensive pressure fr the Local Education Authority whose committee had a firm policy th fuel used in all public buildings should N.P. be coal. As the authority pay for the fuel & the maintenance, it is entirely up to them to ʃʃ accept the consequences of their own policy. Insert 'A'

N.P. The only point th I can add is th the instal- U.C. lation was fully accepted by the authority at the time the school was built. There is no suggestion, as far as I know, th the installation was defective in design, & as far as I can see nothing cd be gained by carrying N.P out a survey. I must emphasize th the ʃʃ financial responsibility rests entirely on the authority.

I do hope th this letter wl prove helpful to you & yr committee.

Yrs ffy

J R Leighton

'A', but if the Managers feel th the whole matter is simply too troublesome then Th / stet we think feel th they shd suggest to th the LEA change the installation over to gas.

Typist: This wl be a 2-page circular letter wh I wl be sending to about 50 selected firms. Put in tomorrow's date, and leave room for name and address of addressee wh you wl type in later. When I have seen yr typed copy, I shall want an offset litho master cut. Better leave out the salutation for the time being.

DRAFT

It is not enough to hv a good product; people buy the branded foods in wh sincere & successful advertising has first given confidence to them. Foodstuffs are sold by the creative ideas wh fix their excellence in the public mind. Yet ideas alone are not enough. The selling 'theme' must be directed by those who understand modern commerce—men w successful experience of the food market.

Advertising, when rightly handled, is no longer a matter of chance; it is the scientific application of creative experience to a tested market.

A market survey is not a hasty glance @ the latest Digest of statistics & a few tentative questions to friends of the family; it is as highly-skilled a part of modern advertising as the etching of colour plates. Indeed, the market must be tested & the campaign controlled @ every step by a team wh specializes in measuring public reaction. (Typist: start new para at "Indeed" & then run on.)

That is a picture of the food manfr's ideal advertg agency. Such an agency can help to inspire yr whole sales effort. (Insert 'A' here) Quality Advertising is such an agency. We hv specialized in food advertg for a quarter of a century—a long time; rich in experience. On many a lesson well learned we hv perfected a service wh can sell confidently.

Those are our credentials—here is what we offer:

1. 25 years advertg & marketing co-operation w. leading manfrs in the food industry (Typist: Please do not put in full stops after the Nos. 1, 2, 3, etc. Leave 4 clear spaces after each no. & use block paras.)

2. An integrated team of artists & writers who specialize in food publicity; men not content

Job 37   Production Target—*12 minutes*

Display the following on A4 paper. Centre vertically and horizontally. Draw a frame leaving 25 mm margin all round.

ST. JOHN/S MUSICAL SOCIETY

Presents

The Pearl Fishers (spaced caps)

by

BIZET

in

ST. JOHN'S CONCERT HALL
KINGSHURST ROAD
WARWICK

Wednesday 17th May 1978

to

Saturday 20th May 1978

commencing at 7.15 pm.

* * * * *

PRICES OF ADMISSION

Wednesday to Friday		Saturday	
Stalls	£1.00	Stalls	£1.30
Balcony	£1.25	Balcony	£1.50

ALL SEATS ARE NUMBERED & RESERVED

* * * *

Applications for tickets should be sent to:

Hon. Sec.
St. John's Mus. Soc.
"   "   Road
Warwick   CV.34 4AA

(a) Display the following Message Sheet on A5 portrait paper. Take an original and one copy.

Message Sheet - spaced caps

DATE _____

TIME _____

TO _____

WHILE YOU WERE OUT.

M _____

of _____

Tel No _____

☐ Called to see you

☐ Telephoned

☐ Will call again

☐ Please phone her/him

Left the following message

Signed _____

On carbon copy type the following
Date 27/10/78   Time 1415   To MRS M PUGH
Miss A Windsor of Sheldon Mfg Co Ltd
Tel No 472 2677   Insert lower case
x in boxes before 'Telephoned' and
'Please phone her' Delete the word 'him'
Message Delivery of their order
No 7689/78 dated 30 September now urgently
required. Promised for 15/10/76.
Sign the form.

Type the alphabet review·*once* for practice, *once* for speed, and finally, *once* for accuracy. Margins: Elite 22–82, Pica 12–72.

Review alphabet keys

The magic of the peace and quietness was broken when an extra noisy jet plane flashed overhead across the azure sky.

Accuracy/Speed Practice	Five-minute timing	Not more than 3 errors

words

AS.18   Why do so many visitors to Britain include in their tour a visit   13
to 'leafy Warwickshire'?   This is a well-wooded area, nearly in the   26
centre of England, and has a maze of narrow, winding lanes of great   40
beauty.   In the summer it is leafy in all truth, as one would expect   53
when one recalls that it is all that is left of the once great Forest   67
of Arden.   This forest was once of great size, and the woods were so   81
thick that they became the home of hosts of robbers, who made the   94
journeys of merchants full of danger.   Even now many ancient trees are   108
to be found, trees which have lived for many times the span of a man's   122
life.   123

The Romans, who had landed on the south shores of the country,   135
slowly forced their way into the centre of the land, and many signs   148
of their occupation can still be found in the country.   Four great   161
Roman roads enter the district at different points — Watling Street,   175
Icknield Street, the Ridgeway, and the Fosseway — all of which can   188
still be traced.   It is easy to follow, at least for parts of these   201
roads, the course along which Roman soldiers marched forth into the   215
unknown.   216

There are 2 great feudal castles within its borders — that at   229
Warwick, from the outside scarcely changed since the Middle Ages, and   243
that at Kenilworth, once a great regal building, but now just a heap of   257
ivy-clad ruins.   260

These things, however, are not the reason for so many people from   273
so many lands making this journey.   They come to honour the memory of   287
William Shakespeare, called the world's greatest poet, who was born and   301
lived for most of his life at Stratford-upon-Avon.   His works are known   315
and admired all over the world, and it is no wonder that people from   329
afar should want to see where he lived and worked, and to take the walks   343
he quite likely took in his lifetime.   350

A lot of villages around Stratford are mentioned in his works,   363
and students of the poet, as well as many others, get much pleasure from   378
finding these places and building mental pictures of the days of long   392
ago.   This, truly, is Shakespeare's country.   400

short phrases or simple words. Many ready-made phrases are still current. Lavish use of them robs a letter of meaning or personality & makes it needlessly long.

	Instead of	Use
Typist – insert & display in single spacing	In the near future	Soon
	Wholly at a loss to comprehend	cannot understand u.c.
	Institute enquiries	ask, enquire u.c.
	In a large percentage of cases	Usually, as a rule
	Use our best endeavours	Try

COURTESY & CORRECT TONE Courtesy is more than the use of a
○ ~~correct~~ polite word or phrase. The reader's response shd be constantly borne in mind & tactful phrasing ~~used~~ sought. The purpose of good letter-writing is to convey information. ∧ or ask for

A good letter is more than ∧ communication of facts. The lay out shd be correct and pleasing∧ the presentation∧ facts gives ~~so~~ it scope for style Business ltrs. help to create good public relations: they indicate an efficient organisation. ;however,

Ⓐ It will not impress yr reader.
Business jargon is an artificial vocabulary .... now
○ becoming obsolete∧Some of the worst examples occur in∧ introductory & concluding paras. of letters.

✱ Extract from SECRETARIAL TYPING
By kind permission of the authors
D. M. Sharp
and
H. M. Crozier
Book published by
McGraw-Hill Book Company (U.K.) Ltd.,
Shoppenhangers Road, Maidenhead, Berks.

125

Personal letters

(a) *Personal Business Letters:* Used when writing to an unknown person or firm about a personal business matter. The layout is similar to that of a business letter. If your home address is not printed on your stationery, type it about 13 mm from the top and centre on page, or in such a way that the last line ends flush with the right-hand margin. Date in usual place. Name and address of addressee may be typed in usual place or at bottom left-hand margin, two spaces below your name.

(b) *Formal Personal Letters:* Used when writing to someone older than yourself or to whom you owe respect. Layout as for Personal Business Letter. Salutation is formal, e.g., Dear Miss Brown, Dear Mrs. Taylor, Dear Dr. Emery.

(c) *Personal Letters:* Used when writing to a personal friend. Your address and date as in a Personal Business Letter. No name and address of addressee. Salutation is informal, e.g., Dear Mary, Dear Arthur, Dear Uncle George.

1. Practise typing Personal Letters. Type the following personal business letter on A5 (148 × 210 mm) paper, using suitable margins.

> 12 Warwick Road,
> Kenilworth,
> Warwickshire
> 14th May, 19--

H. M. Inspector of Taxes,
Coventry 3rd District,
94 Gosford St.,
Coventry CV1 5RS

Dear Sir,   Your Ref. 70/75 O/D 2116

N.P/   I hv today recd Form P2 (notice of Coding) & find th an error has bn made in allowances. [In the past 2 yrs I hv bn given an allowance for my widowed mother w whom I
N.P/   live + whose annual income for last yr was £800. [Please be kind enough to include this allowance + amend my code no. accordingly.   Yrs ffy   Doris McLean

2. Type the following Formal Personal Letter on A5 paper, using suitable margins.

> 25 Warwick Road,
> Hampton-on-the-Hill
> Warwick
> 14th June 19--

Dear Mrs. Ingram,
   Thank you f yr letter abt the Club's visit to
(C) Chatsworth House on Sat. 2nd July f my mother + I wl look fwd to this trip ⌐ I enclose a Postal Order for £5.3.
   Yrs sincerely,
Mrs. J. Ingram,
The BUTTS, Warwick.

Enc

Type the following on A4 paper, using shoulder headings and block paragraphs. Use double spacing except for paragraphs lettered (a) and (b) or unless otherwise instructed.

LETTER WRITING. ✗

Typist – use this para. + use block style

u.c. Simple concise English is best for writing letters. In this unit you will learn ⟨techniques required for⟩ ⟨,which,⟩ modern letters, while vigorous in style, maintain a good tone, and are courteous in their wording.

PLAN THE LETTER Make a note of points ⟨you wish to include⟩ then arrange them in the most effective order. ✗ ⟨Lack of⟩ ⟨Deal with ea. point once only⟩ planning leads to afterthoughts...... ✗ indicates careless thinking.

USE ACTIVE CONSTRUCTIONS Active constructions are more forceful than passive, + save words.

⟨passive:⟩ (b) The goods wh were ordered by us a considerable time ago hv. not yet bn. received. (16 words)

Inset Active: We hv. not yet recd. ⟨gds. ordered on⟩ 3rd March. (11 words)

(a) + (b) USE SINGLE WORDS INSTEAD OF PHRASES & CLAUSES

please (a) In event of yr. absence continuing for more than three days, you shd. submit a med. cert. (18 words)

absence After three days forward a Med. Cert. (8 words)

(b) He made a decision wh it was impossible to justify. (10 words)

He made an unjustifiable decision. (5 words)

OMIT NEEDLESS WORDS

Please see text book.

AVOID BUSINESS JARGON Insert 'A' here

H AVOID READY ⟨⟩MADE PHRASES

H These hackneyed or long winded expressions only hide yr. meaning. Omit them or replace them by suitable

⟨(a) passive:) I understand it he is at present
⊙ employed by ⟨you as a sales Manager⟩ (14 words)
Active:) I understand they employ him
so a S. Man. (10 words)⟩

It is customary to use formal wording when sending out invitations to weddings, twenty-first birthday parties, etc. The invitations are written in the third person with a blank space left for the insertion of names of the guests in ink. The invitation begins with the name(s) of the writer(s) whose address is placed at the bottom left-hand margin. The date and R.S.V.P. are at the lower right-hand margin. Invitations are not signed.

3. Practise typing formal invitations. On postcards, or postcard-size paper, type the following invitation from Mr. and Mrs. Hubbard and the reply from the Facchino family. Use double spacing and centre each line.

(a) **Formal invitation**

> Mr. and Mrs Eric Hubbard request the
>
> pleasure of the company of
>
> [ENRICO] Mr. & Mrs. Enrico Facchino & Jane   (Write this line)
>
> at their daughter's twenty-first birthday
>
> party on Saturday 20th September, at 8 p.m.
>
> The Croft,   1st September 19--
> Newbould-on-Stour,
> Warwickshire   R.S.V.P.
> CV37 8UA

(b) **Reply to formal invitation**

> Mr. & Mrs. Enrico Facchino and Jane
> have pleasure in accepting the kind invitation
> of Mr. & Mrs. Eric Hubbard to their
> daughter's 21st birthday party on
> Sat., 20th Sept., @ 8 p.m.
>
> 7th Sept., 19--

A further exercise on personal letters and invitations is given on page 41 of **Practical Typing Exercises, Book Two**.

Variable line spacer

You will find the variable line spacer (sometimes called platen release) on the left cylinder knob. By pressing in (or pulling out on some machines) the variable line spacer, you release the spacing mechanism, and the platen roller can be moved to any desired position.

It is used for:
Filling in form letters;
Typing on ruled lines;
Finding the correct alignment when paper has been reinserted to make a correction.

UNIT 15

One of the essential things that each of us must keep in mind when we work in an office is that we are responsible not only for the final product, but also for the work of all persons who share a job with us. Thus a typist may feel that all she has to do is to copy an invoice, quotation, pay-roll, etc., and that it is not her fault if the totals, which someone else has added, are wrong. But this is not the case. It is just as much the responsibility of the typist to see that the totals are right as it is the duty of the person who first added the figures and wrote in a wrong total. Check all totals by adding up the columns before you type the total.

If you do find a mistake, needless to say you do not shout about it and wait to be patted on the back; instead, you go quietly to the person who may have made the mistake and ask whether *you* are wrong in wondering about something that seems out of order.

Composing at machine

Type the following in double spacing, filling in the correct preposition in the blank space.

I am grateful — you — your help. I am not prepared to part — the box. We were annoyed — them because they acted contrary — our instructions. The girl was indebted — her teachers — the success she had. He is responsible — the cashier — the most unsatisfactory state of the books. He was quite oblivious — what was going on around him. This student is always amenable — discipline. This desk is different in size — all the others. Do you agree — me, and are you ready to agree — my proposal? The director is well versed — mathematics.

Review Quiz No. 4

Type the following on A4 paper in single-line spacing, with double spacing between each item, filling in the correct word or words in the blank spaces. Do not write on your textbook.

1. When typing on ruled lines, type very slightly . . . the line.

2. Headings (except column headings) typed in lower case must be . . .

3. When typing a circular letter leave . . . spaces before the salutation for insertion of name and address if required.

4. Do . . . leave a space before a footnote sign in the body of the text but leave . . . space after sign in the footnote.

5. A key which can be depressed without causing the carriage to move forward is known as a . . . key.

6. An ornamental arrangement at the end of a section or chapter is known as a . . .

7. If a tear-off section on a circular letter is required, ... or . . . must be typed from . . . to . . . of the paper.

8. When preparing a skeleton form letter, leave . . . space for insertion of the details.

9. When using a catchword, this is typed . . . the last typed line on the page.

10. The page number must . . . be used as a catchword.

11. If matter is continued on the back of the first page, the margins are . . .

12. Footnotes are always typed in . . . spacing with . . . spacing between each.

Turn to page 211 and check your answers. Score one point for each correct entry. Total Score: 18

4. Type the following on A4 paper in single-line spacing with double between lettered and numbered items and for the memo headings. Keep your typed copy for future reference in Folder No. 2.

INTER—OFFICE MEMORANDA

The memorandum (usually referred to as 'memo') is one of the most convenient ways of sending messages from one person to another in the same firm or from the head office to a branch office or agent. A memo may be typed on any size of paper, and firms have the headings printed and the paper cut to the size required. The layout of headings varies, the following being one example:—

(1)

MEMORANDUM

(3)   (4)
FROM   (5)   REF. (5)

TO   DATE
(2)   (2)

(1) Word MEMORANDUM centred on page.

(2) Margins — 25 mm on left and 13 mm on right. Where headings are printed, it is normal practice to set the left margin to coincide with the beginning of the headings. Remember that the right margin must never be wider than the left margin.

(3) When typing in the headings, start left-hand side at 25 mm. Headings are ALWAYS typed in double spacing.

(4) Right-hand headings start at approximately 50 Pica and 60 Elite.

(5) Insertions start two spaces after end of heading. It is absolutely essential that these are consistent throughout.

Other points to remember

(a) No salutation or complimentary close. (b) Body. Single spacing with double between paragraphs. Block or indented paragraphs used. (c) Some firms have the writer's name or initials typed two single-line spaces after the last line of the body. Do not do this unless specially instructed to do so. If they are to go in, then they end level with the right-hand margin. (d) If there are dotted lines after the headings, then you must type slightly above these. If there are no dotted lines, align paper by means of variable line spacer, so that insertions are in alignment with headings. (e) Continuation sheets. When you need to use a continuation sheet, turn up 4, type name of addressee, centre page number, and type date to end at right margin. Turn up 3 and continue with body. ALWAYS use PLAIN PAPER for continuation sheets. (f) If a subject heading is required, turn up 3 after last line of heading and type subject heading in upper case or in lower case with underscore.

5. On memo paper prepare an original and one carbon copy of the headings set out above. On the original insert the following:

To: Managing Director. From: Sales Director. Subject: SALES—JAN.–JUNE 1977. Suitable date. The following are the sales figures for the first 6 months of this year. January £10,750, Feb. £9,830, March £11,620, Apl. £14,560, May £14,000, June £19,740. (Typist: Set out these details in 2 columns.)

On the carbon copy insert: To: Chief Cashier. From: Man. Dir. Subject: Overdue A/cs. Suitable date. Please let me have a list of overdue a/cs as at 30th June.

Further exercises on memoranda are given on pages 48–49 of **Practical Typing Exercises, Book One**, and pages 15, 33, 40, 43 (2-page), 50, 55, 57, and 66 of **Book Two**.

Job 49

On A5 paper type an original and two carbon copies of the following form letter from Newbury's Limited, 79 Victoria Street, London, WC2 8ND.

Dear Sir(s),

v.c.l We thank you f your order No.

dated   for

These gds wl be despatched as requested.

yrs. ffy

Job 50

(a) Address the top copy of form letter (Job 49) to E. G. HALL & CO LTD, King Charles St., Surbiton, Surrey. KT5 9AG. Insert Ref. FIB/OP; today's date; Order No. 1516/70; dated (insert suitable date). For: One Motorist's Holdall

(b) Address first carbon copy to: H. TIBBETT & SONS 4 Glovers Court, Preston, Lancs. PR1 2RL. Insert Ref. SC/BY; today's date; Order No. 6154; dated (insert suitable date). For: 4 only HI-FI Equipment Cabinets (Teak).

(c) Address second carbon copy to: F. L. BRIDGES & CO. LTD, 45 Sackville St., Manchester. M60 3BB. Insert Ref. DBL/40; today's date; Order No. PUR/15/70; dated (insert suitable date). For: One Tubular Trolley with Formica Trays - No. V.306, size 915 × 458 mm

Job 51

Type an original and one copy of the following form on A5 paper. Use double-line spacing. On the carbon copy insert suitable details.

Hon. Sec., Birmingham Indian Assoc.,
156 Orphanage Road, B'ham. B24 6EU

Please reserve   seats for members, and   seats for guests for the Dinner to be held on 26 Jan 19.. The names of those attending are:

———————————————
———————————————
———————————————

Cheque for ——— enclosed.
Signed ———————————————
Address ———————————————
———————————————

UNIT 17

Type the following memo on suitable paper.

To   All Sales Reps   17 Aug '78
From Sales Director
Subject   <u>Sales Meeting</u> caps

1. A meetg of sales reps wl be held in/
Sales Director/s. office @ Head office @
0900 hrs on Mon 28/8/78
<u>AGENDA</u> (spaced caps)
    1 To discuss new lines to be offered
       next month
    2 To consider the question of discounts
    3 To   "   "   activities of competitors
    4 Any other business

Type the following memo on suitable
                                      paper.
Please insert paragraphs and suitable
                                      date
FROM Robert P Freeman To Sales Director.
Subject: Canning & Co, 34 Frederick Str.
          [CANNING]   Sth Shields
Thank y f your memo dated 14 Aug.
I called on Friday last to see
Mr. P. Scott, Chief Buyer at Canning & Co
& he informed me th a cheque in/settlemnt.
full/of their A/c was sent on Aug 9th.
   Please let me know whether or not the
cheque has been received
<u>Typist</u> 2 carbon copies please - one for 'file'
& one for Graham Green (District Manager)

Using postcard-size paper, type one original and three copies of a formal
invitation asking friends to attend a dinner at your home next Friday evening.
After typing the invitations, write your friends' names in ink.

2. Practise typing on ruled lines. Read the explanation on page 120 and then type the following form letter on A5 portrait paper in double spacing, taking a carbon copy. Take both copies out of your machine, reinsert the carbon copy and fill in the details given below. Use margins of Elite 12–62, Pica 5–55. Turn up 9 spaces before typing the reference.

Ref. _____   Date _____

_____

_____

_____

Dear

_____

Note: In normal circumstances the name and address are typed in single spacing. In this case, because the under-score has been used, they must be in double spacing.

On the _____ we quoted you
____ for carrying out the necessary repairs to the above appliance. Please let us know whether you accept our quotation, so that we may proceed with the repairs which will take about __ days.

Yours faithfully,
ELECTRICAL SERVICES LTD.

Details to be inserted on carbon copy: Ref. RT/0/46. Today's date. Addressee: Mr. H. Wadsworth, 40 Chapel Street, Liverpool. L4 6BJ. Heading: Electric Iron. Date of quotation: First Friday of last month. Amount £9.25. Time: 3 days.

3. Type the following order form on A5 portrait paper. Then take it out of the machine. Reinsert it and fill in the details given below.

ORDER (spaced caps 1" (25mm) from top of paper)

Block 1" (25mm) from left edge of paper.

JAMES H. WILKINS LTD
Great Winchester Street
LONDON   N6 6RT

Order No. _____

_____   Date _____

Dear Sirs
Please supply us with the under-mentioned goods
(Typist - leave 6 clear vertical spaces)

Delivery _____
Carriage _____
Terms of Payment _____
Yrs ffy, JAMES H. WILKINS LTD

Details to be filled in: Order No. 546/78. Today's date. Addressee: Office Equipment Ltd., 10 Leahe Str., Bristol BS1 5TN Goods: 1 14-tray Kardex Visible Index Cabinet for 204 × 127 mm cards @ £87.50. Delivery: 7 days. Carriage: Paid. Terms of Payment: Nett Cash.

Further exercises on forms and form letters are given on pages 40–42 of **Practical Typing Exercises, Book One**, and page 19 of **Book Two**.

It is a well-known fact that a good personality is an asset to the office worker. She must be a person who is liked by her employer or supervisor, by her fellow-workers, by the salesmen who call at the office, and by the public who are the customers or clients of the business of which the office is a part. You should know yourself, not as you think you are, but as other people think you are. If you find that your personality is less pleasing to others in some respects than you had thought, you should remedy the defects.

It is not assumed that the following characteristics are the only ones that make for the best personality, but they are important:

Punctuality: You must always be on time, and begin work at once.

Cleanliness: Clean hair; clean, well-kept hands and finger-nails; clean, well-brushed clothes suitable for an office; clean teeth.

Courtesy: Say 'please' when asking a favour; 'Thank you' when one has been granted. Do not interrupt the work or conversation of others.

Co-operativeness: Maintain team-work with your supervisor and other members of staff; assume responsibility for everything you do.

Cheerfulness: Respond to questions and requests with a smile, and cultivate a bright and happy disposition.

Composing at machine

Type the following in double spacing, correcting any errors.

We have no demand from our customers for these kind of materials.
In unity consists the welfare and security of society in general.
If I were him, I would not let anything come between you and I.
These two girls do good work, but the eldest is the most careful.
Neither the boy nor his brother were able to find their way home.

Review Quiz No. 3

Type the following on A4 paper in single-line spacing, with double between each item, filling in the correct word or words in the blank spaces. Do not write on your textbook.

1. In an indented paragraph the first line is indented . . . spaces.

2. In a hanging paragraph the first line is typed . . . spaces to the . . . of the rest.

3. In a fully-blocked letter all lines start at the . . . margin.

4. The complimentary close is typed . . . single-line spaces after the last line of body.

5. An enclosure in business letters is indicated either by typing . . . at . . . margin below . . . or by typing . . . in left margin . . . point of mention in text.

6. When typing sums of money the . . . sign and . . . sign must . . . be used together.

7. Inset matter in a letter is usually . . . on writing line with a space . . . and . . . it.

8. A continuation sheet for a business letter contains . . . name, . . . number, and . . ., all usually typed on . . . line in a semi-blocked letter.

9. When addressing an envelope the post town must appear on a . . . line.

10. When addressing an envelope the postcode should be typed on the . . . line without . . . and with a space between the 2 halves.

11. Do not type signature or initials on a memo . . . instructed to do so.

12. 'For the attention of' is typed on the . . . single-line space after the last line of address and at . . . margin.

13. Invitations to weddings, etc., are written in the . . . person.

Turn to page 211 and check your answers. Score one point for each correct entry. Total score: 27.

Form letters

Form letters are printed or duplicated forms or skeleton letters, the object of which is to save the typist time when dealing with routine correspondence. As a general rule, all that the typist has to do is to fill in the date, name and address of addressee, and insert a few details in the body of the letter.

When preparing form letters for duplicating, care must be taken to see that the type on the machine to be used for inserting the particulars is the same size and kind as that used in the duplicated portion, and that the ribbon matches in colour and depth the duplicated part of the letter. (A different colour, e.g., red, is better than a bad match.)

The following steps should be taken when you fill in a form letter:

1. Insert the form letter into the machine so that the first line of the body of the letter is just above the alignment scale.

2. By means of the paper release, adjust the paper so that the base of the entire line is in alignment with the top of the alignment scale (this position may vary with certain makes of machines) and so that an 'i' or 'l' aligns up exactly with one of the guide lines on the alignment scale.

3. Set margin stops and paper guide. The margin stops should be set to correspond to the margins already used in the duplicated letter.

4. Turn the cylinder back two single-line spaces, and, if not already typed, insert salutation at the left-hand margin.

5. Turn the cylinder back a sufficient number of line spaces to provide the correct space for the reference and name and address of the addressee, and the spaces between, to reach the line for the reference and date.

6. Type the reference at left-hand margin.

7. Type date.

8. Type name and address of addressee

9. Insert any details required and delete any unnecessary letters and/or words.

10. Check carefully.

11. When preparing a form letter, always leave sufficient blank space for the details that have to be inserted. In business this is not always easy to decide and it is better to be over generous. However, if you have a form letter in an examination and have to insert given details, then it is obvious you study the insertions when deciding on the number of blank spaces to leave.

1. (a) Practise filling in form letters. Read the above explanation and then type the following form letter on A5 portrait paper in double spacing. Take an original and one carbon copy. Leave 9 single-line spaces at top to represent heading and, in addition, leave sufficient space for the date and name and address of addressee. Use margins of Elite 12–62, Pica 5–55.

```
Dear

We acknowledge receipt of your cheque for (leave blank)

in payment of our account to the end of (leave blank)

Yours faithfully
W A FOSTER & CO Ltd
```

(b) On the original insert:

Today's date.   Salutation: Dear Sirs.   Addressee: Chichester Stationers Ltd   7 Manchester Square   CHICHESTER   West Sussex PO19 1BE
for £981.52.   End of — insert month prior to today's date

(c) On carbon copy insert:

Today's date.   Salutation: Dear Sirs.   Addressee: M Burton & Co Ltd   81 St John's Street   HEREFORD   HR2 1PS
for £873.22.   End of — insert month prior to today's date

Display the following on A4 paper as a folded leaflet.

Front page   THE MAYOR'S   *(spaced caps)*

↕ *(Leave 4" (102 mm) clear for Coat of Arms)*

CIVIC BALL   *(spaced caps)*

1977 *(spaced)*

Page 2   M E N U   *(spaced caps)*

Minestrone Soup
Croutons
Crusty Rolls & Butter
*   *   *   *(Leave 3 spaces between ea. asterisk)*

Roast Sirloin of / Beef   English /
Baked York Ham Cornettes
Roast Norfolk Turkey & Savoury Stuffing

Hot Minted Potatoes
Fresh Salad in Season
Coleslaw Russian Salad
Pickles & Savouries
*   *   *

Meringue Shells
Fresh Fruit w. Fresh Cream
*   *   *
Cheese & Biscuits
*   *   *
Coffee & Mints

Skill building

Type each line or sentence (A, B, C, and D) *three* times. If time permits, complete your practice by typing each group once as it appears. Margins: Elite 22–82, Pica 12–72.

A. Review alphabet keys

1.   The block pavement is extremely uneven, and many of the children, jumping quickly, fell down and grazed their knees.

B. Build speed on common suffixes

2. being, going, making, showing, getting, shipping, regarding.
3. Are they going to return the damaged crate during next week?
4. They are making enquiries about hiring a hall for the dance.
5. Are you showing anything of your own making at the carnival?

C. Build speed on common phrases

6. you can, you may, you are, you will, you should, you are not
7. If you are not too busy, you may call when you are in Devon.
8. You must not delay; otherwise, you will miss the next train.
9. You should ask if you will be required after the usual time.

D. Build speed on fluency drill

10. John says they went down this lane past that path each time.
11. That poor girl will soon need some help with such hard work.
12. They will only wait till next week when that tour then ends.
13. When they come back home from that long trip they must rest.

Accuracy/Speed Practice	Two-minute timing	Not more than 2 errors

words

AS.21   Years ago, when education was reserved for the rich, and life moved · 13
more slowly, a 'good hand' was an accomplishment. For the daughters of · 27
gentlemen, it was rated as high on the social scale as music and paint- · 42
ing, and examples of some fine handwriting may be seen in most art · 55
galleries. In these days, life is much more hectic, and typewriters are · 69
in common use, so that there is less need to write well, and writing by · 84
hand is not of such great importance. The typewriter is the main cause · 98
of handwriting's fall from status, but the fountain pen and, worse still, · 112
the ball-point, have added to this decline. As a result, handwriting is · 127
now quite illegible in some cases. Yet, although it is not so necessary · 141
as it was in the past, it is still required. So you must try to write in · 156
a neat and clear style.   (S.I. 1.30) · 160

7.30–8.00   RECEPTION
by the
Worshipful the Mayor & Mayoress
Councillor & Mrs Peter Braithwaite

BRAITHWAITE

8.00–8.30   DANCING
led by the
Worshipful the Mayor & Mayoress

8.30–10.00   SUPPER

10.00–11.00   DANCING

11.00–12.00   CABARET
London's Premier Floor Show

12.00–12.30   GRAND DRAW
made by the
Mayoress, Mrs A Braithwaite

12.30–1.30   DANCING.

Job 42   Production Target—*5 minutes*

Type each of the following verses in correct form on A5 paper.

She is not fair to outward view
As many maidens be;
Her loveliness I never knew
Until she smiled on me.
O then I saw her eye was bright
A well of love, a spring of light.
H. Coleridge

To Anthea
Bid me to live, and I will live
Thy Protestant to be;
Or bid me love, and I will give
A loving heart to thee.
R. Herrick

R. HERRICK

In Secretarial Aid No. 1, page 29, we drew your attention to the importance of always proof-reading your work. We cannot stress too strongly the necessity of reading through your typescript and making any alterations before a document is removed from the typewriter. Look particularly for the following types of errors:

1. Mis-spellings, including misuse of the hyphen in compound words.

2. Incorrect division of words at line-ends.

3. Wrong choice of words when there are two or more words of similar sound, such as plain, plane; already, all ready; advice, advise.

4. Incorrect punctuation.

5. Incorrect use of capitals.

6. Failure to correct obvious errors in grammar.

7. Wrong use of abbreviations.

8. Inconsistencies of all kinds.

9. Typing errors, such as: (a) mis-strikes; (b) over-typing; (c) transposition of letters; (d) faulty erasures; (e) errors in spacing; (f) faulty shift-key operation for capitals, resulting in bad alignment; (g) irregular paragraph indentations.

10. Names, addresses, and figures need special attention.

Practise proof-reading. Read the above, and then carry out the instructions given.

The following letter contains a number of errors.

(a) On A4 paper write down the numbers 1 to 20, and opposite each number make a note of the error(s) to be found in that line in the letter. Check your list with the one given on page 211.

(b) Type a fair copy of the letter.

1 Barrett & Patterson
2 Newport.

3 Dear sir.

4   It has bn. kindly sugested to us by the Oldham Manufacturing
5 Co. of Oldam, Lancs. that we invite your advise on the following
6 prolbem. —

7   We are re-modeling out 2 storey factory in Cardif and wishto
8 instal the most up to date automatic sprinlker equipment procure-
9 able. We should appreciate your answer to the folowing questi-
10 ons:— 1. What would be the approx. cost of instaling a satis-
11 factory sprinkler systerm on both flors. (2) How soon after you
12 recieve your order could instalation be completed? 3. Judge-
13 ing by our experiance what is the average %-age of saying in
14 insurance costs resulting from such instalations.

15   we are encl. the floor plans of the Factory. If you re-
16 quire further information in order to anser the forgoing
17 please le us know.

18   You early reply will be apreciated.

19   Yrs. Faithfully,
20   J. Haywood — Sec.   J. M. Steel & Co.

Type the following exercise on A4 paper. Use a dropped head for the chapter, and blocked paragraphs. Please use double spacing.

CHAPTER 4 (1)   '4' to be typed as a Roman Numeral

Centre both lines

MONTE CARLO

What strangely varied pictures are conjured up in the mind by the words MONTE CARLO, (2) especially f those who hv never seen Monte Carlo, nor even visited the Riviera. *Insert 'A'* A town built on solid rock that is in fact a mountain side that stretches almost *perpendicularly* down to the edge of the blue mediterranean. Would it not surprise them to cast their eyes upwards to the rugged *jagged* peaks of the huge mountain range that constitutes the Maritime Alps? And, on the way up, wd it not amaze them to find, a mile above Monte Carlo and crowning it, a a marvellously preserved Roman village w statues in an extra- ordinary state of preservation? *— a fantastic relic of civilisation 2000 yrs old*

They will also find in this place a very *beautifully* delightfully kept gardens in which children romp and play happily a mere stones throw from the Casino itself, while gardeners tend untiringly to every palm and plant, covering each small stem tenderly w a plastic muff every night, lest the chill wind sweeping down fr the mountain peaks shd kill the delicate blooms on those frail stems.

Insert 'B'

The charms of Monte Carlo are forgotten in the glamour and fascination of the Casino w its appeal to millions from every quarter of the globe. To the student of Human nature the Casino is most fascinating, for there one meets people of all types and of scores of nationalities.

The last time I entered its portals I moved near the first Roulette table to observe the play, *to study types,* and to absorb the odd, exotic atmosphere that pervades this place. *& no other*

I looked round the table at the many nationalities represented there & guessed at their countries. All were intent, absorbed, oblivious of all but the game, all that is save one solitary figure, a middle-aged woman at the other end of the table. She puzzled me, for she did not conform to any of the normal types one saw in the Casino. She was plainly, even austerely, dressed. This in itself was odd,

RULE 31a

The funds available for grants in any financial yr sh be limited, after deductions [stet] of all management & salaries expenses, to the following sources wh sh be applied in order h (a) Supplies income accumulated fr the previous year. (b) Investment & financial income for the current year.

(Typist — inset (a) & (b) above & use single spacing)

Rule 31
To be omitted

Typist do not start a new sheet for Chapter XI but leave 3 clear spaces

CHAPTER XI

Suggestions for appointment of an Assistant Administrator

(who sh act as Treasurer)

RULE EIGHT

[stet] The officers from the Board f. the management &c of the affairs of the Assoc. sh be an Administrator & an Assistant administrator, a secretary & a representative from ea. deanery.

RULE 9
Take in 'A'
"h The Assistant Administrator sh be chosen by l Board fr among their own members." inset, please

RULE TEN

h, The Administrator h if present h st take l chair at all meetings; in his absence the Board wl elect a chairman from the meeting.

'A' The words Assistant Administrator cd be inserted after Administrator in the 1st line, or the rule modified to read as follows:

for all sorts of strange and extravagant attire is on display
at the Casino. Even I wore a few sparklers in order not to feel

l.c. undressed or out of setting. ↓Her hair was as plain as her dress.
However, what intrigued me most of all was the absence of any
chips in front of her, coupled with the fact that she took no
notice of any of the game, but wore a far-away, vacant expression.
Could she have lost all her money? Had she become dazed in her

plight? If so, was she too paralysed to leave the table?

'A' They might be surprised to find one of
the lovliest towns in the most picturesque
setting in Europe —

N.P. *'B'* [For me, there always comes to mind the
tiny stream that trickles down among
the palms almost to the entrance of the
casino, & where I once saw a baby water-rat
climb up the bank to sun himself luxuriously
in the open air.

But the French woman wore
not even a brooch, &

(1) Fourth chapter of the book *TRAVELLERS' TALES*
by Norah Holt-Turner.
(2) Monte Carlo - A popular centre for tourists of all
nationalities.

Job 44 Production Target—*7 minutes*
The following is an extract from an examination paper. Type it on A5 paper.

1. Simplify (a) $4\frac{1}{4} - 3\frac{1}{3} - 2\frac{1}{2} + 5\frac{1}{5}$

(b) $5\frac{1}{4} \times 4\frac{1}{5} \div 2\frac{7}{10}$

(c) $\left(1\frac{1}{2} + 1\frac{2}{5} + \frac{1}{6}\right) \div \left(2\frac{3}{4} - \frac{5}{6}\right)$

2. Calculate (a) $\dfrac{37 \cdot 26 \times 72 \cdot 6}{3 \cdot 63}$

(b) $\dfrac{2\frac{2}{3} + 3\frac{1}{2} - 1\frac{5}{6}}{2\frac{2}{3} \times 3\frac{1}{2}}$

(c) $\dfrac{4 \cdot 4 - \cdot 018}{5 \cdot 6 + \cdot 04 + 3 \cdot 094}$

Mechanical + Electrical Engineering. The entry qualifications for this competition are 4 subjects in the GCE Exam at 'O' level. These must include maths, + either Physics or mechanics or Physics w. Chemistry or Engineering Science or Science (Building + Engineering) wh wl enable the candidate to enter the first year of the Ordinary National Certificate Course. The age limits for this competition are over 16 + under 17½ yrs of age on 1 September. [Details + entry forms are now available. [The Official Regulations are enclosed, + Entry Forms are obtainable from the Industrial + Technical Education Officer, Room 503, 55 High Holborn, London, WC1.

Yrs ffy ~~Iam, Sir, yr obedient Servant~~, A. W. Walker
Secretary

Production typing

Job 48   Production Target—*12 minutes*

Type the following exercise on A4 paper in double spacing, making any necessary corrections.

CHAPTER VIII   (Typist - dropped head, please)

Grants   ← caps

Proposed modifications in rules   lc

RULE 30

lc   The funds of the ~~society~~ sh be applicable of the relief of infirm, sick + aged members of the Society. [Relief may be voted + pd by the Committee in such manner + to such amt and as the Committee may (of such periods) fr time to ~~time~~ direct, having regard to the circumstances of ea case, the funds available, + the calls or probable calls thereon. All reliefs.
lc   so voted sh be reported to / next general meeting.

Job 45   Production Target—*10 minutes*
Type the following letter on A4 paper ready for despatch today. Take 2 carbon
copies: one for FILE and one for Mr. P. Palmer. Type an envelope.

Our Ref **R** HC/OSS.

L. S. Davis & Sons Ltd.

30 Highland Way, WESTBURY, WILTS BA13 3BE.

For the attention of the Office Manager

OFFICE FURNITURE

The enclosed catalogue has been specially compiled to assist our customers in making

⊙ their selection of ∧ metal furniture ∧ wooden & N.P. [Space does not permit us to illustrate all the items in our large & varied range ∧ of ∧ and ∧ therefore, we suggest th you communicate w us if y are unable to find in our NP cat. the partic article y are seeking [We

specially ∧d like to draw yr ∧ attention to the following cabinets., illustrations of wh.

(:) wl be found on p. 12 of the cat]

HEAVY DUTY STEEL CABINETS.

Inset & Display #1

	SC/64	1.5 m wide × 1 m high	... £110
SC/65	2 m " × 1.5 m "	... £120
SC/66	2.5 m " × 1.9 m "	... £130

As there are only a few of these cabinets available, we recommend y to place yr order w'out delay

Yrs ffy. W. A Foster & Co Ltd

Roger H Campbell

Sales Director

3. Type the following official letter in correct form on A4 paper. Insert date and paragraphs. Address to R. W. Herdman, 214 Bath Street, Birmingham B31 2JB. Use today's date and type an envelope.

Ref no. 4065/5A Dear Sir, With ref to yr enquiry of the (insert suitable date), I am directed to give you the follow^g information concerning the changes in arrangement for recruitment in connection w the Student Apprenticeship

N.P. Scheme in Research & Developments Establishments. [The 2 main streams of entry to Student Apprenticeships wl be at G.C.E 'A' Level & G.C.E 'O' level, but there are 2 important changes : (a) The age limit for the 'A' level entry is now 19½ yrs instead of 19 yrs. (b) The entry requirement for the 'O' level stream is now 4 'O' level subjects instead of five, & a pass in English

NP/ Language is not a requirement. [The examination requirements referred to are normally applicable to England & Wales. Equivalent qualifications for Scotland & N. Ireland are acceptable. Details of these equivalents are given in the regulations for the competitions, wh are now available

NP ['A' Level Entry – Mechanical, Electrical, Chemical & Metallurgical Engineering The entry qualifications for this competition are a minimum of 5 subjects in the G.C.E Exam., of wh two, maths & Physics, must hv bn passed at 'A' level. English Language must be one of the other subjects. The age limits for the 'A' level entry, are over 16 & under 19½ yrs of age on 1 Sept. Industrial scholarships are granted to student apprentices as part of their apprenticeship to enable them to study for a Degree in Enging or metallurgy at a University or a Diploma in Technology (equivalent to a

NP Degree) at a Polytechnic. ['O' Level Entry –

Type the following letter on suitable paper ready for despatch today. It must be sent Air Mail.

Our ref. WH/HS

Miss M Jack,
1483 Mexico Way, MIAMI, Florida, 33133 USA

Dear Madam,

Thank you f yr. letter dated 19 Oct asking

wall / if we could supply a / plaque with the
v.c. Cotton coat of Arms. We do not carry
this plaque in stock, but we will be
pleased to hv one made for you.

and / We enclose a leaflet / showing a variety
price list of plaques and look forward to hearing
further fr. you.
yrs. ffy The International Heraldry Co.
W. Henderson, Director.

Type the following on a postcard ready for mailing. The postcard is to be addressed to J F Bird & Co   High Street   Ware   Herts SG12 7DT

H. H. BRAY & Co. LTD
84 KINGSTHORPE ROAD   l.c.
CALLANDER, Perthshire FK17 8BA

Suitable date

Thank you for yr order no 125/78 dated
3 Nov. The garden ornaments the y require
will be despatched on Wed Nov 22 by
British Road Services. We understand
delivery will be made on 27 Nov.

2. Practise typing Official Letter. Study the instructions on page 113, and then type a copy of the following on A4 paper.

No. 56497/1964

A W Tennant Esq
20 Miller Street
Manchester
M4 8AA   5 October 1978

Dear Sir

With reference to your application of the 30 September,
I am directed by the Commissioners of Customs and Excise to
inform you that the authority granted to you by their letter
of the 9 July, 1965, No. 45500/1955, has been extended to
cover the use of the Industrial Methylated Spirits at your
premises at 20 Miller Street, Manchester, in making a Liniment
in accordance with the following formula:—

Oil of Eucalyptus   142 millilitres

Oil of Turpentine   142   "

Compound Liniment of Soap
(made with Industrial
Methylated Spirits)
sufficient to produce   2841   "

This extension of your authority is granted subject to com-
pliance with the appropriate provisions of the Methylated
Spirits Regulations, extracts from which are reproduced in
the enclosed Notice. It is not to be taken as implying that
the above formula, or any of its constituent parts, complies
with the provisions of any non-Revenue Act or Regulations.

Yours faithfully

H J Ward
Secretary

Enc 1

Further exercise on Civil Service Letters is given on page 47 of **Practical Typing Exercises, Book Two.**

Skill building

Type each exercise (A, B, and C) *once* for practice, *once* for speed, and finally *once* for accuracy. Margins: Elite 22–82, Pica 12–72.

A. Review alphabet keys

1. Even in her wildest dreams she had not expected such an amazing stroke of luck by the sale of her queer lot of junk.

B. Improve control of figure keys

2. w2 e3 r4 t5 y6 u7 i8 o9 s2 d3 f4 g5 h6 j7 k8 19 12 34 56 788

3. Tariff (1970): 7 days £20.50; 14 days £27.80; 21 days £38.70

4. Dividend increased by 1½% to 15%. Profits £96,250 higher at £10,304,000. Shares rose by 7p to £1.40 — 2p up on 1969/70.

C. Build accuracy on common letter combinations

5. in ink into find line kind thing think going indeed interest

6. Indeed, if they follow the thing through, we think they will find that line of thought interesting. The ink dripped from the pen into his pocket — in minutes his pocket was stained.

Accuracy/Speed Practice

You should now aim at increasing your speed by 5 words a minute.

One-minute timings   Not more than 1 error

words

AS.19   We often have a warm spell in March, sometimes earlier, sometimes   13
later, but when it arrives it means for many of us that spring is not   27
far away.   This is a comforting thought, for we know that the weary   40
winter, with its snow and ice and biting winds, is at last drawing to a   54
close, and a feeling of hope is awakened in our hearts. No wonder that   68
spring is the season of hope and all things look brighter.   (S.I. 1.26)   80

AS.20   A flower delivery service is a useful method of sending flowers to a   14
sick friend or as a present, but it does mean that you do not see the   27
flowers sent, so that, unless your friend tells you what she received, and   42
in what state these reached her, you will never know whether the flowers   56
sent were worth the money paid for them.   You can only depend on the   70
honesty of the florist to whom you gave the order.   (S.I. 1.29)   80

DATE

(a) Unless otherwise indicated by the letterhead, the date is typed on the right-hand side at a standard tab. stop—if possible the same one as is used for typing the writer's telephone extension number —opposite the last line of the address.

(b) To be simplified to 19 October 1971, instead of 19*th* October 1971. Dates in the text should be similarly simplified.

REFERENCES

Unless the placing of 'Our Reference', and 'Your Reference', is indicated by the printed letterhead, they should be placed at the left-hand margin.

NAME AND ADDRESS OF ADDRESSEE

(a) To be positioned at the top left-hand side of the letter, and blocked; i.e., all lines starting at the left-hand margin.

(b) Full stops (after initials, etc.) and commas to be omitted entirely.

(c) Officially recognised abbreviations for departmental and establishment, etc., titles (like HMSO, UKAEA, LOB, etc.) should normally be used in addresses, instead of the full names.

(d) Postcodes to be typed as the final line of an address, with a single space between the two parts of the code.

SALUTATION

At left margin. No final comma.

SUBJECT HEADING

(a) Start at left-hand margin.

(b) Typed in capitals rather than underlined lower case letters.

BODY

(a) Blocked paragraphs.

(b) No full stops after, or unnecessary spaces between the separate letters of contractions and familiar abbreviations; e.g. Appx, Sgd, SEO, NATO, DTI, etc, eg, ie, para.

(c) Sub and sub-sub-paragraphs to be indented from the left-hand margin only and typed in blocked style.

(d) Spacing after punctuation—after a comma, a semi-colon or colon: one space; after a full stop, question or exclamation mark: two spaces.

(e) In the absence of clear directions to the contrary, paragraphs should be numbered '1.', '2.', etc. (figures followed by full stop) rather than '(1)', '(2)', etc. (figures in brackets). In subparagraphs 'a.', 'b.', rather than '(a)', '(b)'. Paragraph numbers should start at the left-hand margin and the full stop should be followed by 3 clear spaces.

(f) Catchwords should not be used.

(g) Pages should be numbered at foot of the page and centred where there is more than one sheet.

(h) The second page is typed on the back of the first and the margins are reversed.

COMPLIMENTARY CLOSE

(a) Typed at left margin; or

(b) at the same right-hand tabulation stop as the date.

(c) No comma at end.

NAME OF WRITER

(a) Typed under the signature space and without brackets.

(b) Either at the left-hand margin; or

(c) at the same right-hand tabulation stop as the complimentary close.

(d) Omit full stops after initials of name.

TITLE OR BRANCH/DIVISION, ETC., OF WRITER

Typed immediately under the typed name of writer. (The Branch, etc., may of course already be included in the printed letterhead, or it may not be needed at all.)

ENCLOSURES

To be indicated by typing ENC or ENCS (no full stop) followed by a figure denoting the number, at the bottom left-hand side of the letter, rather than by typing dashes or dots in the margin opposite the mention.

AMPERSAND

To be used instead of 'and' in such branch, etc., titles as 'O & M', 'Messrs. Jones & Smith'.

SECURITY CLASSIFICATION

Typed (in capital letters and not underlined) at the centre of the top and bottom of each page, if neither pre-printed paper nor stamps are available.

Technique development

Circulars or circular letters are letters (the contents of which are the same) which are sent to a number of customers or clients. The original is usually typed on a master sheet (stencil or offset litho) and a quantity is 'run off'.

1. REFERENCE
In usual position.

2. DATE
Typed in various ways; e.g.,

21st October 1978
October 1978 (month and year only)
Date as postmark. (These words are typed in the position where you normally type the date.)

3. NAME AND ADDRESS OF ADDRESSEE

(a) Space may be left for this, and in that case the details are typed on individual sheets after they have been 'run off'. When preparing the master (or draft) turn up 9 single-line spaces after the date (leaving 8 clear) before typing the salutation.

(b) Very often the name and address of addressee are not inserted and, if this is so, no space need be left when the master is prepared. Turn up 3 single-line spaces after date.

4. SALUTATION

(a) Dear — the remainder of the salutation is typed in when the name and address are inserted.
(b) Dear Sir, Dear Madam, Dear Sir(s), Dear Sir/Madam.

5. SIGNATURE
The person writing the letter may or may not sign it. If the writer is signing, type the complimentary close, etc., in the usual way. If the writer is not signing, type Yours faithfully and company's name* in the usual position, turn up 2 single-line spaces and type the name of the person writing the letter, then turn up 2 spaces and type designation.

* If the company's name is not being inserted, turn up 2 single spaces after Yours faithfully and type the name of the writer, then turn up 2 spaces and type the writer's designation.

6. TEAR-OFF PORTION
Sometimes a letter or circular will have a tear-off portion at the foot so that a customer may fill in certain details and return the tear-off portion to the sender.

The typing on the tear-off section should end about an inch (25 mm) from the bottom of the page and any space not required for the tear-off should be left after the complimentary close or the name of the signatory if this is given.

The minimum space to be left after the complimentary close or signatory is 4 clear spaces. In other words, turn up a minimum of 5 spaces and then type from *edge to edge* of the paper *continuous dots* or *continuous hyphens*; then turn up 2 spaces and type the information on the tear-off portion.

Where blank spaces are left for details to be filled in, use *continuous dots* (or the *underscore*) and *double spacing*. Remember to leave one clear space after the last character typed before starting the dots or underscore and one clear space at the end of the dots or underscore before the next typed character if there is one, e.g.,

Surname .... Christian names .....

7. DELETIONS
It is often necessary to delete letters or words in a form letter or a circular letter. For instance, in 4(b) above, if you were writing to an individual it would be necessary to delete the brackets and lower case 's' in Dear Sir(s). To delete previously typed characters, use a small 'x' aligned precisely with the characters previously typed.

Typing on ruled or dotted lines

In some form letters and forms you may have to type on ruled or dotted lines. In this case you must type slightly above the line: it is recommended that the base of the characters should be about 1 mm above the line.

1. (a) Type an original and one carbon copy of the following circular letter with tear-off portion. Use margins of Elite 12–90, Pica 10–75. Leave space for the name and address of the addressee to be inserted later.

(b) On the top copy only fill in your own name and address before the salutation and also on the tear-off portion. Type an envelope addressed to the Lodgings Warden.

(c) When completing the tear-off portion, be consistent with the starting point after the heading— start typing above the first dot. The insertion over second dotted line of the address may start at the same point as that used after the word ADDRESS or above the first dot.

Date as postmark

Dear Sir/Madam

I am writing on behalf of the University of Newtown to ask for yr help in finding our students somewhere to live during the coming session wh begins in Oct. The University owes a real debt of gratitude to citizens of Newtown who have helped us over many yrs.

This yr we expect to increase our student nos. by over 600 and, altho this increase is being met by building extra student flats, we sh need to place at least 1,500 students in lodgings & well over 4 000 in flats and bedsitters. Therefore, if you have any suitable accommodation vacant in September or Oct, please consider offering it for the use of students.

If you have any queries, please do not hesitate to tele my office, or write to me at the above address.

Should you be able to offer accommodation, please be kind enough to complete the form below and return it to me.

Yrs ffy

M P HERBERT

....

To: The Lodgings Warden and Student Welfare Adviser
     Newtown University Hamnavoe Newtown NO5 6DT

I have accommodation for ..... students and would like one of yr assistants to call and discuss with me the letting of these rooms to University students.

SURNAME .... CHRISTIAN NAME(S) ....

ADDRESS ....

.... POSTCODE ....

Further exercises on circular letters are given on page 63 of **Practical Typing Exercises, Book One**, and on page 46 of **Book Two**.